NORTH POLE LEGACY

North Pole Legacy

BLACK, WHITE & ESKIMO

✳ ✳ ✳

S. Allen Counter

The University of Massachusetts Press

AMHERST

Library of Congress Cataloging-in-Publication Data
Counter, S. Allen.
    North Pole legacy : black, white and Eskimo / S. Allen Counter.
    p. cm.
    Includes bibliographical references
    ISBN 0-87023-736-5 (alk. paper).
    1. Henson, Anaukaq, 1906–   . 2. Peary, Kali, 1906–   . 3. Eskimos—
Greenland—Biography. 4. Eskimos—Greenland—Genealogy. 5. Eskimos—
Greenland—Families. 6. Peary, Robert E. (Robert Edwin), 1856–1920. 7.
Henson, Matthew Alexander, 1866–1955. 8. Greenland—Genealogy. I. Title.
E99.E7C747   1991
998.2'00497102—dc20
[B]   90-11223
                                                                       CIP

            British Library Cataloging in Publication data are available.

Remembered by What I Have Done

Up and away, like a dew of the morning
That soars from the earth to its home in the sun;
So let me steal away, gently and lovingly
Only remembered by what I have done.

My name, and my place, and my tomb all forgotten,
The brief race of time well and patiently run
So let me pass away, peacefully, silently,
Only remembered by what I have done.

Gladly away from this trail would I hasten,
Up to the crown that for me has been won.
Unthought of by man in rewards or in praises—
Only remembered by what I have done.

Not myself, but the truth, that in life I have spoken;
Not myself, but the seed that in life I have sown
Shall pass on to ages—all about me forgotten,
Save the truth I have spoken, the things I have done.

Sincerely yours
Matthew Alexander Henson

Poem found in Matthew Henson's diary, Matthew A. Henson
Collection, Morgan State University, Baltimore.

CONTENTS

FOREWORD

Within the past two decades historians have critically reexamined many of the great moments of exploration and, in a phrase, found them wanting. There is controversy over where and when Europeans first landed in North America; where Columbus first set foot in the New World; what caused the apparent extinction of the first colony of English in North Carolina; and when and by whom the North Pole was first seen by human eyes. The last controversy has generated a spate of volumes—some reasoned, some not. In the beginning decade of this century both Dr. Frederick Cook and Comdr. Robert E. Peary claimed to be the first to have "reached the Pole." Both eventually received a fair degree of acclaim for events that are extremely difficult to verify. Whether Cook or Peary actually accomplished his goal may never be known with certainty.

Into the mélange of confusion and debate about these claims has stepped S. Allen Counter, who, with the gentility and perseverance of a true scientist and scholar, has demonstrated conclusively the validity of certain phases of Peary's exploits. Counter, a member of the Explorers Club, knew that Peary and his black associate, Matthew Henson, both also members of the Explorers Club, had spent several years living in the far north making preparations for their final march to the North Pole. This march is verified, unlike Cook's ostensible trek. Many rumors circulated that both Peary and Henson had lived a communal life with an isolated group of Eskimos near Moriussaq. This small village some one thousand miles north of the Arctic Circle was to be the site of studies by Counter, which eventually untangled many of the complex strands that led back to a comprehensive recognition of the lives of these two explorers in the Arctic.

But Counter then proceeded further. Having established the relationship of Anaukaq Henson and Kali Peary to their noted fathers, he determined to reunite the two Eskimos with their American relatives. This, to say the least, was far from easy. The controversy that surrounded Peary and, to some degree, Henson in their later years persisted down through several generations to living family members.

Again, Counter patiently and sagaciously dealt with all the political, legal, and emotional ramifications of uniting long-lost relatives of totally disparate cultures. It is doubtful that Peary and Henson ever could have imagined the impact their progeny would have on society eighty years after their births in 1906.

The results of some of Counter's efforts are totally unexpected and unforeseen—as is frequently the character of many feats of exploration. Surely the emotional encounters with siblings and cousins whose existence had never been a certainty rival any that ever have been recorded. It may have taken four generations but both Henson's and Peary's descendants should now recognize the greatness of their ancestors. Counter's volume is not easy to categorize. It is about the Arctic; exploration; Eskimo culture; Edwardian traditions; intense family relations; isolation; even the complexities of modern bureaucracy. Counter does not give heed to the demands of our society to put all things in neat cubbyholes. It is the message of affection and perseverance that is of import—and a powerful message it is.

NICHOLAS SULLIVAN, F.S.C.
President, The Explorers Club

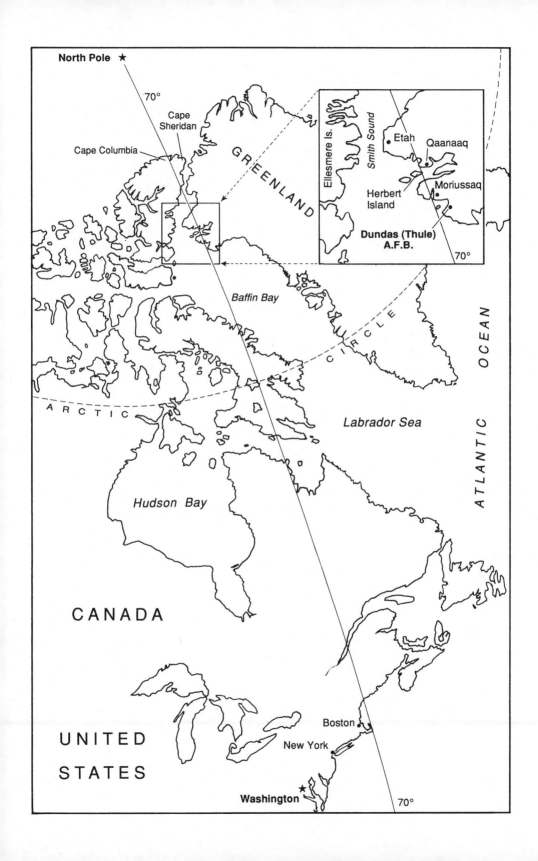

North Pole ★

70°

Cape
Sheridan

Cape Columbia

GREENLAND

Ellesmere Is.

Smith Sound

Etah • Qaanaaq

Herbert
Island

Moriussaq

Dundas (Thule)
A.F.B.

70°

Baffin Bay

ARCTIC CIRCLE

ATLANTIC OCEAN

Labrador Sea

Hudson Bay

CANADA

UNITED

STATES

Boston

New York

Washington ★

70°

NORTH POLE LEGACY

CHAPTER ONE

✳ ✳ ✳

Anaukaq, Son of Mahri-Pahluk

The old Polar Eskimo, bent slightly at the waist, steps briskly across the pack ice toward his team of sled dogs. Curled up like giant woolen balls, partially covered by a recent blizzard, the wolflike beasts come to life in response to his calls, "*Kim-milk! Kim-milk!* [Dog! Dog!]." They shake the crusted snow from their thick coats and yawn with soft howls as Anaukaq greets each of them by name and pats its head. Sensing that they are about to be hitched up for a trip, the dogs wag their tails and begin whining excitedly, for a Polar Eskimo dog would much rather be running than sleeping.

With graceful, measured movements, Anaukaq untangles the traces that tether each dog to stakes driven deep in the hard snow—traces now made of durable nylon rather than of the more perishable sealskin used in his youth. The dogs prance about and snap at one another playfully as he connects them, one by one, to the front of an eight-foot wooden sled with tall rear upstanders. He beckons me to a thick deerskin seat at the rear of the sled and we're off, rushing down the hillside toward the frozen bay with Anaukaq cracking his whip above the dogs' ears.

As we head out of the settlement, Anaukaq's eighteen-year-old grandson Nukka runs from his house and jumps on the sled, whip in hand. The family has assigned him to chaperon his grandfather over

3

the dangerous mounds of broken ice scattered across the bay—
subtly, of course, so as not to hurt the old hunter's feelings.

The eight dogs pull us much faster than I had thought possible.
"Wock, wock, wock, wock," the old man yells, directing the dogs to the
left. *"Ahchook, ahchook, ahchook"* and, like the turning wheels of a car,
the dogs and sled move to the right. Anaukaq looks back at me and
laughs as he detects my admiration. Dogsled driving is considered a
Polar Eskimo's most valuable skill, and Anaukaq is exceptionally
good at it.

No doubt this skill was learned, yet perhaps he was born with a
talent for it. For if he is who he says he is, his father was reputed to be
among the greatest dogsled drivers in the world. Anaukaq has told
me that he is the son of Matthew Alexander Henson, one of the first
two Americans to reach the North Pole. This claim has been corroborated by other Polar Eskimo elders, who still refer to Henson as
"Mahri-Pahluk," meaning "Matthew the Kind One," a name given
him by their forebears nearly a century ago. More telling still, Anaukaq has a much darker complexion than the other Eskimos and very
curly black hair—a trait rarely found among his people. Matthew
Henson, too, was *kulnocktooko* [dark skinned]. He was, in fact, the
only black known to have visited this Arctic region before Anaukaq
was born.

*   *   *

After about a half hour's ride, we reach our destination: the offshore
seal traps set by Anaukaq's son Avataq, who is some hundred miles
away hunting walrus. Anaukaq chops a hole in the ice around a rope,
which is tied to a stake. Once the rope is free, he tugs several times to
see whether there is a seal attached. "No luck," he says. "We'll come
back tomorrow." Anaukaq seems to take great delight in this chore.
As an old retired hunter who now for the most part is confined to his
village, he would feel useless if he did not have some food-gathering
responsibilities, so his five sons permit him to travel up and down
the bay, accompanied by his grandchildren, to examine their traps.

Returning to the warmth of his son Ajako's home, a boxlike wood-
en structure that the Eskimos still call an "igloo," we pull off our

snowshoes and prepare to enter the main room of the house in our socks. Anaukaq leans over and with a pocket knife cuts off a sliver of walrus heart hanging just inside the door. "*Mahmaktoe* [Tasty]", he says, looking at me with an inviting smile. He cuts a second sliver and hands it to me. I reluctantly put the raw, bloody meat in my mouth saying to myself, "It's okay. It's only cardiac muscle," but thinking all along that it tastes simply like dull, uncooked meat. "*Mahmaktoe*," I say, without conviction.

As we enter the central room, Anaukaq's daughter-in-law Puto is scraping the fat from a polar bear skin so that it can be properly stretched to make pants for her son Nukka, who has just killed his first *nanook* [polar bear]. The sweet aroma of polar bear meat in Puto's stew on the stove permeates the house. As a gesture of good will and respect for her father-in-law, Puto pulls a small piece of fat from the polar bear skin and hands it to him.

"Thank you," Anaukaq says. "Mmmm, very tasty!" The old-timers love this delicacy. "For you, here," he says, offering me a slice.

"No, thanks, my friend." I point to the kitchen. "I will wait for the *nanook* that is being cooked out there." I will only eat cooked polar meat because of the high risk of trichinosis from eating it raw. As the Polar Eskimos themselves are aware, trichinosis has been a major health problem within their community for many years, primarily as a result of their consumption of raw polar bear and bearded seal.

Anaukaq laughs politely. "Okay, but it's very tasty."

Eventually the stew is ready, and Anaukaq's granddaughter Malina serves me a portion with some hot tea. The polar bear meat has been boiled thoroughly without any spices, because none grow in this desolate part of the world and so they are hard to come by. Nevertheless, it is quite flavorful.

"Mmm, *mahmaktoe*," I say, to the delight of everyone present. Each nods with pleasure.

As we sit and eat, Puto resumes scraping the polar bear skin with her *ulu*, a small, flat, half-moon shaped utility knife that Eskimo women use for everything from flensing seals to slicing foods. After a while I sense that Anaukaq is watching me closely. I look up, and our eyes meet. He smiles, a little embarrassed that I caught him staring.

He reaches over and rubs my head, then his own hair, and laughs. "Curly! We have the same curly hair. We are the same people, black people."

"Yes, that's right," I agree, as everyone in the room breaks into laughter.

"You must be my relative," he says.

"Well, in spirit, perhaps, but not by family line." He seems a bit disappointed. It is not the first time he has said this to me. He finds it difficult to believe that we are not related, because he has never seen another black person outside of his own family. Can he really be who he says he is? I believe him, but I wonder.

I have come to Moriussaq, this tiny Eskimo village some one thousand miles above the Arctic Circle, because of my special interest in Matthew Henson. For many years he has been my hero, and I have struggled to gain him the recognition he deserved but never received during his lifetime. Henson was among the most successful Arctic explorers of all time, yet he remains relatively unknown in his own country. The reason for this paradox is as clear as American history, and it all comes down to a single world: *race.* Because Henson was black, his achievements were overshadowed by those of his white companion, Comdr. Robert Edwin Peary.

On April 6, 1909, Henson, Peary, and four Polar Eskimos reached a point that the two Americans determined to be the North Pole. During their previous eighteen years together in the Arctic, Henson and Peary had risked life and limb together in over ten thousand miles of exploration. They had made several other attempts at the Pole, coming closer each time but never attaining their goal. They had discovered meteorites, new fauna, and previously unknown geographical features, such as the fact that Greenland is an island rather than a continent that extended to the North Pole. Throughout, Henson had been an invaluable asset to Peary—as dogsled driver, mechanic, navigator, translator, and friend. So it was only fitting, and only fair, that they reached the top of Earth together and "nailed the Stars and Stripes to the Pole."

Once their goal was achieved, Henson and Peary left Greenland for the United States, never to return. But both left behind a legend and a legacy. Anaukaq is part of that legacy.

Anaukaq tells me that since his childhood, he has heard many wonderful stories about the great Mahri-Pahluk. Having no memory of his father, he has only these stories to go by, but the stories have made him very proud. Matthew Henson, he says, was the most popular outsider ever to visit his land. Polar Eskimo legends and songs tell of how masterfully Mahri-Pahluk could drive a dogsled, hunt a walrus, and skin a seal. They also tell of his long trek north across the great sea ice, with Ootah, Seegloo, Egingwah, Ooqueah, and Peary, to the strange place they call the North Pole. The Eskimos, it is said, would never have traveled so far from their land were it not for Mahri-Pahluk's presence and persuasion. Henson knew most of the 218 members of the tribe and spoke their difficult language fluently. Peary was known to the Eskimos as the commander of the expeditions, the one who could provide them with pay in the form of valuable goods. But Henson was known as the man who made the expeditions work. Even the great Ootah said that while the other outsiders were like children in the ways of the Eskimo, Mahri-Pahluk was a natural in their world. He was one of them.

CHAPTER TWO

✳ ✳ ✳

"You must be a Henson"

My trip to Moriussaq had its origins in a conversation that took place some years earlier in Stockholm, Sweden. I was a visiting professor at the Karolinska Nobel Institute at the time, and my colleague Dr. Erik Borg invited me to dinner. Over the years Erik, his wife, Birgitta, and their children had become my adopted Swedish family, and I had often dined at their home in the suburb of Bromma.

On this particular occasion we were joined by Erik's old schoolmate Peter Jacobson and his family. Peter had recently returned from Greenland and was keen on telling us about his trip. After dinner, when the conversation turned to Arctic exploration, I mentioned that a black American had made significant contributions to that field. To my surprise, both the Jacobsons and the Borgs knew about Matthew Henson. The Swedes, like other Scandinavians, are fond of Arctic lore and history. They grow up on stories of explorers such as Roald Amundsen and Peter Freuchen, much as American children do on tales of Daniel Boone and Davy Crockett.

Peter told us of rumors that there were some dark-skinned Eskimos in Greenland who might be the descendants of Henson, as well as others of particularly light complexion who might be the offspring of Commander Peary. The possibility of "white" Eskimos was not surprising, since it was well known that many Danish men stationed in Greenland over the years had fathered children with Eskimo women. But the notion of "black" Eskimos intrigued me. I made a mental note to investigate this matter later.

During the next few years I read everything I could about Henson and Peary, hoping to uncover some evidence that would confirm or disprove the rumors Peter Jacobson had heard. I learned a great deal about the history of polar exploration, the controversy surrounding the conquest of the Pole, and the unique relationship between Henson and Peary, but I found no mention of Amer-Eskimo offspring in Henson's and Peary's own writings, and nothing elsewhere that went beyond rumor or innuendo. In the end I became convinced that the key to this mystery could not be found in any library or archive. If Henson and Peary had in fact left behind children in the Arctic, surely the Eskimos themselves would know. Perhaps only they would know. I decided I would have to ask them.

* * *

The most difficult thing about visiting polar Greenland is getting there. Commercial transportation is limited to southern Greenland, where most of the inhabitants of this sparsely populated island live. Only American and Danish military planes serving the American air base at Thule are permitted in the northern part of the country. Built in 1955 on land traditionally occupied by a large group of Eskimos, who were forced to move, Dundas Air Force Base was established as part of an early-warning system and frontline defense against Soviet air attacks.

Permission for nonmilitary personnel to travel in the area is rarely granted, except for approved scientific studies and exploration. I therefore decided to apply to the Danish government for permission to conduct "a scientific study of ear disease in Eskimos and to interview some of the Polar Eskimos who were familiar with early American explorations in the area." My proposed audiological study was serious. As a neurophysiologist, I had read extensively about the ear problems of Eskimos. Of particular interest to me were studies showing that Eskimos from Canada and lower Greenland suffered an unusually high degree of sensorineural ("nerve") hearing loss. Sensorineural hearing impairment is irreversible and generally results from aging, ototoxic compounds, genetic factors, viruses, or noise trauma. Since no one had ever conducted a systematic hearing study of the Polar Eskimos, who are considered tribally and culturally different from Canadian Eskimos, such an undertaking seemed worthwhile. This way, even if my search for the descendants of Henson and Peary proved fruitless, I would have something to show for my efforts.

In the spring of 1986, at the end of a long trail of formal letters, long-distance phone calls, and lengthy applications, the Danish authorities granted my request. Several weeks later the First Space Wing of the U.S. Air Force gave me special permission to fly to Dundas Air Force Base on one of their C-141 transports. After arriving in Thule, I was forced to delay my journey to the Eskimo settlements because of high winds along the mountainous seacoast. Eventually, however, I boarded a helicopter that carried me to remote Moriussaq.

As the helicopter hovered over the edge of the tiny village, about a dozen young Eskimos ran out of their houses to greet me. The pilot set the aircraft down between two large orange oil drums that marked the landing zone and turned off the rotating blades. The young villagers rushed toward us, eager to collect any mail or supplies we might have brought and to get a look at their visitor. Unpacking my gear with the aid of the Eskimos, I asked if Tobius was among them.

"Yes," responded the short, round-faced man standing next to me, smiling. "I am here. Welcome to my village."

I had been directed to this settlement of about twenty families by a Polar Eskimo hunter named Panigpak Oaorana, who worked for the Danish ministry at Thule. Panigpak, who spoke only a little English, referred me to Tobius, who had previously worked at the base but now lived in Moriussaq. I asked Tobius if there was a family of dark-skinned Eskimos living in Moriussaq who were the descendants of Matthew Henson.

"Yes, there is such a family. Mahri-Pahluk's family lives there, and over there, and over there," he said, pointing to three different "igloos" in the distance.

"Will you take me over to meet them?" I asked.

"Yes, I take you." We headed off in the direction of the houses. "How do you know of this family?" Tobius asked.

"From your friend Panigpak, at the base," I replied.

"Oh, I see. They will be happy to see you."

"Why? Are they expecting me?"

"Oh, no," Tobius said, and then fell silent.

"Or is it because I am black?" I asked.

"I think so," he said with a mischievous grin. "No black person has ever come here before."

As we walked toward the settlement lugging my equipment and heavy backpack, I learned that Tobius had no formal training in English but had picked up the language over the years through his work at the air base. He was disappointed, he told me, that the base was now off-limits to most Polar Eskimos, though he agreed with the government's efforts to preserve traditional Inuit culture by minimizing outside influences, including alcoholic beverages. I questioned Tobius more about the dark-skinned Eskimo family.

"The old father lives there, just over there, in that igloo," he said, pointing to a small wooden structure covered with faded blue paint that lay just ahead of us.

"Let us visit the 'old father' first," I suggested.

We gave wide berth to the big dogs tethered to stakes along the way and zigzagged around their large droppings, which seemed to be strewn everywhere. Many of the fierce-looking canines howled or yelped at our approach. When we finally reached the cottage, built in the style of a New England "saltbox," Tobius climbed the steps and knocked loudly on the door. We could hear noises inside, and the voice of a man saying in Eskimo what must have been, "I'm coming." Soon a dark-complexioned, elderly man with curly hair, high cheekbones, and Eskimo eyes appeared in the doorway. He was wearing a gray flannel shirt with its collar exposed under a bulky white sweater, gray wool trousers, and sealskin boots. Tobius, a big, full-toothed grin on his face, said something to the man in Eskimo and then turned to me. I smiled, extended my hand, and said (in the rehearsed Eskimo that I had learned from Panigpak), "*Hi-nay* [Hello], I am Allen Counter, from the United States." The old man turned to Tobius, who translated. With a pleasant smile and soft laugh, the old man turned back and carefully examined my face.

"I am looking for the family of *Myee-Paluk*—Matthew Henson," I continued.

Tobius quickly corrected me, *"Mah-ri Pah-luk."*

I tried again, this time to the satisfaction of both men, *"Mahri-Pahluk."*

"Hi-nay," the old man said, cheerfully grasping my hand. "I am Anaukaq, son of Mahri-Pahluk."

"Son of Mahri-Pahluk?" I said incredulously, turning to Tobius. Could this be true? Offspring, yes, but could it be possible that this man is the *son* of Matthew Henson? His dark hair, smooth skin, and muscular frame did not appear to be those of a man old enough to be Henson's son. Henson had left Greenland for the last time in September 1909. Any Eskimo child of his would therefore have to be at least seventy-seven years old, yet this man looked to be in his sixties, at most. Perhaps he is a grandson, I thought, and Tobius erred in his translation. After all, Henson and Peary had been in the area since 1891, sometimes up to four years at a stint, so they certainly could have fathered children who begat other children. But Tobius made it clear that there had been no mistranslation.

"Yes, he is the son of Mahri-Pahluk," he said. "All of us up here know that."

I studied Anaukaq's face in detail. Everything about the appearance of the man said that I was looking at a descendant of Matthew Henson. Even his laugh and gestures were curious, somehow different from those of Panigpak and Tobius. Then again, I thought, maybe I was seeing what I wanted to see.

He tried to communicate something to me in his native tongue. I turned to Tobius. "What did he say?"

"He says you must be a Henson, and you have come to find him," Tobius said with an inquisitive smile on his face. I could see in Anaukaq's expression that he was elated by the thought and anticipated an affirmative response.

"Unfortunately, I am not a member of the Henson family," I said and then added, "but I have come here as a friend, looking for any Polar Eskimo descendants of Mahri-Pahluk."

Tobius translated. "I am Anaukaq, son of Mahri-Pahluk," the old man proudly reiterated. "I am pleased that you have traveled to Moriussaq to see me."

* * *

We spent the next few days getting acquainted. Using his cane, Anaukaq walked me about the village, introducing me to his relatives and neighbors. One day, as we sat drinking some spiced tea that I had brought along, we talked at length about Anaukaq's early life. What he knew of his father he had learned from his mother and the older Eskimos who had known Mahri-Pahluk. To their knowledge, he was the only child Henson fathered in the Arctic. Anaukaq said that he was born on Peary's *omiak* [ship] in 1906. He then went on to tell me numerous stories about his life, particularly his childhood. As I listened, I became increasingly convinced that this vigorous, eighty-year-old "black" Eskimo was in fact the son of Matthew Alexander Henson. And I had found him—alive and well. I felt good inside.

In subsequent conversations, over the next couple of weeks, Anaukaq talked with me more and more personally, as if I were the long-lost relative he had hoped for. "You are the first *kulnocktooko* to visit my home," he said. "I never thought anyone who looked like me would ever come to visit. I am very happy you came." From time to time he would ask, "Are you sure you are not a Henson?" then laugh warmly. "You look very much like you could be one of my relatives." He would then rub the hair on my head and say, "Very good," after which he would touch his own hair. "The same. Your hair is the same as mine." It became a kind of ritual between us, and each time we both would laugh. I noticed that he always clapped his hands when he laughed, as I have seen so many black Americans do.

"I have often wondered whether the curious urge to search for Matthew Henson's descendants way up here might not be based on some unknown biological kinship to Henson's family," I told Anaukaq. "But I don't think we're related."

Yet even if I were not his relative,' what about other relatives? Anaukaq wanted to know. "Did Mahri-Pahluk have any children over there? Do I have any brothers and sisters in America?"

"I do not know," I replied, "but to my knowledge your father had no children by his American wife, Lucy Ross Henson, whom he married after your birth."

"Is that true?" He chuckled. "You mean my father had no American wife when he was with my mother?"

"No, not until after you were born."

He laughed again. "Peary had two wives, one Eskimo and one in his own land. I thought maybe Mahri-Pahluk had two wives also."

"No, he married Lucy in 1908, the year he and Peary left the United States for their last attempt to reach the Pole. They had no children then or later." I could not be certain about other children from other relationships, of course, but I said I would be happy to initiate a search for possible relatives when I returned to the United States. Anaukaq wanted to know more about Lucy Henson, but information about her is so sparse I could only tell him a little about her background. At times he looked so disappointed at my lack of information that I had to reassure him I would do my best to track down his American relatives.

"All my life I have wanted so much to see my father or someone from his family," Anaukaq told me. "When I was young, I would talk with my friends about traveling to the land of my father to visit him, but I had no way to get there. Then one day I realized he must be dead, and I dreamed of seeing his birthplace and burial place." He paused, then continued. "My children too have wondered about their relatives over there. Even if I never meet them, I would like to have my children see their American relatives." The poignancy of his expression was occasionally relieved by an awkward laugh, as if he were a little embarrassed about sharing such deep personal feelings with so new an acquaintance. When he was much younger, he said, he had often wondered why his father had never come back to visit him or sent for him to visit his distant homeland.

I explained to Anaukaq that even if his father had wanted to return to the Arctic, it would have been very difficult for him to do so. I described the obstacles that anyone of that era, and especially an African American, would have faced in trying to make such a journey. Even if Henson had wished to join one of the later expeditions led by his old friend Comdr. Donald B. MacMillan, it is doubtful he could have spared the time or the money. Having secured a minor post with the U.S. Customs Service in New York, he would have risked losing his job by taking an extended leave of absence. As it was, he and his wife both had to work full time in order to make ends meet.

"Akatingwah, my mother, held a special place in my heart," Anaukaq said, after I had finished. "She was a feisty, tough, independent woman and a good mother." She died when Anaukaq was a teenager, but his memories of her remained vivid. He told me, as did some of the older Eskimo women in the area, that Mahri-Pahluk loved Akatingwah but realized that she had been "given" by her family—in the Eskimo way of marriage—to an Inuit man named Kitdlaq. So his mother was technically "married" when she first lived with Matthew Henson in 1902. Her husband was a hunter who traveled regularly by dogsled across the ice between Ellesmere Island in Canada and northwest Greenland. He also worked as a hunter and in other capacities for Peary's expeditionary teams. It was not uncommon then for married Eskimo women to cohabit with men other than their husbands for short periods, though this custom was usually confined to those within the community and was misunderstood by outsiders. What seems to have been unique about Henson's relationship to Akatingwah is that the Polar Eskimos believed him to be a tribal relative and accepted him as such.

Several of the older Eskimo women in Moriussaq later told me that when Akatingwah gave birth to a dark-skinned baby with never-before-seen curly hair, everyone in the village knew at once that it was Mahri-Pahluk's child. Like Anaukaq, they also expressed the belief that Matthew would have taken his "Eskimo wife" to his homeland if she had not already been given in marriage to another man.

Anaukaq himself seemed to have thought little about how different his life might have been if that had actually happened. As it was, he felt fortunate that his Eskimo stepfather had adopted him and reared him. Even after Akatingwah died, Kitdlaq had continued to be a "kind father" to him. Anaukaq loved and admired his stepfather, who taught him how to be a good father and a *peeneeahktoe wah* [great hunter], skilled in the ways of the Eskimo people.

CHAPTER THREE

✳ ✳ ✳

The Amer-Eskimo Hensons

"I was married to Aviaq for fifty-four wonderful years, and we had seven children. My wife died in 1975. She is buried over there." Anaukaq pointed to a small graveyard just beyond the settlement. "I miss my wife dearly. I have been very lonely since her departure."

Like most modern-day Eskimos, Aviaq is buried in a plot marked by a white Christian cross rather than in a traditional Eskimo surface-stone grave. In the past, Polar Eskimos buried their dead by covering the entire body and a few cherished possessions with stones. Men were typically buried fully clothed in their animal-skin garments alongside their sled and lead dog, strangled and tied to the sled for travel in the afterlife. Women were also clad in traditional sealskin attire and were buried with an oil lamp and *ulu* at their side. It is said that before the arrival of Christian missionaries at the turn of the century, a dead woman's youngest infant would be strangled and placed in the grave out of fear of possible disease and because an unnursed infant was a burden to a wandering band of Arctic hunter-gatherers.

Since Aviaq's death, Anaukaq's sons and grandchildren help to look after him, stopping by his house whenever they can to make sure that he is all right.

"It is still not the same as having a wife for company," he told me.

"She used to go on hunting trips with me, and some years we traveled by dogsled hundreds of miles up and down the coast."

On more than a few occasions, Anaukaq remembered, he and his wife had come close to death while out on the ice.

"I shall never forget the time Aviaq and I were out on a hunting trip, many days north of here, and I left her and the children behind at the igloo while I headed out to hunt seals. I located several seal breathing holes and a few seals on the ice, basking in the sun. As I crawled across the ice behind a white cloth screen, stalking the animals, I decided to climb up on a large hummock of ice to get a good aim. I never noticed that the ice was slowly shifting. After a few minutes, the ice hill cracked under my weight, and I went tumbling into a gaping crevasse, about two-men high. When I didn't return to the igloo, Aviaq became worried. She left the younger children in the care of the older ones and set out looking for me. I heard her calling my name and I yelled back 'Aviaq, my wife! Aviaq, my wife! Here!' She found me and helped me out of the crevasse. I was so happy with my Aviaq. She saved my life."

Some of the women of Moriussaq commented that Anaukaq and Aviaq had a model relationship. In fact, Aviaq had confided to several of her friends that she and Anaukaq had had only one fight in all their years of marriage. One old woman, Kayqeehuk, reminisced about her first meeting with Anaukaq:

"When I was a young girl of about fifteen, living with my parents near Savissivik, some people visited our settlement and stopped to speak to my father. There was a young boy, also about fifteen, with them named Anaukaq, who looked unlike any Inuit I had ever seen. He was very dark with the most beautiful curly hair. I wanted to touch his hair. I had never seen anything like it. I thought he was such a handsome man, the handsomest man I had ever seen. I and several of the other girls in my settlement wanted to marry this boy. Years later, we were a bit jealous when we learned that he had chosen Aviaq as his wife."

* * *

Matthew Henson was sixty-two years old and residing in New York City when, unknown to him, his first grandson was born on December 3, 1928, in polar Greenland. Anaukaq, then about twenty-two, and Aviaq, about seventeen, named their first son after Anaukaq's beloved stepfather, Kitdlaq. This, Anaukaq said, was his greatest tribute to the man who had accepted him as his own blood-kin and had been a wonderful father to him.

Anaukaq took great pride in teaching his firstborn son to become a *peeneeahktoe wah*. Like most Eskimo men, he wanted his son to learn to be a good provider for his family and his village and to earn the respect of his peers. Early on Kitdlaq proved to be a quick learner and a skillful hunter. Like his father before him, he killed his first polar bear at the age of thirteen. By the time he was sixteen, he was a master kayaker and had developed an excellent reputation as a walrus hunter. He would approach the walrus prey by kayak and thrust his harpoon into the lung area from a few meters away. The injured walrus would then dive deep, carrying the harpoon tip and attached rope with it. A ballooned sealskin float attached to the other end of the rope prevented the walrus from diving too deep and served to mark its location. After a prolonged struggle, Kitdlaq and his companions would kill the walrus with their harpoons or guns. One large walrus could feed a family and their vital sled dogs for many weeks.

Then tragedy struck. Hunting alone, Kitdlaq one day approached a large bull walrus that appeared to be sleeping on an ice floe. Creeping up on the animal in the silent kayak, he got within a few meters before he raised his harpoon and prepared to hurl it into the animal's body. Just as he let go of the harpoon, the animal was aroused by another walrus, and it turned its head toward Kitdlaq. The harpoon missed its mark and only grazed the beast's neck.

The bull quickly slid from the ice floe into the water, where walruses can move with incredible speed. Kitdlaq tried to flee as fast as he could, but the wounded walrus overtook him and struck his kayak savagely with its head and tusks. The mighty blow split the kayak in half, sending Kitdlaq flying into the frigid water, head first. Some say that the walrus then struck Kitdlaq with its pointed tusks, killing him instantly. Others believe that he simply froze to death in the icy water. In any case, Kitdlaq, the first grandson of Matthew Henson, died a terrible death when he was sixteen years old.

The loss of their first child devastated Anaukaq and Aviaq. Not since his stepfather, the first Kitdlaq, died had Anaukaq felt such pain and sadness. According to Polar Eskimo tradition, a death should not be openly mourned for more than a few days. But the deceased's name is not to be uttered again in the settlement for an indefinite period. During this time everyone in the community bearing the name of the deceased must give up his or her name until a new child is born in the settlement. The child is then given the name of the deceased, at which point all others may resume using their original names. Anaukaq told me that he had mourned his son's death for years and still had not gotten over it fully.

In the weeks that followed, I met most of the other members of the Amer-Eskimo Henson clan: sons, grandsons, and great-grandchildren. We talked at length about the family heritage, and they made it clear that they felt very special to be the progeny of Matthew Henson, about whom they knew much more than I had anticipated. Like Anaukaq, many expressed a desire to visit the United States and meet their American relatives. Like Anaukaq, too, they found it difficult to believe that I was not myself a Henson. They questioned me incessantly: Would their relatives look like me? Were they all *kulnocktooko?* What did Mahri-Pahluk's wife look like?

For the moment, I had too few answers.

* * *

Bam! Bam! Bam!

A loud, frantic noise at the door of my little wooden hut awakened me from a sound sleep around 2 A.M. I poked my head out of my sleeping bag and tried to orient my senses. "Allen! Allen! Come, Allen! Avataq! *Ahvuk!* Avataq! *Ahvuk!*" the voice at the door was shouting excitedly. Dogs behind the hut were barking wildly and growling at each other. I could hear a gruff voice yelling at them, as if trying to bring them under control. The door flew open and the freezing air rushed into my already cold room, causing me to shiver as if I had been splashed by icy water. In the doorway stood Nukka, Anaukaq's grandson. He hurriedly beckoned me to come outside with him. "Allen, Avataq. *Ahvuk.*" As I rushed to put on my boots and down parka (I had been sleeping fully clothed because of the room's cold temperature), I realized that Nukka was calling the name of Avataq, Anaukaq's oldest son. But the other word, *ahvuk,* I did not understand.

At first I thought that perhaps Avataq had taken ill or been hurt, and they wanted my help. Then, as Nukka and I dashed off toward Anaukaq's house, I began to worry that something had happened to Anaukaq. Just behind the house, I could see the silhouette of a broad-shouldered, stocky man trying to untangle his sled dogs. Moving closer, I saw that he was dressed in a thick, thigh-length leather parka with a fur-lined hood to protect his head and face. His knee-length trousers were made entirely of polar bear fur and his boots were traditional high-top sealskin *kamiks.*

It was Avataq. He had just returned from a hunting trip and was working by the light of a kerosene lantern, tethering his dogs and preparing to remove his quarry from the sled. He turned to me and smiled. "*Ahvuk,*" he said proudly, pointing to his sled. I walked over to the sled and removed the deerskin cover to reveal three large walrus heads with long ivory tusks, as well as slabs of bloody meat stacked two feet high, filling the entire eight-foot sled. To the Polar Eskimos, who prize the walrus particularly, it was an impressive harvest.

"Avataq, *peeneeahktoe wah,* huh?" said Nukka admiringly.

Avataq stored most of the *ahvuk* meat in a small wooden shed, similar to a chicken coop, just behind his house—a natural, year-round refrigerator. Other slabs were placed on racks some four feet above the ground, high enough to be beyond the reach of the dogs.

Born in 1933, the second child of Anaukaq and Aviaq, Avataq is about five feet four inches tall, with a stocky build, dark complexion, and straight black hair. His big, warm smile is a bit comical because of a missing front tooth. With his high cheekbones, Eskimo eyes, and straight hair he reminds one of a Southeast Asian, perhaps a Java-nese. As a child, Avataq briefly attended a Danish missionary school, where he learned to speak some Danish and do simple arithmetic. Yet in most respects he has remained faithful to the traditional Es-kimo way of life. Registered with the Greenlandic authorities as a full-time hunter, he earns his livelihood by hunting narwhal, seal, and rabbits in the summer, and walrus, polar bear, and seal in the spring and winter. He is, in fact, the most celebrated hunter in the area, renown for his courage and expert techniques. Walrus hunts are his specialty, but he is equally adept at hunting seals and polar bears.

Avataq and his wife, Minaq, have five children: three girls, Malina, Louisa, and Cecilia; and two boys, Jakub and Magssanguaq. Though he is only ten years old, Magssanguaq, the youngest, is already an accomplished hunter in his own right. During my stay I saw him return from the hunting grounds with four large seals and numerous birds.

* * *

Our vigil on the rock-strewn, desolate mountainside had been long and uneventful. Rising up from the shoreline of Wolstenholm Sound to the craggy peak where we sat, the terrain reminded me of a moonscape or the surface of some unknown, lifeless planet. Not far from me, a man wearing polar bear pants and an anorak sat atop a large rock, peering through binoculars out over the distant waters. Suddenly the quiet was broken by the roar of a huge iceberg thundering down a nearby glacier and hitting the water with the force of a bomb. The sentry did not stir. He had been there many times before, and he knew that when nature spoke, all a man could do was listen. He was searching the bay for schools of *kahlayleewah* [narwhal]. He must not lose his concentration. The vigil could go on for hours, even days. One must be patient.

Below us, just above the shoreline, sat a fifteen-foot kayak made from a light wooden frame and covered with off-white tarpaulin material. A few decades ago this kayak would have been constructed from whale and walrus bones and covered with stitched sealskin. In the center of the kayak was an opening, just large enough to accommodate the slightly built Eskimo. At the stem was a neatly coiled nylon rope connected to the removable tip of a seven-foot wooden harpoon, which lay parallel to the line of the craft within reach of the pilot. Attached to the other end of the rope and placed behind the hunter's seat was a large, balloonlike sealskin float that looked like a stuffed seal with feet when fully inflated. To the left of the seat, a high-caliber rifle sat on the flat part of the stem, balanced precariously and pointing forward. Lying perpendicular to the long axis of the boat, just behind the seat, was the kayaker's distinctive double paddle. Although even the slightest swaying motion of the boat can cause a hunter to lose his rifle and gear, the expert Eskimo kayakers can travel long distances at impressive speeds with remarkable balance and stability.

There were only three tents on the mountainside, including my own. The sentry, and the leader of our expedition, was Ussarkaq, Anaukaq's third son. Like his brother Avataq, the fifty-year-old Ussarkaq is a full-time hunter, best known for his skill as a hunter of narwhals and for his ability to handle a kayak. In fact, he is the kayak-racing champion among the Polar Eskimos, often competing with young men in their teens, twenties, and thirties. A respected leader within his family, he is also well known for his sense of humor.

"Do you want to become a great narwhal hunter?" he asked me, seemingly serious. "Then take off that red parka. You'll scare off the narwhals." I looked at him incredulously, having no intention of taking off my parka for any reason. But Ussarkaq just laughed. "Come over to the tent for some tea, and we will teach you some funny Eskimo words."

He called down to his eighteen-year-old son, Massauna-Matthew. Ussarkaq had been on watch for three hours; it was time for his son to relieve him. Massauna-Matthew, named for Matthew Henson, emerged from the tent. He is much darker in complexion than the other Eskimo Hensons and has spirally curled hair. Anaukaq says that he is "my favorite grandson because he and I have the curliest hair in the family."

Ussarkaq gave Massauna the binoculars and returned with me to the tent for some hot tea that his son had prepared. After drinking a cup, he rubbed his eyes, now aching from the long watch, and promptly dozed off. But not for long.

"*Kahlayleewah! Kahlayleewah!*" shouted Massauna-Matthew, running down the mountainside to the sea. Ussarkaq sprang from his deerskin mat, rushed out of the tent, and headed down the slope to his kayak. There he met Massauna, who was pointing in the direction of four large narwhals in the center of the bay, breaching the surface like dolphins. Ussarkaq and Massauna quickly but carefully lifted the kayak and carried it to the water's edge. Ussarkaq slipped into the tightly fitting seat and pulled a rubber sealer over the remaining open space surrounding his body. Massauna then gave the stern of the kayak a shove, and Ussarkaq pushed off with his paddle.

Once in the water, Ussarkaq paddled rapidly with the classic, rotating movements of the Eskimo kayaker. He moved with grace and speed through the bay, gliding toward the narwhals. The kayak moved through the water so quietly that it slipped up on the school of narwhal before they could detect it. Ussarkaq tried to head the single-tusked mammals off before they could reach the mouth of the bay. The hunter and kayak became smaller and smaller in the distance, soon visible only through the binoculars. When he reached the narwhals, they appeared confused as they scattered about the kayak, their blowholes spouting water and air all around him.

Ussarkaq selected a large male that had breached right in front of his kayak. His harpoon found its mark in the animal's head, causing it to thrash about wildly before submerging. The attached rope lying on the kayak uncoiled in seconds as the animal dove deep into the water, trying to free itself. The sealskin buoy flew off the kayak into the bay when all the rope had run out. The buoy disappeared beneath the surface, then reappeared, traveling away from the kayak at high speed. This was a good sign and meant that the harpoon tip was fixed securely in the narwhal's flesh. Ussarkaq paddled frantically after the moving float. When it changed direction, he changed direction. After about forty-five minutes of chasing the buoy, Ussarkaq was exhausted. His strokes became slower and more labored, but he could not stop to rest. Finally, the buoy, too, began to move more slowly, and Ussarkaq moved in on it. He picked up his rifle and steadied his aim in the direction of the buoy, waiting for the narwhal to surface for air. Moments later the big, gray-black mammal broke the water's surface, its spouting blowhole marking the spot. Ussarkaq fired two rounds. The water all around the thrashing animal turned bright red. Then the movement stopped. Ussarkaq quickly paddled to the narwhal and plunged a metal pipe down its throat.

Placing his mouth around the open end of the pipe, he blew air into the animal's lungs and stomach, bloating it so that he could keep it afloat and tow it more easily behind his kayak.

The half-ton narwhal would feed Ussarkaq's family for more than a month. Ussarkaq and his wife, Simigaq, have seven children—four boys and three girls—ranging in age from seven to twenty-four. The girls are named Arnakitsoq, Aviaq, and Eqilana. The boys are Massauna-Matthew, Thomas, Avatak, and Peter. The family lives in Siorapaluk, the northernmost settlement of Greenland.

* * *

Anaukaq's fourth son, Ajako, is a part-time hunter who lives near his father in Moriussaq. Forty-eight years old, about five feet seven inches tall, with dark curly hair and deep brown skin, Ajako is considered very handsome by the villagers. The manager of the local government-run general store, he serves as a sort of unofficial mayor of the settlement. His store, which also functions as a post office, bank, and transport service, is restocked once each year when a Danish ship laden with food and dry goods comes to Moriussaq during the summer thaw.

Ajako and his wife, Puto, have five children: three girls, Nadiketchia, Sabina, and Aviaq; and two boys, Jens and Nukka. Like good parents everywhere, Ajako and Puto try to provide as much as possible for their children and take great pride in their children's achievements. One day, for instance, I found them out on the frozen bay, commemorating Nukka's first polar bear kill by preparing the skin so that it could be made into trousers for their son.

Dressed in his own polar bear pants, deerskin parka, and sealskin mittens trimmed with polar bear fur, Ajako chopped a hole about three feet in diameter in the ice using a spearlike metal tool. Puto stood beside him, dressed in native sealskin boots and an imported gray down-filled jumpsuit that she had purchased through the local trade cooperative. Ajako dunked the huge skin in the icehole, moving it up and down in the frigid water, much as one washes a shirt by hand in a tub. After a few minutes of washing, he took the pelt out of the water and spread it over the snow. He and Puto then threw some snow on top of the bearskin, after which they began stomping and dancing on it with their boots. They repeated the process several times until they were satisfied. Ajako then beat the skin repeatedly with a stick to remove the residual water, snow, and ice. *"Daymah!* [It is finished.]" He threw the limp skin over his shoulder, and we headed for home.

*   *   *

Vittus, Anaukaq's fifth son, lives a life much different from his older brothers. Trained as a machinist by the Danes, he works on various kinds of equipment now making its way into the Eskimo settlements. Forty years old, he is physically well built and about five feet nine inches tall, making him the tallest of Anaukaq's five sons. "I am a black man," he is fond of boasting, though in fact he looks more "pure Eskimo" or Asian than any other member of his immediate family. He is said to take after his mother more than his siblings, in temperament as well as physical appearance. He is very soft-spoken but at the same time friendly and outgoing. Vittus and his wife, Cecilie, have five children: three boys, David, Avatak, and Anaukaq; and two girls, Lila and Aviaq.

When Anaukaq's sixth and youngest son was born, he and his wife decided to name their new baby after the son they had loved and lost and the stepfather Anaukaq had so revered. Young Kitdlaq was raised in much the same way as the other children in the family, yet in some ways he was given special treatment. Ever conscious of the fate of their eldest child, Anaukaq and Aviaq were more protective of their youngest. He was not permitted to hunt alone, as the other boys were at his age. He was forbidden by his father to use a kayak until far beyond the age when most Eskimo boys learn to do so, and even then he was required to have a companion at all times.

Kitdlaq succeeded in becoming a good hunter, but he also excelled in the Danish missionary school. Anaukaq and Aviaq moved the family from Savissivik to Moriussaq when Kitdlaq was ten so that he and the other children could get some schooling. Now thirty-eight, Kitdlaq is a part-time hunter and a teacher in the small elementary and junior high school in the Eskimo village of Qaanaaq. Kitdlaq is about five feet six inches tall; he is dark-complexioned and could easily pass for a black American. He and his wife, Kista, have three young daughters: Tina, Avortungiaq, and one-year-old Aviaq.

"When we were growing up, we were a typical Eskimo hunter family," Kitdlaq told me one day as he worked on his kayak. "We, all five sons, traveled from place to place with our parents in search of the good hunting grounds. We all slept together in one igloo. We ate together and sang together. We also played together as friends, and we learned hunting skills from each other and our father. My big brothers really took care of me. They treated me kind of special because I was the baby of the group. But they also taught me to be strong and to provide for myself.

"When I was a child, some of the other children who wanted to be mean would occasionally taunt me by saying that my skin was dark and dirty. They would say, 'Go wash your face.' At first this hurt me very much. But my big brothers would tell me not to worry about the teasing. They would support me and tell me to be proud of my *kulnocktooko* heritage. My father too would say that we should be proud to be the descendants of Mahri-Pahluk.

"As I grew older, I thought a lot about my grandfather. My family used to say that we must have relatives in America, but they never did anything about it. We couldn't. Anaukaq, my father, used to say that he wanted more than anything to travel to Mahri-Pahluk's homeland and meet his American relatives. He thought that he must have relatives in America, maybe some half brothers and half sisters. He would say to us children, 'If I don't live to meet Mahri-Pahluk's American relatives, I want you to travel there one day to meet them.' I always hoped we could fulfill his dream as a family, especially before my mother died."

Between the birth of Vittus and Kitdlaq, Anaukaq and Aviaq had a baby girl whom they named Akatingwah. She died at age six of unknown causes. Each brother told me of his profound sense of loss at the death of his only sister.

* * *

Anaukaq enjoyed introducing me to the members of his family and instructing me in the ways of his people. But most of all, he enjoyed talking about the old days. As he reminisced, he mentioned another relative whom he referred to as "Cousin Kali." He told me that Kali— pronounced "Karree" by many of the Eskimos—was the son of Robert Peary and his best childhood friend.

Taken aback, I asked Anaukaq if he was certain that Kali was Peary's son.

"Oh, yes," he said seriously, "Kali is the son of Peeuree and an Eskimo woman named Ahlikahsingwah." He stretched out each syllable so that I would better understand the pronunciation.

"Most Americans do not know that Peeuree fathered children in Greenland," I said.

Anaukaq chuckled. "Yes, Peeuree had two wives, a Peeuree wife in America and Ahlikahsingwah up here." He laughed again and clapped his hands.

"Did Peeuree have other children with Ahlikahsingwah?" I asked.

"Oh, yes," he replied. "He had another son with Ahlikahsingwah named Anaukaq, like me."

"Older or younger?"

"Older. Oh, maybe five or six years older. But he is dead now."

Anaukaq said that Kali was also born aboard Peary's ship, the *Roosevelt*, in 1906. In fact, Anaukaq and Kali were born within days of each other. Yet the reason they called each other "cousin" had less to do with the circumstances of their birth than with the fact that their mothers married two Eskimo brothers, Kitdlaq and Peeahwahto. Both men, he said, worked for Peary as hunters. Kitdlaq later adopted Mahri-Pahluk's son, Anaukaq, while Peeahwahto adopted Kali and his older brother, also named Anaukaq. After Peary and Henson left Greenland for good in 1909, Kitdlaq and Peeahwahto took their wives and children to the island of Qeqertarsaaq, now Herbert Island, where they lived between hunting trips for about fifteen years.

Young Anaukaq and Kali became the best of friends. They played together as children and hunted together as young men. According to Anaukaq, Kali was "a great seal hunter, and like a brother to me." Although they had not spent any time together since becoming adults, they still referred to each other affectionately.

Anaukaq said that Kali still lived on Qeqertarsaaq, about forty miles north of his settlement. When I expressed an interest in visiting him, Anaukaq implored me to do so, in part because Kali would be able to provide additional information about the North Pole legacy of Robert Peary and Matthew Henson.

"You will like my cousin Kali," he said. "Give him my best regards."

CHAPTER FOUR

❋ ❋ ❋

Cousin Kali

Approached from the southeast, Qeqertarsaaq looks much like an ancient castle rising from the sea—an isolated, snowcapped mountain surrounded by barren white plains. Located some twenty-five miles off the coast of northwest Greenland, it is a well-known hunting ground for walrus and seals, just as it was when Robert Peary camped there in the late 1800s. Today it has few human inhabitants. The only settlement, if such it can be called, consists of a few scattered dwellings. It was there that I found the man Anaukaq called "Cousin Kali," son of "Peeuree."

As I neared my destination, I saw a young man of about twenty years old bending over a freshly killed seal, methodically slicing it to pieces. Using a large hunter's knife, he made a small incision just under the mouth and then cut the skin vertically in a single line from chin to tail flipper. He next peeled away the animal's skin in one piece, much as one would remove a diver's wet suit. He walked a few paces to a platform made of old timber and placed the valuable pelt on a wooden rack, well beyond the reach of his dogs, tethered a few yards away. The pelt would be stretched later and made into boots, gloves, or possibly a woman's hooded jacket or *amaut*.

Returning to the skinless animal, the hunter began to flense its fleshy pink blubber, tossing some of the scraps to the dogs. The dogs caught the chunks in the air and gulped them down. He made sure that each dog got a piece, then stored the rest of the blubber on the rack. Another vertical incision, this one deep into the seal's throat and down to the tail, spilled its innards over both sides of the carcass. He carefully removed the liver, stomach, intestines and other organs. The intestines would be dried and used for tubing or, perhaps, for a shirt. The undesirable innards would be fed to the dogs, the rest would be eaten by the hunter and his family.

The young man then quartered the animal, saving every piece of flesh for food. Nothing was lost. With blood covering his hands and a few spots on his face, he turned and smiled at me as he passed on his way to store the meat. It was the first time he had acknowledged my presence. He had a round face with perfectly even white teeth. His skin was pale and only his eyes and high cheekbones suggested that he was Eskimo. His smile was difficult to interpret, at once friendly and cautious, warm yet reserved. Still, I smiled back and then moved on.

Entering the tiny settlement, I spotted a rather fit-looking, slightly graying "white" man with animated eyes, standing in the entrance of a small wooden house. He was wearing a tan pile-and-wool turtleneck sweater, heavy dark trousers, and sealskin boots. Wanting to know who the visitors were, he came out of his house to meet me, smiling cheerfully, and graciously greeted my translator Navarana Qavigaq-Harper, the great niece of Ootah. He was lighter in complexion than the other Eskimos I had met but similar in stature. His eyes were more Asiatic than Anaukaq's, and his gray-black hair much thinner.

Before I left the United States, I had carefully studied photographs of all the men who accompanied Commander Peary on his various Arctic expeditions. Right away, I could see a striking resemblance between "Cousin Kali" and Robert Peary. Still, I could not be certain that the man who now stood before me was Peary's son, since other white explorers in the region had reportedly fathered children with Eskimo women. By comparison, verification of Anaukaq's identity had been much simpler because Matthew Henson was the only black explorer to visit northern Greenland in the early 1900s.

Like Anaukaq, Kali assumed that I must be a Henson. Why else would the first black American he had ever seen have come so far to meet him? I explained to Kali that I was not myself a Henson but had come to the region in search of the progeny of Matthew Henson and Robert Peary.

"I am Kali Peeuree," he said.

"Are you the son of Robert Peary, the explorer who came to this area many years ago to reach the North Pole?" I asked.

"Yes, I am the son of Peeuree, the friend of Mahri-Pahluk," he responded, with a smile and obvious pride. "You know, it was Mahri-Pahluk who took my father to the North Pole," he said. "My father could not have reached the pole without Mahri-Pahluk."

Kali invited me into his igloo, where we sat down and talked over some tea I had brought along. "Don't you have anything stronger?" he asked with a mischievous grin.

"No, only tea and coffee," I said.

Kali laughed. "How are you going to tolerate the cold up here without some good whiskey to keep you warm?"

I told him I shared his sentiments, but that the Danish government prohibited the transport or use of unauthorized alcoholic beverages in the area.

Again he laughed. "What do they know? Every man needs a good drink once in a while."

Kali said that he was eighty years old. He did not know the exact date of his birth but knew that he was born in the late summer of 1906. I tried to get him to talk about his father but he seemed somewhat reluctant. He preferred to talk about other matters.

"How is my cousin Anaukaq?" he asked.

"He is very well, and he sends you his regards," I replied.

"I have not seen him in many years, but I have thought of him often," Kali said. "I heard some years ago that he was very ill. Then later I learned that he had overcome this illness."

"Well, when I visited him, he was in good health and eating well," I said. "In fact, a few days ago, he and I ate *ahvuk* together."

"You have eaten *ahvuk?*" Kali asked with apparent amazement. "Did you like it?"

"Yes," I said. "It was tasty."

"That is wonderful. You should have brought me some. Did Ana-ukaq hunt this *ahvuk?*" he said, smiling as if he were teasing me.

"No, his son Avataq killed the *ahvuk,* but I am sure that Anaukaq is still a great hunter, just as you are. Both of you could still hunt the *ahvuk* if you so desired." This evoked a proud laugh. I had evidently said the right thing to flatter the old hunter.

"Oh, maybe," he said. "I try to shoot a seal now and then if I pass one on the ice, but I leave the hunting to my son, Talilanguaq, and my grandson Ole. They are both *peeneeahktoe wah.*"

"Where do you come from?" Kali inquired.

"The United States. Boston," I said.

"How far away from Qeqertarsaaq is that?" he asked.

"Several thousand miles away. Here, I'll show you." I drew a rough map of Greenland and the United States on my interview notepad. "You are here, and Boston is here," I said, pointing to marks on the map.

"Mmmm, seems very far away. Is that where Mahri-Pahluk's fam-ily lives?" Kali asked.

"I'm afraid I don't know. But I would think they might live in Maryland, about here on the map," I said, pointing. "That is where Mahri-Pahluk was born."

"What about Peeuree. Where was he from?" Kali asked.

"He was born in Pennsylvania, about here on the map, but he grew up in Maine—here, north of Boston."

"Is his family still there?" he asked.

"I honestly don't know where his family lives, but I can try to find out when I return to the United States," I said.

Kali said nothing. He just stared at the map for a while, expres-sionless.

In subsequent conversations, Kali opened up to me and talked about his own family. Kali and his wife, Eqariusaq, had five chil-dren—two boys and three daughters. Like Anaukaq, Kali had suf-fered the loss of his first son. Peter (his Christianized name) had died some years earlier from a gunshot wound which the authorities ruled to be self-inflicted. Some family members and other local Eskimos suspected that Peter had been the victim of foul play following an alcohol-related argument with a close acquaintance. Whatever the truth of the matter, it was clear that his death remained a source of profound grief. "It hurts when I speak of him," Kali said.

Everyone I spoke with had nothing but praise for Peter, who is survived by his wife and three children. He was, by all accounts, handsome, charming, bright, and a natural leader. He was also a skilled hunter. As a young man he traveled throughout northwest Greenland with Ussarkaq Henson, Anaukaq's third son, who eventually became his best friend. Peter and Ussarkaq hunted together and even courted their respective wives together. According to Ussarkaq, they often discussed their common dream of one day visiting America to search for their relatives, but Peter died before they could make any concrete plans.

After Peter's death, Kali's second son, Talilanguaq, assumed responsibility for supplying the family with most of its food. Now forty-five years old, Talilanguaq bears a remarkable resemblance to photographs of young Robert Peary. He is reputed to be one of the best all-round hunters in the region, just as his father had been in his younger days. On occasion he has also worked as a guide for the European adventurers who regularly visit the area. Hoping to secure some niche in history or simply to live out their fantasies, these would-be explorers hire highly skilled Eskimo dogsled drivers such as Talilanguaq to take them to the North Pole. The Eskimos joke about their employers, many of whom treat the journey as if it were a long taxi ride. Others end up traveling part of the distance by plane. Nevertheless, Talilanguaq himself seemed proud to have followed in his grandfather's footsteps. I later learned that both his brother Peter and Avataq Henson had journeyed to the Pole at some point in their lives.

Talilanguaq's son Ole, who is nineteen years old, also works as a hunter, having chosen to follow the traditional Eskimo way of life rather than attend school and take a job with the Danes. It was Ole I had seen carving the seal when I first reached the settlement. Talilanguaq has one other son, Ossmus, and three daughters, Paulina, Tukumaq, and Om'ayekeycho.

Talilanguaq's eldest sister, also named Paulina, is a teacher in the village of Qaanaaq and a well-known figure in local Greenlandic politics. She is the mother of three sons, one of whom recently committed suicide. Another son, named Sip'soo, has worked around the American air base at Thule and speaks some English. Now in his thirties, he changed his name to Robert Peary II a few years back, ostensibly in defiance of taunts at school about his racial mixture.

Kali's other daughters, Marta and Mikissuk, are the wives of hunters and also live in Qaanaaq. Marta bore no children of her own but has adopted three Inuit orphans, while Mikissuk has five children.

Although Kali clearly preferred to focus on the present, the longer we talked, the more he reminisced about the past. He retained especially fond memories of Anaukaq. "Cousin Anaukaq is one of the greatest men I have known," he said. "Perhaps there has been no greater hunter in our country. Until he injured his eye in a hunting accident some years back, he was the best hunter around."

"We were the best of friends in our youth," he continued. "We always felt that we belonged to the same family because our Eskimo fathers, Kitdlaq and Peeahwahto, were brothers, and we lived together as one family for most of our youth. As young boys, we always called each other's father 'uncle,' and we called each other 'cousin.'"

Kali reiterated what Anaukaq had told me about Ahlikahsing-wah's relationship with Robert Peary. He said that his mother was already married to Peeahwahto when she first became involved with Peary in 1896, and that she worked as Peary's personal maid or "laundress." At the same time, Peary hired Peeahwahto as a hunter for his expedition, supplying him with a rifle and sending him away from the camp for extended periods. Peeahwahto and the other Eskimos were apparently aware that Peary was having sexual relations with Ahlikahsingwah. No one knows how Peeahwahto felt about this relationship, but many of the other Eskimos resented it.

In 1900 Ahlikahsingwah gave birth to Peary's first son, whom she named Anaukaq. Peary called the child "Sammy." Little Anaukaq Peary later developed the nickname "Hammy" among the Eskimos, many of whom have difficulty pronouncing the "s" sound. According to Kali, his brother Hammy died at the age of twenty-seven after developing "a hole in his stomach," most likely a perforated ulcer.

In 1903 Ahlikahsingwah gave birth to a daughter name Ahveahkotoo, who is believed to have been fathered by Peeahwahto. She, too, died many years ago.

Peeahwahto adopted Anaukaq-Hammy and Kali Peary and raised them as his own sons. He took them everywhere, especially on his long hunting trips across the great ice to the northern parts of Ellesmere Island, where game was abundant. He taught both boys to hunt and provide for themselves. If he had any ill feelings because they were fathered by another man, Peeahwahto never evinced this to Hammy or Kali. Peeahwahto died when Kali was about twelve years old. Ahlikahsingwah remarried, this time an Eskimo named Ulloriaq. At first Kali got along well with his new stepfather, but as time went on their relationship deteriorated, and, eventually, at age sixteen, Kali left home.

Kali's feelings about his real father, Robert Peary, were complicated. "I don't have much feeling for him," he told me. "But I have nothing against him. Peeuree did nothing for me when I was growing up. He did not help me or my mother in any way. It was my mother who meant everything to me. She raised me and looked after me like a good mother. Some of the Eskimo people used to call her a cheap woman because of her relationship with Peeuree. This kind of talk caused her great pain and sadness. I never thought anything was wrong with her. I loved my mother. But I was ashamed of the name-calling she had to endure after Peeuree abandoned us. The other children often teased me for being part *kadoona* (white-skinned). This used to hurt me. [But] my mother was very protective of me."

Not surprisingly, Kali never identified with the Danes or other white Europeans with whom he occasionally came in contact. Like Anaukaq, he thought of himself exclusively as an Eskimo. When our discussion turned to the conquest of the North Pole, a subject in which he professed little interest, Kali made it clear that his own hero in that saga was neither Peary nor Henson, but Ootah. "Without Ootah and the other Eskimos," he said, "they never would have made it to the North Pole."

Kali's regard for Ootah is shared by most Polar Eskimos, including the Hensons. Renown for his dogsled driving and hunting skills as well as for his bravery, Ootah was thirty-one years old when he accompanied Peary and Henson on the 1906 polar expedition that fell short of its goal by some 120 miles. Witnessing the dejection of the Americans, he promised that if they ever made another attempt, they could count on his participation. True to his word, he was there to greet Peary's ship when it returned to Etah two years later.

By all accounts Ootah was on particularly friendly terms with Matthew Henson, whom he seems to have genuinely liked and admired. Together the two men prepared for the final assault on the Pole, hunting game and setting up the advance camp that would serve as the launching point. Once the expedition was underway, Ootah joined Henson in breaking the trail. Even when some of the other Eskimos turned back out of fear of the "ice devil," Ootah stayed on.

Henson later reported that on April 3, 1909, three days before they reached the Pole, he was pushing his sled across a lane of moving ice when the ice slipped from beneath his feet, plunging him and his sled into the frigid water. Struggling frantically to pull himself out, but unable to grip the ice with his gloved hand, he had just about given up hope when Ootah grabbed him by the neck of his parka, pulled him to safety with one hand, and with the other hoisted the dogsled out of the water. He had saved Henson's life as well as the sled carrying the expedition's vital navigational and scientific equipment.

As a tribute to Ootah's contributions to Arctic exploration, the northernmost point of land in the world, an island just off the coast of northern Greenland, was recently named in his honor.

Yet if Kali thought of himself first and foremost as an Eskimo, he was still curious about his American relatives. He knew that he had had an older half sister whom the Eskimos called *Ahnighito* (Snowbaby). The daughter of Robert Peary and his wife, Josephine, who accompanied her husband on one of his early expeditions, she was believed to be the first white child born in the Arctic. But she had been taken back to the United States long before Kali was born. Kali later learned that some of the American Peary family had visited the Cape York region of Greenland in 1932 to dedicate a monument to their father. According to some of the Eskimos who went to meet them, Ahnighito was among those present. Kali hoped that I could tell him more about the American Pearys, but unfortunately I knew little about them. I did tell him, however, of Anaukaq's interest in meeting his American relatives and of my plans to assist him in achieving that goal.

"When we were young men," Kali remembered, "Anaukaq and I talked about going over there to find our fathers, but it was never possible for us to go. If cousin Anaukaq goes over there to visit his relatives and see Mahri-Pahluk's grave, I would like to join him. I would like to meet my father's other family."

I gave him my word that I would search for his American relatives as well and would see whether I could arrange for him to meet them.

I stayed with Kali and his family for several weeks. During that time I became convinced that he was indeed "the second son of Ahli-kahsingwah and Peeuree." In part I was persuaded by a physical resemblance to Robert Peary and in part, by his own testimony and that of other older Eskimos in the area. But most of all, it was the way he talked more than the words he spoke that erased any lingering doubts: the sorrow that filled his eyes when he described his mother's relationship with "Peeuree"; his insistence that he was not a *kahdonah* but an Eskimo; the longing he expressed to see his father's grave and meet Peary's "other" American family. Intuition may be an unreliable guide, but if this man was not the son of Robert Peary, it was clear that he had spent his entire lifetime believing he was.

* * *

Before leaving Qeqertarsaaq, I tested Kali's hearing as part of my audiological study. Like Anaukaq and other hunters I had examined, he too had a degenerative nerve-hearing loss caused by the repeated use of high-powered rifles. Otherwise, he was in excellent health.

"Perhaps we could get the Greenlandic government to provide you with a hearing aid," I suggested.

"Oh, I hear what I want to hear," he joked. " I would rather have them give me a good bottle of whiskey."

Kali was not a heavy drinker, but he enjoyed a glass of spirits now and then. Active and spry for his age, he was continually joking and telling stories. As I had with Anaukaq, I felt that with Kali I had made a new friend.

CHAPTER FIVE

✳ ✳ ✳

"Hallelujah!"/"Not interested"

Determined to keep my promise to Anaukaq and Kali, I began my search for their American relatives as soon as I returned to the United States. I started by working my way through the telephone directories of New York City, Matthew Henson's home for more than fifty years, and Charles County, Maryland, his birthplace. My efforts produced no leads, however, until several newspapers printed the story of my journey north.

"Hallelujah! God bless you, son, for finding our relatives," shouted Olive Henson Fulton, rushing forward to embrace me. "We never knew Uncle Matt had any children."

By now she was squeezing me with excitement. She gave me a big kiss on the cheek, and as she stood back to look at me I could see the tears streaming down her cheeks. "I can't believe it," she said again and again. "Uncle Matt has children in the Arctic."

Olive is a brown-skinned woman of sixty years with a round face, wavy white hair, and a warm, sincere demeanor. About five feet four inches tall and full-figured, she is the image of everyone's favorite aunt. After reading about my discovery of Anaukaq and Kali in the *Boston Globe*, she had called my Harvard office and excitedly told me that her grandfather, David Henson, was Matthew Henson's brother, and she, Matthew's great-niece. She also said that she had photographs of her grandfather and her Uncle Matt, which she would be happy to show me. We arranged to meet at her home in the Roxbury community of Boston.

Concerned about my ability to locate her house as well as for my safety in her neighborhood, Olive had come out to the corner to meet me. I spotted her from a distance, waving her arms above her head. She then led me to her first-floor apartment in a modest two-family house situated at the edge of a train track. We sat down in a small, quaintly furnished living room, surrounded by shelves of books that extended from floor to ceiling.

After some small talk to get better acquainted, we began to review the history of the American Henson clan. We talked at length—at times laughing together, at times choking with emotion—and the more we talked the more convinced I became that I had indeed found a consanguineous relative of Matthew Henson. Olive showed me photographs of several family members, including her grandfather, David Henson, who bore a clear resemblance to Matthew at the same age. She explained that her grandfather had migrated to Boston from Maryland around the turn of the century. There he had married and raised five children, one of whom was her father, George.

As a young girl, Olive had traveled with her family to New York on many occasions to visit with her great-uncle Matt. During these visits he would talk with his curious little niece about his trip to the North Pole, showing her photos, maps, and artifacts from the Arctic.

"I felt so proud when I saw Uncle Matt," she recalled. "He was always impeccably dressed and dignified, and he spoke so humbly of his achievements. Uncle Matt had a love for children, although he had no children with his wife Lucy. He would always give me a big hug, sit me on his knee, and tell stories about his life with the Eskimos in Greenland.

"I remember that one time I couldn't wait to return to my school in Boston to tell the other children about my great-uncle who had gone to the North Pole with Admiral Robert Peary. But when I told my classmates and teachers, no one believed me. In fact, one teacher scolded me and called me a liar in front of the class and sent me home from school. This crushed me. When my father came home I told him what had happened. He held me in his arms and said, 'Don't worry, dear. We know the truth. In our hearts, we can keep the truth even if they don't want to know it.' This memory has stuck with me throughout my life and made me determined to share with everyone the stories that Uncle Matt told me."

A clerk at a nearby Veterans Administration hospital, Olive had volunteered some of her off-duty time to work with youngsters from inner-city neighborhoods. Hoping to instill in them a sense of cultural pride, she taught them about their African-American heritage and the contributions made by black Americans in all walks of life. She taught them about Martin Luther King, Jr., about Malcolm X, and, of course, about her own great-uncle, Matthew Henson.

Now, with my discovery of the existence of Anaukaq, a new chapter had been added to her great-uncle's story. When I showed her photographs of Anaukaq and his family, Olive's eyes welled with tears. "My goodness, Anaukaq looks just like Uncle Matt. Incredible!" she said. "I can still see him in some of the grandchildren and great-grandchildren as well. Are they okay? Do they have enough food and clothes and things?"

"Well, they do not have many material things," I replied, "but they are fine. They all have jobs as hunters to provide food for their families, and some have jobs with the Danish government."

"Can I do anything for them?" she asked. "I don't have much but I could send them something, you know, to help them if they need it."

I told her I didn't think that would be necessary, but that I would be returning to Greenland in a few months and would tell Anaukaq about her. I knew Anaukaq would be thrilled to know that I had found his cousin Olive.

"Is there any way I can go up there with you?" she asked. "I don't mind the rough travel if you get me there."

"That may be possible in the future," I told her. "But first I would love to bring Anaukaq and Kali here. Both have told me that their lifelong dream has been to visit America to meet their relatives and see their fathers' graves."

"Then please bring them," Olive said. "They can stay right here with me. I can host a big family reunion with all of our relatives. They all want to meet our Eskimo relatives. There are about thirty-five of us here, and others you might find in other parts of the country. They can all come to Boston. We can invite the Peary family, too. I'll cook some good American soul food for them: fried chicken, ham, sweet potatoes, cornbread, black-eyed peas, homemade ice cream—everything."

I laughed. "Did you know that they eat most of their food raw?"

Olive paused, then said, "Well, I'll prepare something raw on the side. But *everybody* likes soul food."

As we bade each other an emotional farewell, Olive began searching among her things for a gift to send Anaukaq. After considering several articles, she settled on a beautiful multicolored wool blanket that she had recently knitted.

"Please tell Anaukaq that his cousin Olive wants him to have this," she said.

We also selected several family photographs for Anaukaq—one of Olive, one of her grandfather David, one of her father, and a few of other members of the American Henson clan. I knew that Anaukaq would love all these presents. I could imagine his reaction and could even hear his infectious laughter ringing out over the tiny village of Moriussaq.

*   *   *

I had no idea which Peary family members were alive or where they lived, although I knew that Peary and his wife, Josephine, had had several children. Marie Ahnighito Peary, their eldest child, had gained early notoriety as the first white person born in northwest Greenland. The story of her birth in 1894 was later recounted in a popular book entitled *Snowbaby,* written by her mother. A second child, Francine, had died in infancy. Their third child, Robert E. Peary, Jr., was born in 1903.

My search for Admiral Peary's descendants began at his alma mater, Bowdoin College in Brunswick, Maine. Bowdoin is the home of the Peary-MacMillan Arctic Museum, which I had visited previously to collect photographs of Peary, Henson, and other members of their expeditionary teams. It was there that I learned that Marie Peary had married Edward Stafford and had two sons, Edward P. Stafford, Jr., and Peary Stafford.

I decided to try to track down the Staffords, but, as it turned out, they contacted me first.

"Are you Dr. Allen Counter?" the caller asked, identifying himself as "a member of the Peary-Stafford family."

"Yes, I am," I replied. "I'm so glad you called. I have been trying to locate some of the American Pearys." There was silence at the other end of the line. "Well, what do you think about the news of Kali?" I continued excitedly.

"I have read articles about your work in the Arctic and your statements about the so-called offspring of Robert Peary," he said in a cold, flat voice.

I assured the caller that I had indeed "found a man and his family in Greenland who say they are the descendants of Admiral Robert E. Peary."

"Why are you doing this?" he asked accusingly.

"I beg your pardon?" I said.

"Why are you doing this?" he repeated. "Why are you bringing this out?"

I explained that I simply wanted to share with members of the Peary and Henson families the fact that I had found two families in northwest Greenland who had convinced me they are the descendants of Robert Peary in one case and of Matthew Henson in the other.

"I thought that perhaps you might like to make contact with them," I said somewhat uncomfortably. "Have I upset your family by revealing information about Kali? I mean, if I have, I have certainly not done so intentionally."

"Our family just wondered what your motives are for making this thing public," he responded. "We are not pleased with all of this."

I reassured him that I meant no disrespect or harm to the family. When he indicated his desire to end the conversation, I asked him whether he thought that there were people in the American Peary family who might be willing to meet Kali, and if so, would he give me their names.

"Not interested," he said.

Hoping to elicit some sign of compassion, I offered to send some photographs of Kali and his family and asked whether someone might be willing at least to write to them. "They are a very lovely family," I said.

The caller then told me that one member of the Peary-Stafford family had been designated as "our representative" to handle all public information on Robert Peary and his memorabilia. "I'll give you his telephone number. You should call him," he said. He gave me the number and said good-bye. Before he could hang up, I quickly asked him if we could discuss the matter again. I emphasized that it had been Kali's lifelong dream to meet his American relatives.

"I don't know," he said, politely but coolly. "I will call you if I think we should talk."

I never heard from him again.

My first contact with the Peary family left me shaken and depressed. Amid all the excitement of my discovery, I had never considered the possibility that the Pearys might not welcome the news I was bringing them. Upon reflection, however, I came to realize that the Pearys' mistrust was understandable, if not fully excusable. There was, to begin with, the issue of "legitimacy." The Pearys were probably embarrassed by the fact that the admiral had fathered a child out of wedlock, perhaps believing that it tarnished his image and compromised his achievements. In addition, they might have suspected financial motives. Both Kali and Anaukaq were, technically speaking, Americans. Both were born on an American ship, the USS *Roosevelt*, to American fathers undertaking a mission in the service of their country. Robert E. Peary held the rank of commander in the U.S. Navy at the time, while Matthew Henson was officially listed as Peary's "valet," which was, in most cases, the highest naval rank then attainable by a black. Maybe, I thought, the Pearys suspected that Kali intended to lay claim to a share of the family inheritance or seek some other form of recompense. Although I couldn't be certain that such fears underlay their rejection of Kali, I knew that neither Kali nor I had ever considered asking the Pearys for anything but a warm and friendly welcome. I just needed to convince the Peary family that this was the case.

The Peary-Stafford family's designated "representative" was no less cold and guarded than the first person I had spoken with. I introduced myself, this time mentioning my work at Harvard in an effort to convey credibility. I told him I was calling at the suggestion of one of his relatives. He seemed to have been expecting to hear from me. He began by raising the same question I had encountered before: "Why are you bringing this out before the public now?"

I repeated my story to him.

He told me that his family already knew about Peary's Eskimo offspring and that his "Uncle Bob," the explorer's son, had met one of his relatives on a trip to Greenland in the 1920s. I told him that I found this rather odd because Kali had said that he'd never met any of his American relatives.

"Maybe," I suggested, "your uncle met Kali's brother Anaukaq who, the Eskimos say, was also Peary's son."

"Don't believe everything the Eskimos tell you," he responded brusquely.

I was surprised to learn that the American Pearys already knew something about the admiral's Amer-Eskimo progeny. But I was equally intrigued to learn that Robert Peary, Jr., was still alive. My quick calculations told me that he must be around eighty-three years old. The family representative confirmed this and informed me that Robert Jr. was currently living in Augusta, Maine.

Wouldn't it be great, I thought to myself, if Kali and Robert Jr., half brothers who had been separated throughout their lives, were at last brought together? I shared the thought of a brother-to-brother meeting with the family representative.

"I will speak to him about it," he promised, adding that he personally believed "such a meeting is out of the question. We're not interested."

I decided to press the issue. "Why is your family so opposed to meeting this kindly old man who does not have many years left and who simply wants to meet some of his American relatives? Why are you and your family reacting this way?"

"Dr. Counter, you don't understand," the family representative said. "Let me share a story with you." He proceeded to tell me a long story about a film on the North Pole discovery that had appeared on

American television some years ago, featuring Rod Steiger as Robert Peary and Richard Chamberlain as Frederick Cook. (He never mentioned Matthew Henson or who played his role.) "When we saw that Richard Chamberlain was playing the role of Cook, we knew the film was going to do our grandfather in," he said. The film had "totally distorted my grandfather's image and discredited his name," he continued, leaving his family "greatly disturbed." He then drew an analogy between the film and my own efforts to bring Kali and Anaukaq to the United States. While he understood that "these Eskimos would welcome a free ticket to America," he also believed that the publicity attending their return would tarnish the Peary family image.

When he finished his story, I told him in a conciliatory tone that I was sorry the television show had been so negative in its portrayal of his grandfather's achievements. "I am in no way trying to discredit that legacy," I assured him, "but to validate it. And I appeal to you and your family not to view me or Kali in the same light as this movie. I would simply like for you to see Kali as a human being who has a genuine desire to meet his American relatives before he dies. He has said that to me."

Apparently unmoved by my words, the family representative reaffirmed that the Peary-Staffords had no interest in meeting with Kali and his family. He again reminded me of the still-extant "supporters of Peary's adversary Frederick Cook, who liked this kind of information and who would use it as ammunition against Peary's credibility as the discoverer of the North Pole."

I made further appeals, but to no avail. No matter what I said, I could not break the link in his mind between my own motives and the machinations of those who sought to discredit Admiral Peary. Frustrated as I was, I became even more unsettled when the suggestion was made that Kali might not actually be Robert Peary's son, but rather the son of some other member of his expeditionary team. I was convinced that if the Pearys would only agree to meet the man, to see his face and listen to his story, any doubts they might have about his paternity would quickly be erased. Additional evidence could be found in the testimony of those older Eskimos who knew about the relationship between Peary and Ahlikahsingwah.

"Well," the family representative groaned, "we can't be sure of this or just what all went on up there."

"If you have such strong doubts about the validity of Kali Peary's claims, sir, we can easily settle this question beyond a shadow of a doubt with a relatively simple new blood test called a DNA fragmentation analysis—that is, if Kali and his half brother would agree to such a test."

"No," he answered. "Such a test would be demeaning for both men."

The family representative then fell back on another argument, claiming that Peary had been forced by local custom to engage in sexual relations with the indigenous women, including Ahlikahsingwah. "That was a condition of Peary's association with the Eskimo villagers who served his expeditionary interest. He had to have sex with the women before he could gain their confidence."

This contention was based on a long-standing myth about polar Eskimo culture, the notion that men routinely offered their wives to outsiders. This was not the case. Within the Eskimo community, men and women alike exchanged spouses with one another for reasons of fertility and, in some cases, pleasure. But non-Eskimo men who engaged in sex with Eskimo women usually exchanged Western material goods for favors. At times the women's husbands also derived some material benefit from such relationships, such as a gun or a hatchet or cooking utensils. Existing records of such liaisons further suggest that the women who consorted with outsiders, and especially with Westerners, were often criticized for their behavior by other members of the community.

Robert Peary's relationship with Kali's mother, Ahlikahsingwah, seems to have fit this pattern. Peary had known Ahlikahsingwah since she was a child and may have developed an intimate relationship with her when she was a teenager. Peary employed his mistress as his laundress and bodyservant and hired her husband, Peeahwahto, as a hunter, supplying him with a rifle. According to Kali, his mother subsequently fell into disrepute within the Eskimo community because of her relationship with Peary.

As my conversation with the Peary family representative came to a close, I asked him to find out whether any of his relatives felt differently from him about meeting Kali. I was especially interested in talking with Robert Peary, Jr., although I was also concerned about the emotional impact such a discussion might have on him. The spokesperson said he would pass along my request and even agreed to send me the names of some family members so that I could contact them myself. I suspected that his willingness to provide such information reflected his certainty that all the Pearys shared his views.

In the weeks that followed, I spoke with many more members of the Henson family, all of whom seemed delighted to learn of their Amer-Eskimo relatives. Like Cousin Olive, they wanted to send gifts to Greenland and to help in any way they could to bring about a reunion in the United States.

Meanwhile, I called various members of the Peary family and told them of my plans for another visit to northern Greenland. I wanted to know if I could take Kali some word or letter or anything that would indicate that his American relatives were now aware of him and that they cared about him. Some of those I contacted refused to discuss the matter, while others made it clear that they were not interested in communicating with Kali.

During the same period, I received a discouraging letter from someone claiming to be related to a member of one of Peary's early expeditionary teams. Hostile in tone, the letter stated baldly that I was off the mark in my efforts to "exalt" Henson and to "question" Peary. The writer accused me of using "bastardy" as a way of discrediting Peary.

A short time later, a letter from one of the Peary family members similarly charged me with exalting Henson at the expense of Peary. This second letter arrived soon after I gave a lecture at the Woods Hole Oceanographic Institution and Marine Biological Laboratories for scientists and local citizens. After the lecture, I was interviewed on a local radio program about the significance of Matthew Henson's contribution to Peary's Arctic successes. My comments had apparently been reported to the Peary-Staffords. The same letter once again tried to explain away Peary's sexual relations with Eskimos as cultural rituals in which he had reluctantly engaged in order to advance his nobler mission.

Despite such criticism, I still hoped to persuade the Pearys that they were wrong about me and, more important, wrong in refusing to get in touch with Kali. After learning that Robert Peary, Jr., had a son who lived with him in Augusta, Maine, I decided that I would broach the subject of a reunion with him. When I reached Robert Peary III by telephone, I found him pleasant and soft-spoken. He expressed the now familiar concern about the effects of media reports of Kali on his grandfather's image and reminded me that the designated Peary-Stafford representative spoke for him, too. Yet unlike the family representative, he seemed willing to consider my point of view and showed some sensitivity to what I was trying to do. Nevertheless, he was still opposed to any further publicity about the "so-called" Peary Eskimo offspring and unwilling to arrange a meeting between Kali and his father.

As I prepared to set out again for the Arctic, I wrestled with the question of what I would tell Kali. I knew that telling him the truth would hurt him deeply. Yet I could not conceive of lying to him either. I could certainly leave out parts of the story in good conscience. He did not need to know, for instance, that some of the Pearys had apparently known about him for years but had never seen any reason to contact him or even to acknowledge his existence. But I would have to tell him that I had spoken with some of his American relatives and that they had expressed no interest in meeting him, at least not in public. I would try to explain why they reacted as they did, and I would continue to hold out hope that they might eventually change their minds. Finally, if I could arrange for the Amer-Eskimo Hensons to visit the United States, I would give him the opportunity to accompany them so that he could at least visit the grave of his father. Beyond that, there was little that I could offer Kali other than the knowledge I had gained through my own research into the lives of Robert E. Peary and Matthew A. Henson, the fathers that he and his "cousin" Anaukaq had never known.

CHAPTER SIX

* * *

Black and White Partners

Matthew Henson was born on August 8, 1866,[1] in Charles County, Maryland, the son of freeborn sharecroppers who worked on a large farm near what is today the town of Nanjemoy. When he was about four years old, his parents moved the family some thirty miles north to Washington, D.C., where jobs for blacks as servants and technical workers were available. Within a few years, however, both of his parents died, and Matthew and several of his siblings were taken in by an uncle who also resided in Washington.

In 1879, at the age of thirteen, Henson left school and went to Baltimore, hoping to land a job on one of the many ships leaving port. Throughout his young life he had been fascinated by stories of life at sea and had marveled at the men who worked the steamboats on the Potomac. He later told a biographer that he was fortunate enough to meet an elderly sea captain in Baltimore who was looking for a cabin boy to assist him. Given the job, Henson set out on voyages that would take him around the world in the years that followed. Bright, eager to learn, hardworking, and exceptionally strong for his age, he became "an able-bodied seaman" and sailed to such exotic venues as China, Japan, North Africa, and the Black Sea. During his years at sea he continued his education, studying geography, mathematics, history, the classics, and the Bible under the cap-

tain's tutelage. He also displayed a knack for learning foreign lan-
guages, a talent that would serve him well throughout his life.

When the captain of the ship died in 1884, Henson, now eighteen
years old, gave up seafaring for a time and returned to the United
States. During the next two years he traveled up and down the
eastern seaboard, taking on whatever odd jobs might be available to a
young black man in need of work.

In 1886, Henson returned to Washington, D.C., and moved in
with his sister Eliza and her family at 3003 West P Street in the
northwest section of the city. Soon thereafter he found a job as a clerk
at F. W. Stinemetz & Sons, an exclusive capital furrier. Charged with
responsibility for storing furs, recording sales, and keeping an accurate inventory of goods in the warehouse, Henson quickly earned the
trust and respect of his employers.

Yet while he continued to work diligently at his job, he was in fact
biding his time. Already a seasoned world traveler, he longed to
resume the adventurous life he had known. All that was needed was
the right opportunity.

The man who would afford Matthew Henson that opportunity
had led a far different life. Born on May 6, 1856, in Cresson, Pennsylvania, Robert Edwin Peary was the only child of Mary Webster Wiley
and Charles Nutter Peary. Following his father's death in 1858, Peary
and his mother had moved back to the family's home state of Maine.
It was there that Robert Peary was raised and educated.

A bright and physically active child, Peary performed superbly in
school and soon developed a reputation as a dedicated achiever. His
academic successes eventually earned him a scholarship to Bowdoin
College in Brunswick, Maine, where he majored in civil engineering
and also participated in a variety of sports and social organizations.
He graduated from Bowdoin second in his class, with a Phi Beta
Kappa key, in 1877.

No matter how much he accomplished, however, Peary always
seemed to aspire to more. From an early age he had made it clear that
he intended to make his mother proud of him. He wanted to achieve
great things. He wanted the world to know his name.

Grand as his ambitions were, Peary's professional career began
modestly enough. After graduating from Bowdoin he moved to

Washington, D.C., to work for the U.S. Coast and Geodetic Survey Office. In the next two years he came to be regarded as one of that agency's best draftsmen, enabling him to become an officer with the rank of lieutenant in the U.S. Navy Corps of Civil Engineers. Both of these jobs gave him access to the resources of the government's civil engineering offices and the opportunity to travel widely.

It is difficult to say just when Peary developed an interest in Arctic exploration. Some believe that it was a long-standing interest that can be traced back to a childhood fascination with the adventurous accounts of the Arctic explorer Elisha Kent Kane. Others contend that it was Baron Nordenskjold's book on Greenland that initially aroused Peary's curiosity about the far north. In any case, the first clear expression of Peary's interest in the Arctic occurred in 1886, when he requested and received a six-month leave of absence from the U.S. Navy to reconnoiter the Greenland ice cap east of Disco Bay.

That summer Peary sailed to an area of Greenland some two hundred miles north of the Arctic Circle to determine the feasibility of reaching the North Pole by an overland route. Braving constant danger and surviving a series of narrow escapes, Peary and a Danish assistant made the first recorded journey to the interior ice cap of lower Arctic Greenland, reaching a record altitude of 7,525 feet above sea level on July 15, 1886.

Upon returning to Washington, Peary formally presented his findings, which included excellent maps of the Greenlandic interior. Praised by scientists and laypeople alike, these reports gave him his first taste of popular recognition. Invitations to lecture poured in and he was soon elected to the American Society for the Advancement of Science.

Although the success of the Greenland expedition reinforced Peary's belief that he could reach the North Pole, his naval obligations forced him to postpone his quest indefinitely. During the next two years he worked on several inland waterways projects, performing admirably in each instance. Then, in 1888, he was assigned to an ambitious new government-sponsored project in Nicaragua. The project involved a study of the feasibility of cutting a shipping canal through lower Nicaragua that would connect the Atlantic and Pacific oceans. Mindful of the strategic and commercial significance of the venture, Peary regarded the assignment as another opportunity to win the renown he so eagerly sought.

In preparation for his departure, Peary took a collection of valuable furs he had acquired in Greenland to Stinemetz & Sons for storage. It was not the first time he had visited the firm. On several previous occasions he had brought other Arctic furs, which he eventually planned to sell. Each time, in addition to meeting with the proprietors, he had encountered a young black man who seemed to share his passion for exploration. Intelligent, articulate, forthright, and courteous, Matthew Henson had made a strong impression on Lieutenant Peary. The two men had exchanged travel stories and perhaps talked of future journeys. Now, as Peary readied himself for his new mission, he decided to offer Henson a job as his "personal assistant" in Nicaragua. Henson accepted.

Before hiring Henson, Peary had had little contact with black Americans. Like most European Americans of his time, he seems to have accepted common shibboleths about the "natural superiority" of the white race, views that found backing in much of the "scientific" literature of the period. Yet the state where he grew up had few African-American residents and no tradition of legalized racial slavery. Peary's own understanding of the biological basis of racial difference is reflected in several of his writings. For example, in 1885 he wrote, "If colonization is to be a success in Polar regions, let white men take with them native wives, then from that union may spring a race combining the hardiness of the mothers with the intelligence and energy of the fathers."[2] Another writing refers to "the mixed race in South Greenland, which, in spite of the fostering care of the Danish Government, is still like most half-breed human products, inferior to the original stock."[3]

Some of Peary's other writings, however, suggest that he believed that members of all races were human beings first and foremost. His upbringing had taught him to be charitable to his less-fortunate, though "inferior," brethren. In a culture steeped in racism, Peary's racial attitudes might thus be described as sympathetic, even "liberal," if not truly enlightened.

Whatever Peary may have thought about blacks in general, it is clear that he developed a sincere respect for Matthew Henson. During the year the two men worked together in the steamy jungles of Nicaragua, Henson's multiple skills as a mechanic, carpenter, and navigator proved invaluable. Peary later lauded his assistant for his "intelligence, faithfulness, and better than average pluck and endurance"[4]—qualities usually attributed at the time exclusively to white males. Henson reciprocated by praising Lieutenant Peary's fairness, noting that "it was with the instinct of my race that I recognized in him the qualities that made me willing to engage myself in his service."[5]

Although Peary and Henson went their separate ways after returning to the United States, their shared experience in Nicaragua forged a bond between them that would not be easily broken. In the context of the time, their relationship was as close to a friendship as one could imagine between a white boss and a black assistant. They also complemented each other. In Henson, Peary had found an experienced, multitalented aide willing to travel anywhere in support of his ventures. In Peary, Henson had found a well-disposed white sponsor, without whom he had no hope of satisfying his own thirst for travel. Of more immediate and practical importance to Henson, Peary also represented a potential source of continued employment. It was with this in mind that Henson wrote to the lieutenant soon after arriving back in Washington.

West Washington D.C.
Aug 1st 1888
Mr. R.E. Peary

Dear Sir
   I write you these few lines hoping that they may find you enjoying the best of health and that you are having a good time. I arrived in Washington all safe last Saturday at 11/30.
   Mr Peary please let me know when you are going back to Nicaragua, for I will be pleased to go with you again. I have not had any work yet. I now come to a close hoping to hear from you soon.

M.A. Henson
#3003 P Street. Georgetown D.C.[6]

Still unable to find work, Henson wrote Peary a second letter some months later.

Dear Sir

 I write you a few lines to let you know that all is well at this present time. As I had written to you before I am not doing any work yet and if you want me to go back with you when you go back to Nicaragua I will be pleased to go with you indeed sir. And if you want me I would like to know as soon as I can. And I would like to stay for a year or more or as long as you stay, if I pleased you with my work when I was with you before.

 And I hope to hear from you soon.

From a friend,
Matthew Henson

When he did not hear anything from Peary, Henson returned to his old job at Stinemetz. Then, in early 1889, Peary wrote to ask if Henson would be interested in working as a "messenger" at the League Island Navy Yard in Philadelphia, where Peary had recently been reassigned. Though it was not the opportunity Henson had hoped for, he quickly accepted. What he did not yet know was that Peary had already begun making plans for his first polar expedition and intended to take Henson along.

Peary moved to Philadelphia soon after his marriage in 1889 to Josephine Diebitsch, the daughter of a prominent Washington professor. Henson followed in the spring of 1890, taking up residence at 1524 Burton Street in the heart of the city's black community.

Philadelphia was widely regarded at the time as one of the better American cities for blacks. For much of the nineteenth century it had boasted the largest freeborn black population in the United States. Until they were displaced through the organized efforts of Irish and German immigrants, blacks dominated many of the city's trades, including carpentry, masonry, and blacksmithing. As a result, many black Philadelphians had achieved a level of economic prosperity and social respectability uncommon, if not altogether unknown, among African Americans elsewhere.

Yet as young Matthew Henson discovered, gaining entry into the city's black community was not easy. Despite his wide-ranging experience and respectable position as an employee at the navy yard, he was still considered an outsider. He had little in the way of formal education and did not belong to any of the trade organizations that served as the main source of employment for many black men.

Hoping to gain acceptance and get ahead, Henson joined a local church and began attending Sunday outings in the influential Juniper Street area of the black community. It was on one such occasion in late September 1890 that he met Eva Helen Flint, a twenty-two-year-old sales assistant in a local store. Henson was charmed by the attractive Eva, and she by him. He began to frequent the store where she worked, bringing her small gifts to show his affection. From time to time, he would see her strolling through the park on Sunday evenings with the other young African-American Philadelphia ladies. Eva was a fabulous dresser whose passion for fine clothes complemented Henson's own dapper style. The two seemed made for each other. After a month of secret meetings, Eva invited Matthew home to meet her family.

The Flints were a large, educated, and conservative family that had moved to Philadelphia from Washington, D.C., to work in the thriving trades. Although inclined to be skeptical of a young man pursuing the hand of any of the Flint women, they were thoroughly charmed by the twenty-three-year-old Henson. The men, especially, were captivated by his tales of travel and adventure. In addition, his position at the navy yard was considered auspicious, since government jobs often carried pensions that could guarantee a family a modicum of economic security for a lifetime.

Matthew and Eva courted for several months, seeing each other as often as possible after work and on Sundays. By now, they were very much in love and seriously considering marriage. But Henson wanted to wait until he had saved enough money to purchase a home, ideally in the Juniper Street community. He also worried about his ability to support Eva's love of material things. Perhaps most important, his desire to settle down with Eva conflicted with his lust for adventure, and he knew that it would be difficult to reconcile these two impulses. Eva, on the other hand, was convinced she had found the right man and was eager to get away from the rigid control of her parents and brothers at home.

The issue of marriage was still unresolved when Robert Peary summoned Henson to his office in late February 1891. Peary had just received a letter from the navy granting him a long-sought leave of absence for the purpose of exploring northwest Greenland. He asked

Henson to come along as his personal assistant. Flattered by the invitation, Henson immediately accepted. This was, after all, the opportunity Henson had been waiting for, a chance not only to resume his travels but to distinguish himself and his race in the process. Perhaps no less than Peary, Henson sought recognition, although in Henson's case the goal was not so much fame as social acceptance. He had always admired the educated, successful blacks of Washington and Philadelphia but never felt their equal. Now, given the opportunity to go where no one, black or white, had ever gone before, he could surpass them in achievement. At the same time, he could disprove once and for all the widely held theory that black-skinned people could not survive in the Arctic, thus providing further proof of racial equality.

Acceptance of Peary's offer did present certain problems, however. In the first place, Henson could not obtain a leave of absence from his own position at the navy yard. If he gave up his job, there was no guarantee that he would get it back upon his return. In addition, he would have to give up his regular, fifteen-dollar weekly wage in exchange for an annual salary of fifty dollars. This meant that if he did get married, it would be difficult to support his wife back home.

Not surprisingly, Eva tried to persuade Henson to decline Peary's offer and stay on at the navy yard. Henson in turn tried to convince Eva that if he made the journey with this ambitious young white man, not only would he achieve personal fame, but Peary would take care of him in the future, as well. Such were the arrangements that white men had with their loyal "colored" assistants in those days. Eva was skeptical; her family, even more so. They urged Eva to refuse to marry Henson, at least until he returned.

But Eva and Matthew were in love, and they both thought it was time to make a decision. Henson consulted Peary and his wife, Josephine, and they were encouraging. Peary felt that marriage would give Henson stability, although he was privately concerned about its impact on Henson's flexibility. Already, it seems, he had special plans for young Henson on future Arctic expeditions.

On April 13, 1891, Eva Helen Flint and Matthew Alexander Henson filled out an application for marriage before the clerk of Orphan's

Court in Philadelphia. Three days later they were joined in marriage in the presence of a few friends and family members. During the next two months they lived with Eva's family, drawing up plans for the future and awaiting the departure of Peary's expedition.

In early June, Henson bade his wife farewell and traveled to Brooklyn, where he boarded the barkentine *Kite* and assumed his duties as Peary's assistant. In the late afternoon of June 6, 1891, the *Kite* set sail from Brooklyn. Throngs of well-wishers stood on the docks, waving white handkerchiefs, as the ship moved out to sea via the East River, en route to northwest Greenland.

In addition to Henson, the hand-picked expeditionary team included four other assistants, each selected on the basis of his "mental and physical well-being" as well as for the particular skill he offered: Frederick A. Cook, an affable young physician from New York; Eivind Astrup, an experienced Norwegian Arctic traveler; Langdon Gibson, an ornithologist from Long Island; and John M. Verhoeff, a mineralogist from Kentucky. Also among the passengers was Josephine Peary. As far as the American public was concerned, the presence of "the woman," as Mrs. Peary was commonly referred to, was no less unusual than that of Peary's black "manservant."

Henson, of course, was no mere servant. In addition to his skills as a carpenter and mechanic, he had more experience at sea than any other member of the expedition, including naval lieutenant Peary. He loved sailing in the open sea, and the 280-ton *Kite*, with its vast white sails and seven-knot steam engines, was his kind of ship. During the seven-week voyage, Henson spent most of his time doing inventories of the expedition's equipment and supplies, preparing for the landing.

After struggling through the frozen waters of Disco Bay and Baffin Bay, the *Kite* reached Wolstenholm Sound near the area of Itilleq. On July 26, Peary's party went ashore with pickaxes, shovels, and lumber and began to set up camp at the base of red-brown cliffs near the mouth of an inlet. The burden of work fell chiefly to Henson, whose carpentry skills were called upon to build a spacious two-room house that would serve as the expedition's headquarters. Henson and the other assistants labored long and hard to erect the large rectangular dwelling before the winter set in. Incapacitated by a

broken ankle, Peary could only observe and supervise the construction of "Red Cliff House," as it came to be called.

Completion of construction happened to coincide with Matthew
Henson's twenty-fifth birthday on August 8. In commemoration of
both events, Josephine Peary threw a party at which Henson was the
guest of honor. For his present, he was permitted to select the dinner
menu from their stores and to eat as much as he wished. In *A Negro
Explorer at the North Pole*, Henson later described the occasion as
among the most memorable of his life.

The group spent the fall and winter acclimating themselves to
Arctic conditions and exploring the surrounding area, in the vicinity
of present-day Thule. In the spring of 1892, Peary and his men,
including Henson, set out to accomplish the principal mission of the
expedition, a crossing of northern Greenland from west to east.
Though the ostensible goal was to locate the northernmost terminus
of Greenland, in actuality Peary wanted to determine the shortest
route to the North Pole.

Josephine Peary remained behind at Red Cliff House, as did John
Verhoeff, whom Robert Peary considered to be insubordinate and
undependable in the field. Verhoeff, in fact, had been trouble from
the start, not only for Peary but also for Matthew Henson. A Ken-
tuckian unaccustomed to interacting with blacks as equals, he resented the respect and relatively impartial treatment that the Pearys
accorded their "manservant." He repeatedly harassed Henson, calling him by the most vulgar of American racial epithets and occasionally threatening him.[7] Friction between the two men came to a head
after Henson hurt his heel during the early stages of the trans-
Greenland crossing and was forced to return to Red Cliff. At one
point Verhoeff attacked Henson for resting his injured foot on a table.
On another occasion Verhoeff became infuriated when he discovered, after oversleeping, that Henson had taken over one of his
duties. So frequently did the two men clash that the otherwise placid
Mrs. Peary eventually ordered them out of the house to "fight it out."

In the meantime Gibson and Cook also returned to the camp,
leaving only Peary and Astrup to complete the crossing. Both Gibson
and Cook seemed to share Verhoeff's sentiments about Henson, even
if they didn't imitate his tactics. When Henson asserted in their

presence that black Americans should have the right to vote, for example, they were quick to remind him of his proper "place." Similarly, they joined Verhoeff in deriding Henson's efforts to befriend the Eskimos and learn their skills.

None of this deterred Henson from standing up for his beliefs, however, or from learning as much as he could about Polar Eskimo culture. He hunted with the Eskimos, visited their villages, and eventually became the only member of any of Peary's expeditionary teams to master their language.

By contrast, the other men at Red Cliff seemed to have no interest in the Eskimos beyond taking advantage of the women. According to Verhoeff's diary, Cook and Gibson regularly flirted with the Eskimo women, at times engaging in the practice of "cooney," which involved "putting their faces to the women's faces and smelling them." This intimate behavior apparently offended the local Eskimo men, some to the point of threatening violence. On one occasion Cook and Gibson cited such a threat to convince Henson to take Mrs. Peary farther inland for a few days to a safe, remote location that Lieutenant Peary had arranged for her in case of danger. While she and Henson were away, Cook and Gibson gave a "dinner party" for four Eskimo women, during which they engaged in "cooney," according to Verhoeff, who claimed he was a reluctant participant in the dinner and that he did not take part in the other activities.[8]

Yet in spite of his differences with the other men, Henson enjoyed life in the Arctic. In many ways, he was freer and more independent there than his fellow African Americans were back home. So unusual was Henson's position in Peary's Arctic work that T. S. Dedrick, a white assistant on a later expedition, felt compelled to voice his outrage at Henson's "freedom and insolence" and Peary's apparent "indifference" to it.[9]

The truth of the matter was that Henson had time and again proven his worth and earned Peary's admiration and respect. Henson even managed to win over Frederick Cook, who would later become Peary's archenemy. After their return to the United States, Cook invited Henson to live in his mother's New York apartment while an eye injury suffered during the expedition healed satisfactorily. Ironically, Henson's own chief nemesis, John Verhoeff, never made it back from

Greenland. He was said to have been killed in an accident while exploring a glacier just a few days before *Kite* set sail for America.

Henson spent the better part of the next eighteen years of his life exploring the Arctic with Robert Peary. He returned to Greenland with Peary in 1893 and remained there with him for another year after the other members of the team abandoned the mission and went home. He marched across the entire ice cap of Greenland with Peary and Hugh J. Lee in 1895 and joined in the discovery of the island's northern terminus. He also participated in the 1896 and 1897 expeditions, when Peary removed some of the Eskimos' sacred meteorites and only source of metal, which he later sold to the American Museum of Natural History in New York to finance his subsequent explorations.

Henson also helped raise money between expeditions by donning his Eskimo regalia and accompanying Peary on cross-country lecture tours. He even toured the United States alone in a play of Peary's creation titled *Under the Polar Star*. This latter work proved so physically and psychologically exhausting that on November 7, 1896, Henson wrote Peary complaining of the difficulty in managing the dogs onstage and of poor health. "Mr. Peary," he pleaded, ". . . I don't think that I could stand going around this winter, I have been sick ever since I have been in Chicago and now I am hardly able to get to the theater—but I have to do it, or walk home. Will you please let me know if you can get me a place at the American Museum [of Natural History], for I am afraid that I have to give this job up."

Understandably, Henson's travels put a severe strain on his marriage. Unwilling to play the classic role of the sailor's wife, Eva Henson refused to tolerate her husband's long absences. Henson tried to mollify her, chiefly by requesting more money from Peary "to send home to my wife." But he had no intention of changing his ways. Having established himself as a permanent member of Peary's expeditionary team and, in the process, having acquired a degree of personal fame, he was determined to share in the achievement of Peary's ultimate goal—the conquest of the North Pole. To put it another way, his love for his work eventually surpassed his love of his domestic life in Philadelphia and, apparently, Eva. By 1896, the couple was on the verge of a divorce.

A terse letter that Eva wrote to Robert Peary in June 1896 reflects the lack of communication between Henson and his wife as well as Eva's growing impatience.

Dear Sir,
  I hear you are going to Greenland again. Will you please inform me when you expect to go and how long you are going to stay and oblige yours truly

Mrs. Eva Henson
1240 Rodman St,
Phila. Pa

p.s.
as Matt says he is going with you again.

Henson later accused his wife of infidelity in his absence. She and her family in turn accused him of negligence. The relationship became so bitter that Henson wrote Peary on April 5, 1897, saying that he would like to stay in Greenland "for five or ten years . . . anything to get away from this town."

Peary and Henson returned to Greenland that summer to collect the last and largest of the Inuit's sacred meteorites, which the Eskimos called "The Woman." When they returned to the United States in October 1897, Eva requested a divorce. Henson agreed, and their relationship ended that year.

The years between 1897 and 1902 were the toughest for Henson and Peary. Determined to reach the North Pole, they remained in the Arctic for four uninterrupted years of exploration. During this time they developed the first map of the northern boundaries of Greenland and for the first time traveled out on the Arctic Ocean, reaching a record 84° 17' north. But they did not attain their goal.

In the summer of 1900, Josephine Peary made an unplanned visit to the Thule area aboard a relief ship. To her utter surprise, she found Ahlikahsingwah with a part-white baby that was said to be Peary's. It was probably Anaukaq-Hammy, Robert Peary's first-born Amer-Eskimo son. A woman of great stoicism and devotion to her husband, Josephine accepted the painful reality of the child and kept her marriage intact.

From 1902, when the expedition returned to the United States until 1905, Matthew Henson worked at a variety of odd jobs, first as a porter on the New York Central Railroad and later as a janitor in New York City. Although the cross-country train rides appealed to his love of travel, and his work in New York kept him close to friends, Henson could find little satisfaction in the mundane routines of workaday life. At one point he did seek a job with his old employer, the American Museum of Natural History, but he was unsuccessful. He could only find work as a janitor.

In the summer of 1905 Henson and now "Commander" Peary returned to the Arctic, where they undertook preparations for their historic spring 1906 assault on the North Pole. Though they managed to get as far as 87° 6' north, a new record, delays at open water and dwindling food supplies forced them to turn back about one hundred miles short of their goal. The failure of the expedition crushed both men. Peary, at age fifty, and Henson, forty, knew they were getting too old for the rigors of Arctic work. They also knew that the public was becoming less interested in and tolerant of their misadventures.

Returning to New York in the late fall of 1906 on the badly damaged *Roosevelt*, Peary and Henson agreed to make one final attempt to reach the North Pole the following year. Peary then set out to raise money for the expedition while Henson remained on the docked ship, directing repairs and readying equipment. It was during this period that Henson proposed to Lucy Jane Ross, whom he had been courting for two years while he was a tenant at her mother's house on West 35th Street. Not long before the *Roosevelt* set sail for the last time, Matthew and Lucy were married in a quiet ceremony, with only Lucy's mother and a few friends present.

On June 21, 1908, Henson wrote to Peary.

Mr. Peary, Dear Sir
I am going to ask you for a raise in wages as I think that 40 dollars a month is rather small to maintain a family. I have never asked you before as I did not have any encumbrance. I would like to have sixty dollars a month if that is not asking too much of you.

Respt.
M.A. Henson

Peary split the difference and agreed to pay Henson "$50 a month and keep." In the interest of the greater mission, Henson accepted.

CHAPTER SEVEN

* * *

The Struggle for the Pole

On July 6, 1908, after a year's delay for repairs to the USS *Roosevelt* and amid much fanfare, Henson and Peary departed New York for a final attempt at the Pole. President Theodore Roosevelt was on hand to see the men off, declaring that if any man could succeed, it would be Peary. This time Peary had his finest hand-picked team: Dr. John W. Goodsell, a physician from Pennsylvania; Donald B. MacMillan, an instructor of mathematics and physical training at Worcester Academy in Massachusetts; Ross G. Marvin, professor of engineering at Cornell University; George Borup, a recent graduate of Groton and Yale and an outstanding athlete; Robert Bartlett, the ship's captain; and Matthew Henson, the most experienced Arctic explorer in the group other than Peary.

By the first week of August the expedition had reached Etah, where they took on Eskimo helpers and collected enough coal and freshly killed seal, walrus, and narwhal to last through the winter. The *Roosevelt* then headed farther north, struggling against the barriers of Kennedy and Robeson channels like a modern icebreaker, finally reaching its destination—Cape Sheridan on the northernmost tip of Ellesmere Island, Canada—on September 5, 1908. There the expeditionary team disembarked and prepared for the relay assault on the Pole. Henson and the other men were busy all winter, hunting for musk-ox, deer, and arctic hare, and readying the equipment for the journey north. Team member Donald B. MacMillan would later say that Henson, "with years of experience equal to that of Peary himself, was indispensable to Peary and of more real value than the combined services of all four white men. . . . He made all the sledges, he made all the camp equipment, he talked the language like a native."[1]

On February 18, 1909, Henson, accompanied by a group of Eskimos and laden with supplies, left the *Roosevelt* for Cape Columbia, which had been selected as the jumping-off point for the strike at the Pole. When they reached the tip of the cape, Henson and the Eskimos set about building several large igloos that would serve as a base camp. Then they waited until the entire team could be assembled at "Crane City," as the encampment was named.

On the morning of March 1, 1909, Peary ordered Henson and three Eskimos to take the lead in breaking the trail north to the Pole. For an entire month the Americans and their Eskimo assistants acted as relay teams, setting up caches of supplies along the trail that would support the journey to the Pole and back. Henson and Bartlett did most of the trailbreaking, with Peary's and Marvin's sled teams following.

The American members of the team knew that they could not all accompany Peary to the Pole. Eventually someone would be selected to make the final leg of the journey, and the choice would be made by Peary alone. Donald MacMillan would later say that Peary had remarked to him before they even left the ship that "Henson must go all the way. I can't make it without him."[2]

There were, of course, a variety of considerations weighing in Henson's favor, beginning with his uncommon skills and long experience as an Arctic explorer. For twenty years he had used his talents to support Peary's ventures, proving his loyalty time and again. He knew Peary better, perhaps, than any man living: his likes and his dislikes, his virtues as well as his idiosyncrasies. He also shared one of Peary's most intimate secrets, knowledge of the children Peary had fathered with the Eskimo woman Ahlikahsingwah. Henson and Peary undoubtedly saw their Amer-Eskimo sons when they returned to Etah in 1908, but Henson never breathed a word of this in public, then or ever.

No matter how much he may have deserved the honor of sharing in the discovery of the North Pole, however, Henson himself did not count on it. He remembered that on the historic march across Greenland in 1895, when he had literally saved the lives of Peary and Hugh Lee, Peary had promised both men that they would be with him if he ever reached the Pole. Now there was no Lee, only Henson. But as Henson well knew, even if Peary still intended to keep that pledge, any decision was subject to change out on the treacherous and unforgiving polar ice. Injury, illness, anxiety, or a dozen other things could force a complete rearrangement of even the best-laid plans.

MacMillan and Goodsell were the first to turn back, after ferrying supplies to 84° 29'. MacMillan most likely would have been permitted to travel farther north, but he had injured his heel. Borup and his Eskimo assistants took the next leg, to 85° 23', then returned to the ship behind MacMillan and Goodsell.

The ranks of the expeditionary team were thinned further on March 27, when Peary ordered Marvin back after reaching 86° 30' north. At that moment, Henson later recalled, his "heart stopped palpitating, I breathed easier, and my mind was relieved. It was not my turn yet, I was to continue onward and there only remained one person between me and the Pole—the Captain [Bartlett]." In keeping with his reputation for being a gentleman, Henson "went over to Marvin's igloo to bid him good-by." According to Henson, "In his quiet, earnest manner, he [Marvin] advised me to keep on, and hoped for our success; he congratulated me and we gave each other the strong fraternal grip of our honored fraternity and we confidently expected to see each other again at the ship."[3]

Unfortunately, the anticipated reunion would never take place. Marvin's two Eskimo companions, Kudlooktoo and "Harrigan" (a nickname given Inighito by Peary's group because of his frequent attempts to sing the popular song of the same name), returned to the ship without Marvin, saying that he had fallen through thin ice and drowned out on the Arctic Ocean. Henson, the only man aboard the ship who could speak their language well enough to interrogate them, believed their plausible story. Some years later, however, it was learned during a confession at a Christian confirmation that Marvin had been killed on the return march when he apparently became emotionally distressed after suffering a seriously frostbitten foot and threatened Kudlooktoo and Harrigan for not carrying him on the sled.

The version of the story told among the Polar Eskimos today is that Marvin treated their people brutally and even tried to get Harrigan, the younger of his two companions, to leave Kudlooktoo behind on the ice when their food ran low. Rather than leave his fellow Eskimo out to die, Harrigan shot and killed Marvin, and the two men buried his body under the snow and ice. It is ironic that both Peary and Henson (who knew the tribe even better) had always described the Polar Eskimos as an innocent, childlike people who were incapable of violence. Yet as early as their first expedition in 1891, they had encountered the threat of violence from some of the natives. It is even more ironic that the only other violent incident recorded on the entire North Pole expedition of 1909 occurred aboard ship during the tense months they wintered in Cape Sheridan, waiting for the spring journey to the Pole. This incident involved Harrigan, who was se-verely beaten by one of the more irascible members of Peary's crew who had tired of his "practical jokes." Harrigan protested this physi-cal assault to Peary, but he and his men laughed the matter off and gave the angered Eskimo a cloth shirt to calm him down and make him forget the incident. Apparently, he did not forget about it. He had learned his violence well from the *kahdonah*.

Bartlett broke camp on March 27, and Henson followed about an hour later. After six days of "marches" over treacherous ice, each involving up to fourteen hours of travel from start to rest, the group reached 87° 46' 49" north. It was at this latitude, on April 1, that Henson learned for certain that he had gotten the call. Peary ordered Bartlett back to the ship, leaving Henson as the only other American on the final leg of the historic journey. Recalling the occasion, Hen-son wrote: "I knew at this time that he was to go back, and that I was to continue, so I had no misgivings and neither had he."[4] Bartlett would later say, however, "I don't deny that it would have been a great thrill to have stood at the peak of our globe. . . . It was a bitter disappointment. I don't know, perhaps I cried a little. But . . . Henson was a better dog driver than I."[5] As a kind of consolation prize, Peary let Bartlett travel on five or six miles to 88° north, putting him farther north than any other European explorer had traveled. Peary later explained his decision by saying that "in view of the noble work of Great Britain in artic exploration, a British subject [Bartlett was a Canadian from Nova Scotia] should, next to an American, be able to say that he had stood nearest the Pole."[6] Henson recollected that "Captain Bartlett was glad to turn back when he did. He frankly told me several times that he had little expectation of ever returning alive."[7]

Under pressure to defend his choice of Henson, Peary later wrote that "Henson was the best man I had with me for this kind of work, with the exception of the Eskimos." At the same time, however, he undercut that explanation by asserting that "Henson . . . would not have been so competent as the white members of the expedition in getting himself and his party back to land" because "he had not as a racial inheritance, the daring and initiative of Bartlett or Marvin, MacMillan or Borup. . . . I owed it to him not to subject him to the dangers and responsibilities which he was temperamentally unfit to face."[8]

What prompted Peary to offer such a fundamentally racist rationale for his decision? Did Peary really believe that the man who had spent close to twenty years traveling around the Arctic with him could not find his way back to land—the man who had brought him home safely so many times before? And what about the Eskimos? Did their "racial inheritance" preclude them, too, from following the trail back home on their own?

Perhaps Peary simply intended to mollify those critics who derided his choice of a black man as codiscoverer of the North Pole. Some have speculated that an editor or ghostwriter inserted the statement to make Peary's decision more palatable to the reading public. Still others have suggested that the reason Peary chose Henson in the first place was because he knew a black man would never be accorded equal recognition for discovery of the North Pole. The implicit, though glaring, racism of his subsequent explanation was thus consistent with his intentions.[9]

Whatever one may conclude about Peary's rationale for his decision, his reasons at the time were clear to every man on the expedition, including the Eskimos. As MacMillan, who later became a
famous Arctic explorer in his own right, wrote in a 1920 article for
National Geographic: "And the Negro? . . . With years of experience
equal to that of Peary himself . . . clean, full of grit, he went to the
Pole with Peary because he was easily the most efficient of all Peary's
assistants."[10]

After Bartlett and his Eskimo team turned back, Henson, Peary,
and four Eskimos—Ootah, Seegloo, Egingwah, and Ooqueah—
were all left alone on the frozen Arctic Ocean, more than three
hundred miles from land and more than one hundred miles from the
Pole. For the next five days they raced toward their goal, rarely
sleeping, and stopping only long enough for Peary to take readings
on his chronometer-watch and sextant and to make depth soundings
through the Arctic ice. His calculations confirmed those of Henson
who, knowing the distance and direction they had to travel and the
average distance covered per march, judged from dead reckoning
that they were heading in a straight line toward the Pole.

The almost reckless pace of the final thrust toward the Pole was
dictated as much by fear as by anticipation. The men knew that they
could freeze to death, that they could fall through the thin ice at any
moment and drown or die of hypothermia. Perhaps most terrifying
of all, they faced the possibility that a large lane of water would open
like a river and leave them stranded on the other side to starve to
death.

What happened during the last few days is a matter of some
dispute. Peary reported that it was he who broke trail and reached
the Pole first. Yet after the expedition returned to the United States,
Henson said that it was he, Ootah, and Seegloo who first reached the
point they later determined to be the North Pole. In fact, Henson
maintained that he reached the Pole some forty-five minutes ahead of
Peary after inadvertently disobeying the commander's orders to stop
short of what they judged to be the actual spot. There he was to wait
so that Peary could travel on alóne and lay claim to the honor of being
the first person to stand at the North Pole.

According to Henson, Peary became so angry with him for denying him this long-awaited privilege that he refused to speak to him all the way back to the ship. "It was my boy Ootah who disclosed to me that Peary was to leave me behind in the final few miles of the Pole," Henson recalled, and with Egingwah he witnessed "the disappointment of Commander Peary when a few miles from camp, his observations told the lieutenant that he had overstepped and gone past the Pole, which we had reached the night before. Our camp itself was practically situated at the 'top of the earth.' For the crime of being present when the Pole was reached Commander Peary has ignored me ever since. . . . It nearly broke my heart on the return journey from the Pole that he would rise in the morning and slip away on the homeward trail without rapping on the tent for me as was the established custom. . . . On board ship, he addressed me a very few times. When we left the ship he did not speak. I wrote him twice and sent him a telegram, but received no reply from him."[11]

After studying the personality of both men from documents spanning some fifty years, I would not be surprised if the aggressive and self-assured Henson deliberately charged ahead to beat his old friend and boss to the Pole. Henson might well have reasoned that since he and Peary lived in separate worlds back home anyway, why should he not go for the glory that would be known only among his race back in the segregated America of 1909? After all, this was clearly their last polar expedition. Moreover, at that moment—and for the first time in their twenty-three-year relationship—they were equals. It was no longer them against the world. It was man to man. Peary was crippled and weak. He had lost all but two of his toes to severe frostbite some years earlier and found walking very difficult, especially on the jagged ice trail. He later admitted, in fact, that he had traveled the last hundred miles of the expedition on a sled driven by his Eskimo assistants. Henson, on the other hand, traveled on foot with the Eskimos all the way to the Pole, driving the sled with all the scientific equipment. Ironically, while one of the prevailing "scientific" theories of that period held that dark-skinned people could not tolerate the Arctic climate and conditions, Henson never suffered a permanent injury in all his years in the Arctic.

While we may never know exactly what happened in those last days, we do know that two Americans, one black and the other

white, held the United States ensign at the top of our planet long
before anyone else or any other nation. And in the minds of African
Americans, at least, Matthew Henson was the "Co-Discoverer of the
North Pole."

*   *   *

It was a sad moment for the Eskimos when they learned that Henson
and Peary would leave Greenland, never to return. Ootah later told
Danish explorer Peter Freuchen:

> "If it had not been for Mahri-Pahluk, Peary might have been quite
> another man. Because as both of them came from far away white man's
> country, there were so many things they did not understand.
>
> "Mahri-Pahluk was the only man from Peeuree's land who could
> learn to talk our language without using his tongue like a baby. If a
> strange man walks during the winter when everything is dark and
> some meet him, and ask who is there, the American will always
> answer so one is glad it is dark—because it is difficult not to laugh. But
> Mahri-Pahluk could talk like a full-grown, intelligent person. Besides,
> Mahri-Pahluk showed all his days that he did not look down upon
> people from up here. Therefore, he wanted to learn our ways and he
> sure did. Nobody has ever driven dogs better than he has. And not
> only swing the whip . . . whenever the sled broke down, he could fix it
> like any of us. He could repair the harness or make new ones—and
> none has ever made a snowhouse [igloo] faster and better and bigger
> than him.
>
> "But Mahri-Pahluk could also sing like us, dance like us, and his
> mouth was always full of stories none had heard before.
>
> "Therefore, we liked him, and we all felt sorry when we understood
> that we should never see him again. . . . But we will always tell our
> children about him and we will sing songs about him."[12]

In contrast to Matthew Henson's legendary status among the Polar
Eskimos, his treatment in America was one of "benign neglect" at
best. Few men have given so much to the honor of their country and
received so little in return. When Henson returned to America after
the North Pole discovery, there was, to be sure, a small level of
mainstream press coverage for "Peary's colored servant." But the
America of 1909 found it hard to accept the fact that Peary had

selected a black man over his five white assistants to share in the conquest of the North Pole.

Peary's decision to take Henson to the Pole certainly did not help his case when he returned home to find that Frederick Cook, the former assistant turned archrival, had laid claim to having discovered the Pole a year earlier. Cook took full advantage of the honor system that governed Arctic exploration, where a man's word regarding his achievement was accepted as fact—unless that man happened to be black, or an Eskimo. Cook's two Eskimo companions, Etookahshoo and Ahpellah, later told Danish officials that he had taken them on a circuitous trek around the islands of northwest Canada, not to the Pole. In fact, they reported, they had never traveled beyond the sight of land during the entire trip. There is no land within four hundred miles of the North Pole. The Eskimos added that they had spent most of the year holed up in an earthen shelter in northern Canada with plenty of food stores.[13]

Henson also suspected that Cook's claims were preposterous, not just because of the Eskimos' testimony but because of other, earlier experiences with Cook that had proved him amateurish in the serious business of Arctic exploration. Nevertheless, the conflicting claims created a personal dilemma for Henson. Cook had treated and cared for Henson in his family's home in New York back in 1892, when the latter had temporarily lost much of his vision to snow blindness. Henson never forgot this kind gesture and for a while found it difficult to criticize Cook publicly.

Even when several international scientific societies sided with Peary and denounced Cook as a charlatan, many people refused to accept their verdict. Some still do. Compared to the pompous, if misunderstood, Robert Peary, the charming Dr. Cook would always be a more acceptable American hero.

Eventually, however, Peary received the recognition he sought and deserved. Most of the leading scientific organizations at home and abroad acknowledged him as the "discoverer" of the North Pole, and the National Geographic Society of Washington gave him their highest award, a special gold medal struck in his honor. Henson, on the other hand, was completely ignored by the geographic societies and other prominent mainstream groups. In fact, it must have been very painful for Henson when the National Geographic Society skipped over him and gave their second highest award, another gold medal, to the white man on Peary's North Pole expedition who, next to Peary, got closest to the Pole. That man was Robert Bartlett, who admitted that he never got within 130 miles of the Pole.

Yet if white America ignored Henson, black America certainly did not. By the time the expedition returned to New York City on October 2, 1909, the New York newspapers had named Matthew Henson as Peary's American companion at the Pole. Black leaders around the country who had been following accounts of Henson's explorations sent him telegrams and letters of congratulations for "representing his race well" and organized a celebration in his honor.

On October 19 a group of the most prominent black American intellectuals, politicians, and religious leaders from across the country gathered at the prestigious Tuxedo Club on Madison Avenue in midtown Manhattan for a special dinner to honor Matthew Henson's achievement. There, amid speeches and great fanfare, they presented their hero with a gold watch and chain. The organizers and guests of this impressive affair included Booker T. Washington; the Reverend Adam Clayton Powell, Sr.; John E. Bruce, noted publisher and author; Charles W. Anderson, the highest-ranking black civil service official in New York; Judge M. W. Gibbs of Arkansas; Assistant U.S. Attorney W. H. Lewis of Boston; and many other distinguished leaders. Seldom in the nation's history has such a collection of African-American leaders come together to honor a single person. These men were to the black American community of their day what the highest U.S. government and cultural figures were to the white community. The *New York Times* of October 13, 1909, reported the affair under the heading: "DINNER TO MATTHEW HENSON: Leaders among Colored Race to Give Peary's Aide a Watch and Chain."

Like Peary, Henson had at last achieved his goal: recognition from the leaders of his race. He had risen from the lowly background of a sharecropper with only six grades of schooling to a permanent place in history for his contributions to polar exploration.

Unfortunately, Henson's fame brought him nothing in the way of material reward. In fact, after twenty-three years of service to his nation and to Peary, he found himself without a job or even the prospect of employment. No one came forward to offer the black American hero even a minor position or appointment. For a time he tried to take advantage of the public interest in polar discovery by giving lectures on his North Pole journey with Peary, during which he would challenge Cook's claims. But Peary, fearing that the publicity would cause his adversaries to continually raise the issue of Henson's race, restricted his lecture activities and stopped Henson from showing his own photographs publicly.[14] Henson later wrote, "In my letters [to Peary] I hoped for some understanding. . . . But no reply came until I signed for a series of lectures. When I had given my first lecture I received a telegram from Commander Peary warning me not to use the pictures. At once I sat down and wrote him another long letter. He never replied to it."[15]

On October 15, 1909, Peary wrote H. L. Bridgeman, secretary of the Peary Arctic Club (which had financed his polar expeditions) and the man who had paid Henson his salary:

> *"My dear Bridgeman*
>
> *I have not happened to come across the so called Henson challenge to Cook [Cook's claim of a North Pole discovery], though I note reference to it in the papers.*
>
> *While I can only infer from these references what the challenge really is, it strikes me that anything of the kind would be unwise for three reasons. It is likely to make a fool of Henson by giving him pronounced megalomania; it will put him in a position to be tangled up and made to say anything by emissaries of the Herald [newspaper], and it will introduce into this matter the race issue."*

During much of this time, Henson was working on his own book, which he entitled *A Negro Explorer at the North Pole*. Peary's agreement with members of his expeditionary team precluded the writing of memoirs or other accounts of their Arctic experiences without his approval. After a year or so, as public interest in the subject waned, Peary decided that Henson could publish his book without stirring up too much controversy, but only after Peary had first reviewed the manuscript. Henson was the only member of the 1909 team granted permission to publish an account of the historic expedition. The book was not a best-seller.

In 1912, deeply frustrated and jobless, Henson wrote Peary to request that he use his influence to help him find a job as a "chauffeur or messenger or some other position that I could fill. . . . I am in need of work." Peary responded by writing the secretary of the treasury to recommend Henson for a federal position that carried a lifetime pension. Securing such sinecures was a standard practice among the explorers' fraternity, a way to reward loyal assistants by providing them a measure of long-term security. At about the same time, some of Henson's friends and black politicians were petitioning President William Taft on his behalf for a federal appointment similar to those traditionally given to European American heroes.

About a year later, President Taft signed an executive order granting permission to appoint Henson to "any suitable position in the classified service." Henson was appointed "messenger" in the federal customs house in New York. He remained at the customs house until his retirement in 1937 at the age of seventy. From then until his death in 1955, he and his wife Lucy lived mainly on his small pension of about one thousand dollars a year.

When Peary died in 1920, Henson read about it in the New York papers and, according to a friend, got up, went into his bathroom for privacy, and ran the tap water to mask the sound of his weeping. In spite of their differences of race, status, and condition, Matthew Henson and Robert Peary had become so close during their years of struggle and hardship in the Arctic that they were more like brothers than just friends.

Peary was given a hero's burial in Arlington National Cemetery. The National Geographic Society purchased a magnificent monument to mark his grave. The monument, which was conceived by Peary before he died, is a giant white granite globe mounted on a broad-based pedestal, with a bronze star marking the North Pole. On the base, beneath the globe, is the inscription "ROBERT EDWIN PEARY DISCOVERER OF THE NORTH POLE." Inscribed on another side of the base is a Latin line from Seneca, which his daughter called "his guiding motto": *Inveniam Viam Aut Faciam* (I shall find a way or make one). The monument commands its own hill in the cemetery.

President Warren G. Harding joined hundreds of other dignitaries at the Arlington ceremony. Officials of the U.S. government have said that Henson was also invited to the burial, but he cannot be seen in any of the scores of archival photographs taken of the ceremony that day. If Henson or any other black American was present at the burial ceremony, he must have been seated far away from the official guests.

Yet Henson was not completely forgotten. In 1937, twenty-eight years after the North Pole discovery, he was made an honorary member of the famed Explorers Club in New York City of which Peary had once been president. He was the first and for decades the only black African American so recognized by the club. In 1946, he received a medal from the U.S. Navy in recognition of his contributions to the North Pole discovery. The same medal was given to all members of Peary's 1909 expedition and did not single Henson out for reaching the Pole. Also, Morgan State College in Baltimore and Howard University of Washington, D.C., two predominantly African-American institutions, awarded him honorary master's degrees. Dillard College of New Orleans, to whom he gave the Eskimo clothing he wore at the North Pole, named a hall after him.

By his own account, however, his most prized possession was the gold medal he received from the Chicago Geographical Society. The Chicago award was the work of Henson's old friend Donald B. MacMillan and Comdr. Eugene F. McDonald, Jr., president of the Zenith Radio Corporation and a longtime admirer. To Henson, this medal represented the ultimate tribute to an explorer: recognition by a geographic society. For the entire forty-six years between the discovery of the Pole and his death, he was virtually ignored by the National Geographic Society, a group that had honored and paid numerous tributes to Peary and the other white men on the North Pole expedition.

In 1948 Matthew Henson was "rediscovered" by mainstream America when author Bradley Robinson wrote a biography titled *Dark Companion*. This marked the first time Americans were given a true picture of the role Henson played in the polar discoveries of Robert Peary. Robinson, the liberal son of a member of the Explorers Club, decided to write Henson's story after learning of his crucial role in the conquest of the Pole through extensive interviews and research. Published at a time when American racial attitudes were becoming more enlightened, the book was well reviewed and became a big seller. Henson, now in his eighties, suddenly found himself the object of much attention. Newspapers and magazines interviewed him, and he made guest appearances on radio. He talked about his years in the Arctic and his contributions to the North Pole discovery. Although he had little contact with the Peary family after the admiral's death and felt bitter about the way they had ignored him, he never spoke disparagingly about his old comrade. Throughout his life he would remain faithful to Peary's memory and to their friendship, traveling nearly every year to Arlington Cemetery to place a wreath at Peary's grave.

Matthew Henson died of a cerebral hemorrhage on March 9, 1955, at the age of eighty-eight. Thousands turned out for the funeral five days later at the historic Abyssinian Baptist Church in Harlem, where the Reverend Adam Clayton Powell, Jr., conducted the memorial service. In his eulogy, Powell told Henson's widow Lucy and the large funeral gathering that the "achievements of Henson are as important as those performed by Marco Polo and Ferdinand Magellan." His pallbearers included Arctic explorer Peter Freuchen and other members of the Explorers Club.[16]

No geographic society or Arctic club or any other group offered to help bury Henson among other American heroes in Arlington National Cemetery. With only a modest, fixed income to draw on, Lucy Henson buried her husband on top of her mother, Susan Ross, in the small plot they owned in Woodlawn Cemetery in the Bronx.

Matthew Alexander Henson (1909). *Courtesy of the Explorers Club*

Comdr. Robert Edwin Peary in full Arctic gear (c. 1909). *Peary Collection, National Archives*

Matthew Henson aboard Peary's ship, the USS *Roosevelt*. This photograph is believed to have been taken in March 1909, shortly before Henson and Peary launched their final assault on the North Pole. *Courtesy of Johnson Publishing Co.*

Ahlikasingwah and her baby, Kali, the younger of Robert Peary's two Amer-Eskimo sons (c. 1907). *From* My Attainment of the Pole *by Frederick Cook*

Akatingwah carrying a baby believed to be Matthew Henson's son, Anaukaq (c. 1907). *Peary Collection, National Archives*

Navy lieutenant Peary and his daughter Marie Ahnighito Peary (c. 1899). *Peary Collection, National Archives*

Matthew Henson (*front row, center*) and a group of Polar Eskimo villagers (c. 1900). Deeply interested in the ways of the native population, Henson was the only member of Peary's expeditionary teams who learned to speak the Inuit language. *Courtesy of the Explorers Club*

OPPOSITE:
Taking a break from cleaning a fresh supply of fish, members of Peary's expeditionary team pose alongside their ship, the *Kite*, en route to northwest Greenland in 1891. *Peary Collection, National Archives*

The 1891 North Greenland Expedition. *Left to right:* Frederick Cook, Matthew Henson, John M. Verhoeff, Eivind Astrup, Josephine Peary, Lt. Robert E. Peary, Langdon Gibson. *Peary Collection, National Archives*

GIBSON.

VERHOEFF.

DR. COOK.

ASTRÜP.

HENSON.

Portraits of the members of the 1891 expedition as they appeared in Robert Peary's book, *Northward over the "Great Ice."* What is perhaps most noteworthy about the arrangement of the photographs is the implicitly equal status that Peary accorded to Henson.

Dozens of sled dogs crowd the deck of the USS *Roosevelt* as it steams toward Cape Sheridan, the staging point for the historic 1909 assault on the North Pole. *Courtesy of the National Geographic Society*

Matthew Henson and Polar Eskimos repair a sled used to transport food, supplies, and scientific equipment during the 1909 polar journey. *Courtesy of the Explorers Club*

Particularly during the early stages of the 1909 expedition, the rugged Arctic surface caused repeated delays. Here, members of the team struggle to pull their supply sleds over a small ridge of jagged ice. *Courtesy of the National Geographic Society*

Matthew Henson (*center*) and four Polar Eskimos at the North Pole, April 6, 1909. This photograph was taken by Comdr. Robert E. Peary. *Courtesy of the National Geographic Society*

The four Polar Eskimos who accompanied Henson and Peary to the North Pole. *Left to right:* Egingwah, Ootah, Ooqueah, and Seegloo. *Peary Collection, National Archives*

Five months after the Peary Expedition reached the North Pole, newspapers widely circulated the story that Frederick Cook had accomplished the same feat a year earlier. The front-page photograph shown below purported to confirm Cook's claim, but subsequent investigation proved otherwise. *From* To Stand at the Pole *by William R. Hunt*

HOME EDITION

THE EVENING MAIL

HOME EDITION

VOL. LXXIII. NO. 209.   Fair, cooler.   NEW YORK, WEDNESDAY, SEPTEMBER 1, 1909.   ONE CENT

DR. COOK REACHES NORTH POLE

News of Cook's success was worth an "Extra."

Cook's photograph of his companions at the Pole

EXTRA

GOAL LONG COVETED B' WORLD'S EXPLORERS WON FINALLY BY AMERICAI

Dispatch Received at the Danis Colonial Office from Lervik. Nor way, Says Cook Accomplishe His Great Feat, More Than Year Ago, on April 21, 1908.

Copenhagen, Sept. 1.—Dr. Cook, the American e plorer, reached the north pole April 21, 1908, accordi to a telegram just received at the Colonial office here

The first black to be elected to the exclusive Explorers Club, Matthew Henson poses with other members for the official club portrait in 1947. Next to Henson, in the center of the front row, is the noted Danish Arctic explorer, Peter Freuchen. *Courtesy of the Explorers Club*

Matthew Henson displays a watch and gold chain awarded to him by black American leaders after his return from the North Pole. A medal presented to him by the U.S. Navy in recognition of his achievement is pinned to his lapel (1947).

CHAPTER EIGHT

✳ ✳ ✳

"Now I know I have relatives"

The trip had not been uneventful. It almost never is. The lumbering C-141 military transport lifted off the runway at McGuire Air Force Base in New Jersey at 2300 hours, en route to Thule, Greenland. Before long the aircraft gained cruising altitude, and the military crew, a few other scientists, and I settled into our seats for the long haul. Although the flight sergeant had provided us with ear plugs, the absence of any windows or insulation intensified the high-pitched whine of the jet's engines. Adding to our discomfort, tons of cargo teetered menacingly just ahead of us in the open hold.

Several hours into the trip, I was awakened by the flight sergeant tugging at my arm. He told me that we had developed engine trouble and would be landing at a nearby air base. Despite the momentary surge of adrenaline one feels upon hearing this kind of news, I was more worried about my scheduled connections in Greenland. If we arrived too late, I would be unable to get a helicopter to take me over the mountain range. I would have to travel over the frozen sea by dogsled, a more exciting but more time-consuming means of transportation.

It was pitch black when we landed and disembarked at the air base in Canada. We rushed through the cold night air and huddled into what looked like a small brick bunker while the plane underwent repairs. After a while, the flight sergeant came in to inform us that the mechanics could not repair the plane and we would be returning to the American air base on the next available flight. The news was depressing. It was more than an inconvenience because even a few hours of delay here could result in a layover of several days in Greenland. "Such is life," I reflected, as I began to rearrange in my schedule book my plans to visit Moriussaq. There is probably no sadder or lonelier feeling than being stranded in a bunker on an isolated air base.

A few hours later—just as the full implications of what had happened began to sink in—the flight sergeant reappeared. "I have good news," he said. "The mechanics have repaired the plane and the flight crew is ready to take us to Thule."

"All right!" I shouted. Everyone else in the room just stared at me. Thule, Greenland, it seems, is not the favorite station of our military men and women.

Subzero temperatures and howling winds greeted us on our arrival in northwest Greenland. To minimize our exposure to the dangerous cold, we rushed from the giant green plane into a nearby hangar. I knew that even in the unlikely event that the helicopter was still at the base, it could not take off in these strong winds. I would have to try to get a dogteam to travel north.

* * *

By late fall, the sun disappears at the top of the world, not to be seen again until spring. A kind of twilight appears for several hours during the day, but since the sun never breaks the horizon, the short day resembles an extended gray-blue dusk. By early December, the last vestige of daylight has disappeared altogether, and the area is thrust into total darkness until the sun begins to reappear briefly in mid-February. From March through July, the sun rises higher and higher, eventually circling the sky for twenty-four hours.

The entire settlement appeared deserted as I approached Moriussaq that fall. Although most of the food stores had already been gathered for the winter, I wondered whether the men were out hunting and had taken their families with them. But as I neared the center of the settlement, I spotted several children playing with a bobsled on a small hill. The children rushed forward to greet the visitor, with Ajako's daughter—and Matthew Henson's ten-year-old great-granddaughter—Aviaq leading the bunch.

"Allen," Aviaq shouted, as she and the other children and sled-dog pups ran through the snow toward me. I immediately recognized several of the children whose ears I had examined during my previous visit. I greeted them and Aviaq with big hugs. Hearing the commotion, several older children and adults came out of their igloos to see what was going on. The area came alive. After exchanging greetings of affection, the children and adults helped me with my small packages and bags as I headed off toward the home of Anaukaq Henson.

From a distance, I could make out the figure of a man wearing a heavy blue winter jacket. He walked toward us with the help of a cane in rapid, solid steps. I knew at once it was Anaukaq. I walked forward at a hurried pace, hand extended to meet my old friend. From several yards away, his unmistakable laugh cracked through the cold, crisp air. It lifted my spirits. As we approached each other, he shouted, "Allen, you came back. I did not think you would come back." He then burst into laughter as we shook hands and embraced. The crowd of children and young people gathering around us seemed vicariously to share the old man's delight as they giggled and chuckled shyly at our joyful reunion. We all headed for Anaukaq's igloo.

As we stepped into the warm house, I was greeted by the odor of fresh meat. Just inside the door, a large, freshly skinned bearded seal hung from a rope attached to a ceiling timber. The fleshy mammal was about the size of a small human. A huge bowl on the floor, directly under the seal, collected the blood that slowly dripped from the thawing carcass. Several of the family members cut off small pieces of the raw meat and ate them as snacks as we settled into the central room of the house.

Anaukaq made the usual gesture of offering me tea, which seems to be brewing in almost every Eskimo home one visits. He was all smiles. I had brought along some freshly ground coffee and some spiced tea for him. He suggested that we start with the spiced tea he had been so fond of during my last visit. They don't have such tea in Greenland.

"I am very happy to see you, Allen," Anaukaq said. "We missed your laugh."

"Thank you, Anaukaq, I am happy to see you and your family again," I said, charmed by the idea that Anaukaq and the other Eskimos had discovered my essence and persona in, of all things, my laugh.

"I am so glad you came back," Anaukaq repeated. "Many times I have said to myself and to my children that you would probably not return to this cold land. But you kept your word," he said, patting my shoulder.

By now, all the Amer-Eskimo Hensons were gathering around us in the central room, each greeting me warmly. They were much too modest to ask me questions right away, but I knew what was on their minds.

I had brought along small gifts for the entire family, mainly hunting knives for the men, as well as wool caps and other useful items. I distributed the gifts to the children, and then to the older family members. They accepted the gifts with gracious smiles and soft *kooyounahs* [thank yous]. The polar Eskimos are generally not a very expressive people. Even in joyous moments they typically exhibit a quiet reserve. Anaukaq seemed to be somewhat exceptional in this respect. He was more outgoing, more expressive than the other Eskimos, and endowed with a great sense of humor.

A short time later, Anaukaq asked the question on everyone's mind. "Did you find any of my relatives over there in Mahri-Pahluk's homeland?"

"Yes," I replied. "I have found several of your relatives in America—and they were very pleased to learn about you and your family." The room lit up with a cheer and smiles from the entire family.

"Do I have any brothers and sisters still alive?" Anaukaq asked pointedly.

"No, I'm afraid I did not locate any brothers or sisters, but I found several of Mahri-Pahluk's brothers' and sisters' children and grandchildren in Maryland, in Washington, D.C., and in Boston, Massachusetts, and they are very excited about meeting your family." Again, when my sentence was translated for them, Anaukaq and the family clapped their hands with pleasure.

"Do you mean Mahri-Pahluk and his American wife had no children that I could call brother or sister?" Anaukaq asked.

"No, not that I could find. Matthew and your stepmother Lucy Jane Ross Henson never had children, according to the records I found. But his brothers and sisters had plenty, and you have several first and second cousins still alive and well."

Anaukaq gave a momentary sigh of sadness, partially masked by a smile and a soft chuckle. "It seems so strange to me sometimes—that I have so many parents and yet no brothers or sisters."

Sometimes Anaukaq would say the profoundest things with such simplicity. I felt his sadness even in this moment of joy. He had really hoped for a brother or sister—some close, tangible evidence of a connection to his father. His mother, Akatingwah, had no other children, so he had grown up in Greenland without siblings. In fact, "Cousin Kali" had been the closest to a brother he had known. A true biological brother or sister, albeit a half brother or sister, might even look something like his father, whom he had not seen since he was three years old. A real brother or sister could tell him something about the father he had never known—what he was really like. Anaukaq had always dreamed of meeting a brother or sister. And now, I had to tell him he had none, living or dead.

I did not know at the time, but learned later, that in the spring of 1896, Matthew Henson's first wife, Eva, had given birth to a child, but that Henson had disowned the infant. He later complained to Robert and Josephine Peary that he was "only home [from Greenland] for seven months when the child was born in my family, and they want to say that it was my child. . . . Do you think I ought to live with that woman any longer? I will ask you and Mrs. Peary for your advice." This prompted Eva's brother "Flint" to threaten Henson with plans to write his employers at the American Museum of Natural History in New York and Peary to complain that Henson "did not treat Eva right." Henson continued to support Eva for about another year, but he never claimed the child as his own biological offspring. His belief in her infidelity during his absence caused him to leave her in the spring of 1897.

That summer, Henson went back to Greenland to help Peary collect the last of the Eskimos' sacred meteorites. On October 8, 1897,

Eva wrote to Robert Peary too and asked, "Will you please inform me of the whereabouts of my husband? . . . I did not know that he had been away with you, until I read his name among the crew [of Peary's expeditionary ship]." She asked Peary to "please excuse the liberty," but indicated that she sought no further aid from Henson, only Peary's help in getting Henson to give her a "bill of divorce."

* * *

I reached into my backpack and pulled out the colorful blanket that Olive had sent Anaukaq. "It's from your cousin Olive," I said.

"My cousin?" Anaukaq echoed, with a big smile.

"Yes, your cousin Olive in Boston sent you this blanket. She made it herself."

"*Irriahnocktoe, irriahnocktoe* [Beautiful, beautiful]," Anaukaq declared with a wide grin. "Pretty good," he shouted as he looked around the room, holding up the blanket for the family to see. He patted my shoulder several times with the strong hands of an old hunter, and said, "*Kooyounah,* this is a wonderful day for me. Now I know I have relatives over there!" He passed the gift around the room to his children and grandchildren. They too marveled at the handsome blanket, made even lovelier by the fact that it came from one of their heretofore only imagined relatives in America.

When the blanket came back to Anaukaq, he wrapped it around his shoulders like a shawl, then quietly rocked from side to side and from front to back, humming to himself as if meditating, relishing the moment.

"I also brought along some photographs of your relatives," I said, pulling a stack of old and new photographs out of my backpack. The rest of the family quickly crowded around Anaukaq and me, chattering away excitedly. "This is a photo of your cousin Olive, who sent you the blanket," I said.

"This is my cousin?" Anaukaq asked, holding the photo close to his face and gazing at it with his better eye. "She looks very good. She could be an Eskimo woman," he said with a chuckle.

"Yes, and this is her father David, Mahri-Pahluk's brother."

"Ooh, look at them. They are very good—very beautiful." After examining each print carefully, the old patriarch passed the photos down the line among his children. He continued to rock back and forth, chuckling all the while, as he reached for the next photo.

I had even brought along a few photos of the most recent American Hensons, babies born to Matthew Henson's brothers' and sisters' grandchildren. "Look at them, they are so fat—so cute. They look like Eskimo babies," Anaukaq and his granddaughters were saying. "Oh this baby is so beautiful. I want to keep her," Malina said of one of the American Henson babies.

But one old photograph that I pulled from my collection really caught Anaukaq's eye. It was one of his father at the age of eighty-one—almost Anaukaq's own age—taken in 1947 by the Urban League of New York as part of a new magazine series on black heroes. The photograph showed a distinguished-looking Matthew Henson in a dark three-piece suit, showing an issue of *Negro Heroes* to an African-American boy of about ten, who is sitting on his knee.

"Who is this boy?" Anaukaq inquired right away. "Is he related to Mahri-Pahluk?"

"I really don't know, but I am still trying to locate him through old records," I said. "If he still is alive, he would be about fifty years old now."

"Maybe he is the son of one of my uncles," Anaukaq offered.

"Perhaps. But I shall try to find out who he is when I return to America."

He looked at the photograph, then back at me, and laughed, "My father was a good-looking man."

Anaukaq took this photograph and put it on a shelf behind him in a "special place."

"Do you have a picture of my father's grave?" he asked.

"No. Unfortunately, I did not take a photograph of his grave site. But I can tell you that he is buried in a place called Woodlawn Cemetery, in the city where he spent most of his life, New York."

"Is he buried alone or among others?" he asked softly.

"He is buried among many others, in a large burial ground," I replied.

Anaukaq thought for a moment, looking back at the photograph on the shelf.

"Is he buried next to his wife?" Anaukaq asked.

"No, not exactly," I answered. "She died thirteen years after Mahri-Pahluk's death and was buried in the nearest space available, about thirty meters from Mahri-Pahluk's grave."

"A man and his wife should be buried beside each other. So they can be together again as in old times. So that they can talk about old times. When I die, I will be buried next to my Aviaq."

"I agree," I said. "But I believe Mahri-Pahluk and his wife were poor in their old age. When he died, she had just enough money to bury him in the same grave as her mother, Susan Ross. Then when she died some years later, her friends and relatives buried her in the nearest gravesite available."

Anaukaq sat quietly for a moment, taking this all in. The others in the room, who had been quietly but intently listening to our conversation, now began to talk softly among themselves.

"I would like very much to see my father's grave one day," Anaukaq said, as he took the 1947 photo from the shelf and stared at it again. "I would also like to see my relatives. But I haven't much time. I am an old man now. I have been ill in recent years. I hope I live to see some of my relatives and Mahri-Pahluk's grave. I hope I live to see the day."

"I too hope that you will someday meet your American relatives and see your father's grave. I can only promise you that I will do all that I can to help you."

"Did you find Cousin Kali's relatives too," Anaukaq inquired.

"Yes, I found some of Kali's relatives in the United States also," I responded, somewhat hesitantly.

"Then they must have been happy to learn of Kali," he said, questioningly, then continued. "They say that some of Peeuree's family came up here many years ago, but we never saw them."

"Well, I never really met any of Kali's relatives, but I spoke with them by phone, and they seemed surprised to learn that I had found you and Kali," I said, trying to skirt the issue.

"Did Kali have any living brothers and sisters?" Anaukaq asked.

"Oh, yes," I replied. "Peary had one son in America, and he is still living. He is now eighty-three years old."

"He is eighty-three years old? That is wonderful," Anaukaq responded. "I know Kali will be very happy to meet his brother."

"Well, Robert Peary had a big family in America," I said. "Two children, seven grandchildren, and many great-grandchildren. I told the family about Kali, and I am sure that he will meet some of them."

In spite of my efforts to disguise the reaction of Kali's American family, I had a feeling that Anaukaq detected my reservations. He ended the conversation by saying, "It is good that Kali has a living brother. They should meet. They are brothers and should know one another."

* * *

Over the next few weeks, I followed Anaukaq all about the village, filming him and just observing him as he visited his Eskimo relatives, old friends, and some of the young people of the settlement. He was immensely popular.

He showed the photos of his relatives to almost everyone he met. "These are my cousins from Mahri-Pahluk's homeland," he would say with a big grin. "I'm going to go over there to meet them one day."

His neighbors were invariably gracious. "Oh, what a beautiful family you have," they would say, after looking at the photos. "You must be very happy to have such a beautiful family."

Anaukaq's sister-in-law Mikkisuk Minge, now in her eighties, still wore traditional Polar Eskimo clothing, including hip-length, cream-colored sealskin boots. "Of course, I have known Anaukaq since we were very young," she told me. "Anaukaq has always been known for his very special laugh. No matter how unhappy one felt, when Anaukaq came around and laughed that special laugh of his, your spirits were just lifted in the air."

"One day, when we were young," she went on to say, "I was sitting out in front of the igloo with his wife, Aviaq, cutting some whale meat, when Anaukaq came up and gave her a bottle of wine that he had bought at the Danish trade station. He did not give me one, so I was very jealous. I said to myself, she is married to a *kulnocktooko* man and he treats her very special. He comes here and gives her some good drink. He treats her special, but gives nothing to his sister-in-law. I was jealous." She burst into laughter.

This was an opportunity for me to find out more about the significance of Anaukaq's and Kali's racial differences among the Eskimos, especially among the older people, who were not so much influenced by the world beyond. "You mentioned that Anaukaq was a black man, Mikkisuk. Did the Eskimo people feel that he was different from everyone else because he is dark skinned?"

"Well, yes, of course," she responded, with a big smile. "Up here we all say that Anaukaq and family are a little different from the other Eskimos. Not in a bad way. But different in a good way."

"You mean different because he is darker than the other Eskimos and has curly hair?" I asked.

"Ha, ha! Different in many ways. We always say that it must be because he is Mahri-Pahluk's son."

"How are Anaukaq and his family different? Give me an example," I asked.

"Well, up here we say that his whole family walks different from the other Eskimos."

"Walks differently?" I repeated.

"Yes! You can distinguish a member of Anaukaq's family walking from a great distance. We say that they walk like they are gliding on ice."

Another woman in the room joined in. "It's true what she says. Up here everyone knows this about Anaukaq's family."

Mikkisuk continued. "Anaukaq and his sons could also dance better than the other Eskimos. When we would have our dances, they were always the best dancers."

By now I could no longer contain my laughter. How could these people, who had little or no knowledge of black people, harbor this comical stereotype? I knew they meant no disrespect to Anaukaq and his family. Quite the contrary. They saw these characteristics as desirable traits.

"Most of Anaukaq's family can play musical instruments too. When the *kadoona* missionaries brought musical instruments up here through the trading post, Anaukaq and his family were the only Eskimos to get them and play them well, even his grandchildren."

"Do you really think they dance better than other Eskimos, or did you learn this from the Danes?" I asked, jokingly.

"No! It is true. Everyone up here knows that Anaukaq and his children are the best dancers and the fastest runners among our people—and they walk nicer, so smoothly."

She got up to demonstrate. "See, Eskimos walk like this," she said, taking short, soft steps to imitate their stride and pace. "And the *kahdonah* walk like a stone—like this," she said, now moving from side to side taking long, wide, stomping strides. "Anaukaq and his family walk like this." Her steps were now light touches on the ground, as she glided across the room, slightly twisting her body from side to side, as if riding on a breeze.

Even in my laughter, I had to admit that her imitation of the Amer-Eskimo Henson's walk was unmistakably African-American. Could this be true? I wondered. Amazing! I too had observed that some of Anaukaq's gestures, such as his frequent hand-clapping when he laughed, reminded me of behavior of some older African Americans.

"What about Kali, was he different also?" I asked.

"Yes. Kali was somewhat different from the other Eskimos too. He could dance too, but he could not dance like Anaukaq," she said.

"Well, how was he different from the other Eskimos?" I inquired.

"Kali?" she said, as if rethinking my question. "Kali was a very funny man when he was young. He had a great sense of humor and loved to tell jokes. He also loved to brag about being a good hunter. But he was a good hunter. When he used to have a drink, he would sing and try to dance like Anaukaq."

"What about Kali's children?" I asked. "Were they good dancers and runners like Anaukaq's?"

"Not really. Kali's family is very nice, but they are different—maybe not as friendly as Anaukaq's family. I think when Kali was young he was not as popular as Anaukaq. But everybody up here liked Kali and thought that he and his family were very nice."

* * *

When Anaukaq learned of my plans to travel up to Qeqertarsaaq to visit Kali, he reminded me that he too would like to see his "cousin Kali." "We haven't spent any time together since we were fifteen years old," he said.

I offered to take Anaukaq to Qeqertarsaaq with me, but then thought better of it when I remembered that Kali's island home is not accessible by helicopter. We would have to travel about seventy-five miles over the frozen bay to Qeqertarsaaq. Although Anaukaq appeared in good physical condition, he was still walking with a cane and could tire over long distances. Kali, on the other hand, was in excellent condition. He still frequently traveled by dogsled with his son and grandsons. And yet, I thought, it would be great to see the two old hunters together again after so many years. The stories they could tell would be fascinating, and I could learn much more about their growing up half-Eskimo in Greenland, one half-black, the other half-white.

Anaukaq solved the problem for me. "Why don't you tell Kali that he is welcome to come back with you to visit me? I have plenty of food and tea."

CHAPTER NINE

❋ ❋ ❋

Growing Up Eskimo

Kali and his son, Talilanguaq, welcomed me back as warmly as had Anaukaq and his family.

"Did you have a good trip?" Kali asked.

"Yes. It was a long but safe trip," I replied. "I flew in the big military *cheemeahktoe* [man-made bird] to Thule. I didn't realize it would be so cold up here until we landed. It was warmer the last time I was here."

"Oh, it's only cold outside the igloo," he said with a chuckle. "You just have to stay inside the igloo as much as you can."

"Then I must build my own snow igloo, like in the old days, so that I can really keep warm," I said to his obvious delight.

"Did you find Cousin Anaukaq's relatives over there where you live?" he asked.

I told him that I had located several of Anaukaq's relatives and that they were pleased to learn of their Eskimo relatives.

"That is very good," Kali replied cheerfully. "Does he have many relatives over there—any brothers and sisters?"

"He has many relatives all over the United States, mostly cousins, but no brothers or sisters," I replied.

"I hope they are well," Kali said.

"They are well indeed," I said. "I only met a few of Anaukaq's folks personally, but I talked with most of them by phone. I hope to meet more of them when I return to my country."

There was a long, pregnant pause before Kali posed the inevitable question, "What about my people? Did I have any relatives over there?"

"Yes!" I answered, trying to muster as much enthusiasm as I could in my voice and smile. "I located several of your American relatives, and they all wished you well."

Kali smiled but said nothing.

I told him that I had not met any of his relatives face to face yet, because they all lived in different parts of the country, but that I had talked with some of his nephews by telephone and learned from them that he had an eighty-three-year-old brother living in Maine. "That is in another territory, north of the place where I live," I explained, "and I have not had the opportunity to meet him yet."

"Eighty-three years old," Kali repeated. "We are about the same age."

"That's right," I said. "He is your second big brother."

Kali laughed. "*Eeee* [Yes]! He was born between Hammy and me. What is his name?"

"Robert Peary, Jr.," I replied. "He was given the name of his father."

"He was named for Peeuree?" Kali asked.

"Yes," I replied. "That is a common practice in my country. He has a son named Robert Peary III and a grandson named Robert Peary IV. He has several children and grandchildren, just as you have, but I can't remember how many. He lives with his wife and son in Augusta, Maine, Peary's old home area."

"I hope that he is in good health. I would like to meet him," Kali said. "But we are both getting old."

"I hope you will have the chance to meet soon," I replied.

Since I had received no gifts for Kali from his American relatives, I had brought along a few of my own. I reached into my pocket, pulled out a Swiss Army knife, and handed it to him.

"This is a gift for you," I said.

"For me?" Kali responded.

"Yes, it is for you," I said. "A great hunter always needs a good hunting knife."

"*Kooyounah!*" Kali said with a big smile.

"*Iddigdoo* [You are welcome]," I replied in my best Eskimo.

"Who is this gift from?" he asked.

"It is a gift from me," I said.

"*Kooyounah*," he said again as he examined the knife. I suspected that he would like this gift because such knives are prized among the Polar Eskimos, especially the hunters.

"I have another gift that I brought from America for you," I said, handing him an eight-by-ten black-and-white photograph. "It is a photograph of your father, Commander Peeuree."

"Commander Peeuree," Kali repeated, as if imitating my English.

He studied the photograph for a while. "He looks like he is growing old in this picture."

"I think he was only in his fifties when this photo was taken," I responded, leaning over to look at the photograph again.

"Mmmm. This is my father, Peeuree," Kali said thoughtfully. "It is a good-looking photograph of my father. But I don't remember how he looked. He left when I was a small child. I do remember my mother saying to me that when I was a child, I would hit him about the legs whenever I was near him. I don't know why I would do a thing like that, and I don't remember hitting him," he chortled. "I also remember something else my mother told me many times. She said that when Peeuree was worried, he would take himself like this." Kali grasped the bridge of his nose with his index finger and thumb as he bowed his head over a closed fist and swayed from side to side. "I think maybe I do that, too, sometimes."

Kali continued to stare at the photograph. I wondered whether he could see the remarkable resemblance to himself that was so clear to me. I wondered just how many times during his eighty years he had thought about his real father, or imagined how different his life might have been had Peary claimed him as his son and contributed to his upbringing. I wondered, but I did not ask.

I told Kali that his cousin Anaukaq hoped that he would return with me to Moriussaq. Much to my delight, Kali accepted the invitation. Joined by his son, Talilanguaq, he crossed the bay to Qaanaaq, where he boarded a helicopter. Kali was at first skeptical of the *chemeahktoe*, but once aloft he seemed to enjoy the ride. He grudgingly admitted that this form of travel had its advantages, even if it lacked the adventure and romance of traditional dogsled travel. Even by the fastest dogsled, the trip from Qaanaaq around the mountainous coast to Moriussaq normally took a day. By helicopter it took only an hour.

When he landed in Moriussaq, Anaukaq was there to greet him. As Talilanguaq helped his father from the helicopter, the two old friends began laughing joyously. They shook hands, grabbed each other's shoulders, and stared each other in the eye, chuckling all the while like two young boys.

"*Hinaynukwhonay* [Hello, how are you], my cousin? It is good to see you," said Kali.

"*Aheewhoghia* [I am fine]," Anaukaq replied. "It is good to see you, too, my cousin. Welcome to Moriussaq. You look great!"

"I am good for an old seal hunter. It must be that shot of whiskey that I take once in a while," Kali replied. Again they broke into laughter. "You look well to me," Kali continued. "I had heard from my children that you had been very ill a while back."

"I was very ill last year, but I am much better now," Anaukaq replied. "My granddaughter Malina acts as a nurse for me, and my sons hunt for me. So I am well fed and very *peeshahhah* [strong] today."

"Good," Kali said, as we hurried from under the whirring blades of the departing helicopter, which was blowing swirls of snowflakes all around us.

We collected the bags and headed off in the direction of Anaukaq's igloo. Together for the first time in many years, the two men chatted away. They were a striking sight walking together, proudly leading the small entourage of villagers toward the center of the settlement, ever conscious of my camera recording their interaction. As I watched them step surefootedly over the packed snow—one dark in complexion, the other much lighter—I could imagine that I was looking at Matthew Henson and Robert Peary themselves, hiking together across this frozen land nearly a century ago.

When we reached Anaukaq's home, his sons came out to greet Kali and Talilanguaq and invited all of us into the central room of the house.

"Aah, *keyettoe* [warm]," Kali said. "*Irriahnocktoe* [beautiful] igloo."

Everyone exchanged pleasantries and talked about the two families. Kali was particularly charmed by Magssanguaq, Anaukaq's ten-year-old grandson, who had just returned from a hunting trip wearing his traditional polar bear fur pants and carrying a rifle.

"This is my grandson, Magssanguaq," Anaukaq said proudly, rubbing the boy's head. "He is a *peeneeahktoe* [hunter] at age ten."

"A *peeneeahktoe* already?" asked Kali, making an obvious effort to show the boy that he was impressed. "Maybe he will grow up to be a *peeneeahktoe wah* like his grandfather."

"I hope so," Anaukaq said. "I think he will be a great hunter when he grows up."

Young Magssanguaq smiled, shyly proud at this praise from his revered elders.

Anaukaq served *cobve* [coffee], and the two old-timers sat across from each other, drinking and talking. Later, as a special treat for his guest, Anaukaq brought out their favorite delicacy.

"*Cheemeahk* [Birds]!" Anaukaq announced, displaying a pair of white kittiwakes. These birds, which look like moderate-sized seagulls, are stored in closed sealskin pouches under a rock pile for about a year. During that time they become fully fermented, allowing the Eskimos to eat them raw.

"Aah, *cheemeahk*," Kali exclaimed. "*Kooyounah.* I haven't had any *cheemeahk* since last summer."

"*Iddigdoo*," Anaukaq said. "There is plenty, so eat much. My grandson Magssanguaq shot them."

"Oh, that is wonderful," Kali responded. "That grandson of yours is really a good *peeneeahktoe.*"

Anaukaq and Kali skillfully peeled away the birds' feathers and skin, much as one peels an orange, to expose the red, fleshy meat. Eventually each retrieved from his bird a walnut-sized, membranous sac that looked like a small plastic bag. The sacs were filled with seeds eaten by the bird and stored in its crop. They held the sacs up and commented on their size and contents, which told the old hunters many things about the origin, health, fertility, and general condition of the kittiwake population.

"Here," Kali said to me. "Smell this." He opened the top of the little sac and held it to my nose. It had a fragrance similar to that of fresh flowers, or maybe jasmine.

"It smells very pleasant," I said.

Anaukaq then got up and found a small string of sealskin. He tied one end of the string around the top of the membranous sac and attached the other to the timber in the ceiling. "It will make my igloo smell very good," he explained.

"That is wonderful," I said, once again amazed at the resourcefulness of my hosts. "You have taught me so many things about the Eskimo ways." Both men chuckled with pride.

With their pocket knives, they began to carve their birds in much the same way that we slice apples, putting slivers of the raw, bloody meat in their mouths in between words. Before long their mouths and hands were stained a deep red.

"*Mahmaktoe*," Kali said with a grin, as he handed me a small slice of the delicacy.

Actually, the meat was quite flavorful—somewhat vinegary, but not bad. "Kali. Anaukaq. Which one of you was the better *peeneeahktoe* in your younger days?" I asked. The two men continued eating in silence for a moment, thinking over my question.

"This one!" Anaukaq said, pointing at Kali. "This one! He is probably the greatest hunter of all the Inuit people."

Anaukaq had barely finished when Kali pointed at him and said, "This one! Anaukaq. He is the greatest hunter of all the Inuit people. Before he injured his eye cutting a seal, no one was better."

"Ooh, no," Anaukaq protested. "You used to hunt *pooeehee* [seal] and *kahlayleewah* much better than any of us. You enjoyed it so much."

"Oh, I really enjoyed hunting *kahlayleewah* more than anything," Kali said. "I can remember when I got my first kayak. I was so happy because then I was able to take care of myself. I could be on my own. I liked to sneak up on the *kahlayleewah* by paddling silently," he continued, dramatically imitating the twirling motions of a kayaker.

"Then I would lift my harpoon and thrust it into the *kahlayleewah*, like this." He demonstrated. "All of a sudden, the rope attached to the harpoon tip would start to unwind, and the sealskin float would jump from the kayak into the water as the big *kahlayleewah* struggled against me. We would fight until one of us won. Oh, that was the greatest thrill. I enjoyed that very much."

"You were the best," Anaukaq said, chuckling at Kali's histrionics. "I really miss the old hunting days."

"But you were good at everything, my cousin. I remember how you could run across the ice faster than anyone we had ever seen," Kali said, laughing. "You were the fastest of all the Inuit boys."

Anaukaq's son Ajako, who had just entered the room, chimed in, "Up here they say the men in our family have the fastest legs of all the Inuit, and my *ahtahtah* [father] was the fastest runner."

Kali then turned to me. "Anaukaq could run so fast that I once saw him run after a big *chairreeinyah* [fox], and not only did he catch the fox, but he began kicking him, too, as they ran along."

The old men laughed uproariously at this story.

Changing the subject, I asked Anaukaq and Kali about their up-bringing. "Did you attend missionary schools when you were young-sters?"

"No," Anaukaq replied immediately. "There were no missionary schools in those days when we were young. We could only become hunters. There was nothing else we could do. The women became hunter-wives. Nowadays, the young men and women can go to school and take jobs with the Danes. They can become mechanics, like my fourth son, Vittus. But we enjoyed being hunters. I think a hunter is the best thing a man can be."

"When the missionary schools came along, did you want your children to go to school?" I asked.

"*Eeee*," said Kali.

"Oh, yes," Anaukaq agreed. "We wanted them to have the best advantages. We knew that our traditional world was changing with more of the Danish people coming up here and more modern things reaching this area by ship. But we also wanted them to keep the old ways, too, to become hunters."

"All of our oldest sons were still hunters first," Kali interjected, "even if they attended the missionary schools. But we old hunters had no opportunity to attend school."

"That is right," said Anaukaq. "Even after the air base was built in the 1950s and we saw some modern things come into this area, we were still hunters on the move, so that we could all eat. And our children traveled on the hunt with us."

"Sometimes we would have to take our children out of school so that they could join us on the hunt. We had to have enough food," Kali said. "But we would try not to disturb them while school was in."

"We were happy to be hunters," Anaukaq said. "We could write our names, and we could read our names. That was good. Our children could read and write, so they helped us. But we taught our sons to be hunters so they could survive on their own, look after their families in the traditional ways."

"Didn't the Danes and the Americans provide you with modern food supplies?" I asked.

"They provided some things like canned foods and fish, even frozen chicken lately," Anaukaq answered. "But we preferred our own native foods, like *nanook, kahlayleewah, cheemeahk, ahvuk, pooeehee, tooktoo,* and *ahkahlik,*" he said, listing them in order of Polar Eskimo preference.

"Anaukaq, were you ever treated any differently by the other Eskimos because you were of mixed race?" I asked.

He laughed. "*Nahahn* [No]. Not really. The people up here are too nice for that kind of thing. When I was a youngster, though, if I was too rough with other children, sometimes they would shout, 'You are black! You are black and not clean-faced!' But they didn't mean anything by it, and it was usually my fault for making them say such."

"Did everyone know why you looked different? I mean, why you were darker than the other Eskimos, and why you had curly *newyah* [hair]?" I asked.

"Yes, of course," Anaukaq replied. "All of the Inuit knew I was the son of Mahri-Pahluk and that he was *kulnocktooko.* But I was very happy for that, for being *kulnocktooko* like my father. For many years, though, I was ashamed of my curly *newyah*."

"Ashamed?" I was puzzled. "How so?"

"Yes," he laughed. "As a child, even as a man, I wanted straight hair, like my mother and later my wife. I would say to my wife that 'straight hair is so beautiful, why do I have this unruly curly hair?' Then later all of the young Inuit women started trying to curl their hair. Many of them started to use curlers. I said to them, 'Your straight hair is so beautiful. Why do you mess it up by making it curly?' But they said to me, 'No, your curly hair is beautiful. We want hair like yours.' I was so surprised at them. I thought the idea was kind of silly."

"What about you, Kali? Did the other Inuit treat you very differently as a youngster because you were part white?" I asked.

"Well, sometimes," he replied.

"How so?" I asked.

Kali seemed a bit more reluctant to talk about this subject than Anaukaq had been. "Mmmm, sometimes the other children would taunt my brother and me, call us names, things like that," Kali said.

"What kind of names?" I asked.

"Sometimes they would tell me and my older brother Hammy that we were more *kahdonah* than Eskimo, and that we thought we were better than others. Other times they would point to us and say, 'There, the *kahdonah* ones.'" Kali chuckled. "We used to get very angry, especially Hammy. But our mother protected us."

Kali continued. "This really affected Hammy more than it did me. He used to get so upset inside. He was always very active, doing things to keep his mind off his hurt. Hammy and I tried to be the best hunters we possibly could. That way, we could show them that we were as good as everyone else."

"You mean that you were as much Inuit as everyone else?" I said.

"Yes, that is right," said Kali.

"Do you feel different from other Eskimos because you are part white?" I asked.

"I am Eskimo," he affirmed proudly, still chewing on a piece of raw bird. "I was born and raised Eskimo. I think Eskimo. I was an Eskimo hunter. I did not grow up in the ways of the *kahdonah*. All my children were raised as Inuit. My sons Talilanguaq and Peter and my grandson, Ole, are all Eskimo hunters. My *ahnahnna* [mother] and my adoptive *ahtahtah*, Peeahwahto, raised me to be a good Eskimo," he continued. "That is what they knew. They never told me that I should try to be different from other Inuit because I looked different. And Peeuree did nothing for my brother Hammy and me. There were no other *kahdonah* around. We lived only with other Inuit, traveling from place to place with other families, with the seasons."

"That is right," Anaukaq chimed in. "We are both Inuit Eskimos and we have known only the Inuit life. We had no contact with the *kahdonah* except for the few Danish missionaries at Thule Station, and we would only see them about once a year."

"Sometimes during the summers, whaling ships from different lands would come to Cape York, south of here," Kali added. "Then we would see *kahdonah*, some even from Peeuree's homeland."

"Yes," said Anaukaq. "That reminds me. When we were young boys, MacMillan, who had worked on the North Pole trip, used to come up here to work and travel north on the ice. He would find Cousin Kali and me, and give us gifts and candy. He was very kind to us. He would tell us that our fathers were well and bring us greetings from them."

"MacMillan was good," Kali agreed. "We never saw our fathers up here, but MacMillan came up here several times when we were boys. He was very nice. He always gave us something. It kind of made us feel that we were not forgotten. He gave candy and gifts to other children as well."

"Did he ever give your mothers gifts or anything sent from America personally from Mahri-Pahluk and Peeuree?" I asked, looking at both men.

"Oh, *nahdoohhoyah* [I don't know]," answered Kali. "I can't remember." Anaukaq could not recall either but thought he remembered MacMillan bringing some things from Mahri-Pahluk for his mother, Akatingwah.

Their recollections were certainly consistent with MacMillan's reputation. By all accounts, he was among the kinder, more open-minded members of Peary's party. We also know that after Peary's

last expedition, MacMillan became the preeminent American explorer of the Arctic and made several visits to the area in which
Anaukaq and Kali lived. As one of the few people who knew for
certain of Peary and Henson's "North Pole secret," and as a loyal
friend of both men, MacMillan might well have been asked to look in
discreetly on the explorers' Amer-Eskimo "orphans."

"Did MacMillan ever offer to take you to America?" I asked.

"No," Anaukaq answered. "We were too young then, and we had
to stay with our parents. But later we wanted very much to go to
America and see our fathers and other relatives."

Kali added that when they were young boys, his brother Hammy
used to tell people, especially when they taunted him, that he was
going to go to America to find "Peeuree." And when he found him,
he would stay with his *ahtahtah* in a big igloo. But he and Hammy
were frightened, Kali said, because everyone had heard about the
bad things that had happened to Mene and his family when they
went to Peary's homeland.

"The Eskimos," Kali said, "felt that Mene and his group were all
overcome by bad spirits and died."

Kali was referring to the tragic story of the young Polar Eskimo,
Mene, who, with his father, Kes-shoo, and four other Inuit, was
taken to the United States by Peary in 1897 and later "exhibited" at
the American Museum of Natural History in New York. Some of the
Eskimos had been with Peary that year when he confiscated the last
of the sacred Polar Eskimo meteorites, or "heaven stones," which he
later sold to the museum. Soon after they arrived in the United
States, most of the Eskimos fell ill with pneumonia and other afflic-
tions. Peary and the museum director promptly summoned Matthew
Henson, the only person in the United States known to speak their
language, but there was nothing he or anyone else could do. All but
the eight-year-old Mene and one other Eskimo were hospitalized and
eventually died. Compounding the tragedy, the museum defleshed
the remains of the dead Eskimos and put their articulated skeletons
on display. Upon seeing his father's skeleton in public, the forlorn
Mene became enraged. With the help of others, including some
journalists, he fought to remove his father's remains from the exhibit
for proper burial. Although the noted anthropologist Franz Boas had

come up with the idea of displaying the Eskimos, Robert Peary was roundly criticized for his role in the affair.

After twelve difficult years in America, Mene returned of his own volition to northwest Greenland in 1909 aboard Peary's relief ship, the *Jeanie*. Fortunately, he met Peary and Henson just as they were preparing to depart for the United States. According to Henson, "[Mene] was almost destitute, having positively nothing in the way of an equipment to enable him to withstand the rigors of the country, and was no more fitted for the life he was to take up than any boy of eighteen or twenty would be. . . . However, Commander Peary ordered that he be given a plentiful supply of furs to keep him warm, food, ammunition and loading outfit, traps and guns."[1]

Mene slowly and painfully tried to reacclimate himself to the Eskimo life he had known as a child. He became a pretty good hunter and, with the help of friends and relatives, learned to look after himself. But eventually he abandoned any hope of fully readjusting to his native culture. In the summer of 1916, seven years after his return, he hitched a ride on an expeditionary relief ship bound for the United States and left Greenland for the last time. Unable to reestablish his old contacts, he wandered around the eastern United States for two years, working as an itinerant laborer. Some speculate that he may have been trying to work his way up to Peary's residence in Maine. In any event, in 1918 Mene died of bronchial pneumonia while working at a lumber camp in Pittsburg, New Hampshire. He was buried by friends in a local cemetery, where his body remains today.

"Did anyone besides MacMillan ever bring you word from your fathers?" I asked.

"No," replied Kali. "After MacMillan stopped coming up here, we heard nothing about our fathers. We gave up all hope of ever visiting Peeuree's homeland."

"Did the other white men who came up here know that you were the sons of Mahri-Pahluk and Peeuree?" I asked.

"*Nahdoohhoyah*," said Anaukaq. "No one ever said so. We were treated by outsiders just like other Eskimos. We did not have last names in those days, before the missionaries asked us to take last names in the late 1960s. We were only known by our first names."

"There are other half-white Inuit up here," Kali added. "Maybe they did not know which of us were the children of Peeuree."

"That is possible in your case, Kali," I said. "But Mahri-Pahluk was the only *kulnocktooko* to visit Polar Eskimo lands at that time, and any dark offspring would have to be his."

Both men laughed. "You are right."

"When they built the military base at Umanak," Anaukaq said, "many men came up here from Mahri-Pahluk and Peary's homeland. But they did not know who we were or that we were their [Henson's and Peary's] sons. They just told all Inuit people that they had to move much farther north or south of Umanak mountain because they were going to build a base there. The people did not want to move but were forced to do so."

"One day we heard that some of the Inuit had seen a *kulnocktooko* man while traveling past the base on the way to Savissivik," Anaukaq continued. "My family became very excited because we thought that he might be one of Mahri-Pahluk's descendants—one of our relatives. Maybe he had come up here to find us, we thought. We wanted him to come and visit us, but he never came. A short time later, he left Greenland. We don't know why, but some said that maybe the chiefs at the base would not let him come to see us."

I spent the next few days listening to and recording the two men's stories. They seemed to delight in the opportunity to talk with someone who showed interest in their lives and cultural heritage. The younger family members who joined us also learned from these revelations about their past and ancestry.

I followed them all about the settlement. Anaukaq showed Kali around his settlement much as one does a guest in any culture. Anaukaq proudly presented his eight sled dogs and talked about their strength and breeding. He took Kali to the little general store at the edge of the settlement run by his fourth son, Ajako, and to the grave of his wife, Aviaq.

Too soon the time came for me to return to the United States. I would have to leave the settlement by helicopter while the unpredictable weather was calm, so that I could reach Thule in time for my scheduled flight to McGuire Air Force Base.

On my last evening in Moriussaq, I prepared a big dinner for

Anaukaq, Kali, and their families. The bill of fare was all my remaining food. Though they loved my canned tuna, ham, and other meats, they found other offerings less than appetizing.

"What do you call this stuff?" asked Kali. "It tastes like paper."

"Oatmeal," I replied. "It's a kind of grain, like a bread."

"Why do you have so much of it?" Anaukaq inquired.

"Well, it's easy to carry, it's filling, and it's good for you. All you have to do is add water."

"It is good for people with no teeth," Kali interjected.

Everyone laughed.

In a more serious tone, Anaukaq asked, "Allen, do you think you will be able to arrange for us to go to America?"

"I hope so, Anaukaq," I answered. "But I cannot promise anything, other than that I will try my best to arrange such a trip. There are many difficulties, you know. It will be very expensive. Transportation alone from Greenland to the United States is a big problem. Then we must have food, lodging, and transportation in the United States. It is very difficult and very expensive. I don't know how I can do it, but maybe I can raise the money from your American families. And perhaps I can get the Danish government to help us. I'm just speculating now," I quickly added. "I don't want to get your hopes up only to fail. But I promise you that I will try my best."

"I know you will. We have faith in you," Anaukaq said with uncharacteristic sadness in his voice. "I hope this dream becomes real. It is the last dream I have before I die. You see, I have been ill lately, and I will not live much longer. So if I am ever to see my American relatives and my father's grave, it must be soon."

"I understand, my friend," I said.

"I hope I live to see the day, but if I die before you can arrange such a trip, I hope that you will help my sons and their children meet their American relatives and see Mahri-Pahluk's grave site. That is very important to me."

"You have my word that I will try my best," I said. "Just keep the faith."

"*Eeee*," Kali added. "My cousin has been very ill lately. I now worry for him. I hope we can both go to our fathers' homeland before he becomes more gravely ill. I will help to look after him."

I was deeply moved by Kali's concern for Anaukaq. During the time I had spent with the two of them I had come to believe that they were more like brothers than friends or "cousins." At eighty years of age they were still looking after each other. Their fathers, who also shared a special bond, would be happy to see this, I thought.

"If I can arrange this trip to the United States, how many of your family would you want to go along with you?" I asked both men.

Anaukaq spoke up first. "I would be very happy if my sons could go with me: Avataq, Ajako, Ussarkaq, and Kitdlaq. My other son Vittus is not here. He is in southern Greenland working for the Danes and maybe cannot join us. But I would like to see him."

Then Anaukaq's granddaughter Malina, who had been dancing in African-American fashion to a soul music tape on my recorder, said, "I would like to go, too."

"Me, too," added Anaukaq's ten-year-old granddaughter, Aviaq. "If Malina goes I want to go also."

"What about you, Kali?" I asked. "Which of your children do you want to travel with you to America if we have the opportunity to go there?"

"Oh, I don't know. But I think I would like for my son, Talilanguaq, and my grandson Ole to go with me."

"Let me see," I said, counting on my fingers. "That's Anaukaq, Kali, Avataq, Talilanguaq, Ajako, Ussarkaq, Kitdlaq, Ole, Malina, Aviaq, and possibly Vittus—a total of thirteen, counting myself and Navarana Qavigaq, the translator. That is quite a few people. It will be very expensive. But we shall see. If we have to take fewer people on the first trip, I will let Anaukaq and Kali decide who will join them."

"Maybe we can aim for a date next fall [1987], about a year from now," I said. "But I promise you I will be back in the spring to let you know about my progress in arranging a visit. Just keep the faith."

"Yes, the fall or winter would be a good time because it might be very hot in the other seasons," Anaukaq said.

"I agree with my cousin," Kali chuckled. "You know, Eskimos don't like heat."

Everyone laughed, and on that cheerful note we ended our dinner.

In spite of the enthusiasm I had shown in the presence of Kali and

Anaukaq, privately I was less optimistic. I knew that it would be an enormous task to arrange a trip to America for both families. Just how I was going to do it, I did not know.

As we stepped out into the cold darkness, we witnessed a final, unexpected salute to the end of my visit. At first I was startled. The scene before my eyes seemed surreal, even magical. In the pitch black of the night, as if by some theatrical orchestration, the sky suddenly lit up with lights so bright that I thought they came from unnatural or artificial sources. The lights formed radiant streams of white ghostlike figures, descending from a large circle in the sky directly above me. Some of these luminous apparitions seemed to have long tails and faces on their cometlike heads. As if on cue, the brilliant streams of light would drop straight down toward the ground and then sail back up again. Before long the light forms were all around us, dancing and moving in all directions, like special effects in a Steven Spielberg movie.

Several of the young people ran out of their houses to enjoy what to them must be similar to our Fourth of July fireworks. But I was uneasy. For the first few moments, the lights looked so unnatural that I thought they might be exploding rockets. The fact that we were so close to the air base at Thule, the "northern defense line" of the Pentagon's Early Warning System, only intensified my anxiety. I shivered as my imagination conjured up the ultimate conflagration while I stood at the top of the planet, staring at the night sky.

It took several minutes for Anaukaq and Kali to convince me that I was actually witnessing the aurora borealis. They said that while they regularly see these northern lights, this was one of the grandest exhibitions they had ever experienced. As they explained it, the aurora borealis is a special game played by the spirits of their ancestors, a sport akin to football in which the ancestors kick a walrus's head across the sky.

Curiously and somewhat eerily, Anaukaq and Kali whistled when some especially bright lights appeared in the sky. Several of the youngsters who had joined us also whistled. To my amazement, the sound seemed to bring the lights down like comets, toward the whistler. In each instance, it looked as though there were a direct relation between the whistling and the movement of the light toward

Earth. Groping for some explanation, I thought that perhaps the pitch of the whistle caused the cold air particles to move closer together in such a way as to create a temporarily denser conductive medium of lower resistance for sound and light. Kali and Anaukaq had a simpler explanation. They said that the ancestral spirits simply came to them when they called.

When they were children, walking through a village alone, Kali said, they often were frightened by the aurora borealis if it came too close when they whistled. They thought that the ancestral spirits might come down from the sky and take them away to a strange place.

"Maybe it is a good omen," I said. "Maybe the spirits are telling us something."

The next morning Anaukaq and Kali bade me farewell as I left by helicopter for the Thule air base.

CHAPTER TEN

* * *

Keeping the Faith

Nestled in a fjord surrounded by snow-covered mountains, Dundas Air Force Base at Thule is a colossal sprawl of nondescript military buildings and airplane hangars. Although its strange appearance restores a measure of primal fright even to the most jaded observer, it offers certain conveniences otherwise unknown in this remote corner of the earth. After weeks of melting ice in my "igloo" just to take a "bath," it was therapeutic to step into a shower at the base. The hot, powerful cascade seemed to melt away the dirt, seal oil, and other vestiges of the unusual world I had just left. I let the water run for over an hour, all the while thinking about how I could help Anaukaq and Kali get to the United States—and once there, how I would arrange for their stay and their travel.

Finding transportation to the United States was the first problem. There seemed to be only two possibilities. One was to obtain seats on the weekly, sometimes monthly, military flight from Thule to Copenhagen, and then take a commercial airliner from Copenhagen to the United States. As far as I knew, however, the Copenhagen flight was restricted to the Danish military and staff personnel serving at Thule. Traveling by such a circuitous route, moreover, promised to be not only time consuming but also prohibitively expensive.

The second possibility was to hitch a ride on one of the American

C-141 transports that regularly shuttled between the United States and Thule. Like the Danish flights, however, these too were strictly for military, scientific, and other personnel serving the base. The only difference was that the U.S. Air Force had contracted with the Ministry of Greenland to transport Eskimos between Thule and Sondre Stromfiord Air Base in southern Greenland. Perhaps they could extend this policy to flights destined for the United States, I thought. I decided to meet with both the American and Danish base commanders to explore these options.

In the dining hall at the base, I had a chance meeting with Maj. Quincy Sharp, director of base operations. A tall, statuesque, soft-spoken man in his early forties, Sharp was the lead pilot in a fleet of B-52 bombers. He had flown numerous missions over the North Pole and knew about Matthew Henson and Robert Peary, but he did not know about Anaukaq and Kali, and their story fascinated him. He agreed to help me arrange a meeting with base commander Col. James Knapp, whom I had written earlier for permission to use base facilities.

The next day Colonel Knapp greeted me warmly at base headquarters. He too found the story of the two Amer-Eskimo men fascinating and advised me on the procedures for obtaining official permission from the Department of Defense to use military aircraft. Things were looking up.

I hoped that the Danish authorities would react similarly to my proposal, recognizing it as an opportunity to show some good will toward the native population. Denmark has governed Greenland since 1916, when American control of the territory, first claimed by Peary and Henson, was relinquished as part of a trade for the Danish (now American) Virgin Islands. Yet even before then relations between the Danes and the Eskimos were strained. Early Danish explorers, for example, captured Polar Eskimos and took them back to Denmark for exhibition. To the astonishment of many Danes, some of the Eskimos would steal away from Denmark in canoes in an effort to return overseas to their homeland, only to drown far out at sea.

Some Eskimos still complain, not without reason, about what they regard as a condescending attitude on the part of the Greenlandic Danes. One day during my visit to Moriussaq, I met a Danish technician who had been sent from Thule to repair some downed communication lines in the area. I shared some of my tea with him and inquired about his feelings toward the Eskimos. He said that he and many of the other Danes in Greenland called the Eskimos "junkyard Indians." When I asked why, he said it was because the Eskimos were frequently seen around the refuse and junk heaps of the Danish and American military installations, sorting through the discarded material for wood, metal, and other things. This, he said, was one of the many things that lowered them in his eyes.

But other Danes I met in Greenland, particularly those with whom I collaborated, sincerely cared about the welfare of the Polar Eskimos and treated them as equals.

In the end, the Danish authorities at Thule referred my inquiries about transporting Anaukaq and Kali to their government offices in Copenhagen and Washington.

* * *

When I arrived in Cambridge, an autumn snow had given the old Harvard Yard a picture-postcard beauty. The branches of the huge elm trees strained from the thick, cottonlike snow, and large icicles hung from the roofs of the gracefully aging red-brick buildings.

In my University Hall office, I found stacks of letters inquiring about Anaukaq and Kali. Many of the letters were from Matthew Henson's relatives all over the country. They had read the stories in newspapers and journals about my encounter with their Amer-Eskimo kin, and they wanted to meet them too. I was reminded of the statement Matthew Henson made in 1947, following the appearance of a series of articles highlighting his life. He said that he heard from relatives he didn't even know he had.

I contacted each of the family members and explained my hopes of arranging a visit to the United States for Anaukaq and Kali the following fall. All the American Hensons I spoke with expressed a strong desire to receive their Eskimo kin and to be a part of a general reunion. Some lived in Boston, some in New York, some in Maryland, others in Washington D.C., the Midwest, even California. I later learned that Matthew Henson's eighty-three-year-old niece, Virginia Carter Brannum, the last living offspring of his closest sister,

Eliza Carter, was living in Washington, D.C. A delightful woman of great poise and remarkable memory, she told me how her Uncle Matthew used to send her money to help take care of her mother. When I met and interviewed her, she shared with me her personal letters and other memorabilia from Henson.

In the meantime, following up on my conversations in Thule, I contacted the U.S. offices of the Danish government about possible support for my plans. The Danish officials with whom I spoke expressed complete surprise to learn of Anaukaq's and Kali's existence. I was told that my request would be considered by the proper authorities, who would contact me when a decision was reached.

I also wrote to the U.S. Air Force and the Department of Defense and requested permission to fly Anaukaq, Kali, and their families to America free of charge aboard one of the regularly scheduled C-141 transports. This kind of project, I was told, was unprecedented and would require special consideration.

Anaukaq and Kali had essentially defined an itinerary for their trip when they said that they wanted to visit their fathers' grave sites and meet their American relatives. Matthew Henson was buried in Woodlawn Cemetery in the Bronx, New York. He had lived mainly in New York City, Philadelphia, Washington, D.C., the Maryland area, and, for a brief time, Boston. Most of his closest relatives were in those cities. Robert Peary was buried in Arlington National Cemetery, just outside Washington, D.C. His surviving descendants lived for the most part in Maine, New York City, the Washington, D.C. area, and Maryland.

Though I hadn't heard from any of the American Pearys since my return, I still hoped that eventually they would agree to meet with their Amer-Eskimo relatives. Even if they didn't, I suspected that Kali would want to come and visit his father's grave.

Anaukaq and Kali had given no time limit for their visit but agreed with their sons that about two weeks would be all the time the group could spend away from their families, dogs, and work. This would allow us time only to tour the most important family sites on the East Coast and give receptions at each place.

By now I had determined that the major expenses in the United States would be room and board in each city. If all the Greenlandic family members that Kali and Anaukaq had requested were to come along, this would be a very costly proposition. Most of the American Hensons were working people who had big hearts and a lot of pride but did not have much extra money. They wanted to do all that they could to help me make the Eskimos' visit to America a pleasant one. They offered to contribute what they could to help me bring their relatives to the United States and to transport and house them.

My only complication with the Hensons was that relatives at each location wanted the Eskimos to stay with them longer than with the other kin. In response to this problem, I recommended that we hold a single large family get-together in one city and, from that base, take short excursions into the other cities. I left the choice of the city for the American Hensons to decide, but the relatives and friends could not agree. I then recommended Washington, because it was the city where Henson and Peary first met and it is readily accessible to anyone living along the eastern seaboard.

About a month later, I received a letter from the Danish government indicating that they would not provide support for Anaukaq and Kali's trip to America. This was disappointing. I had thought that at the very least the Danish authorities would have provided us with transportation from Thule to Copenhagen.

Some weeks later, I heard from the U.S. Air Force, my last hope. I nervously opened the letter to read that my request had been turned down. This was a crushing blow. I sat for minutes, just staring at the letter, remembering how optimistic Anaukaq and Kali had been when I last saw them and trying to decide how I would break the news. But after a while, I pulled myself out of my depression and started to write to the air force and the secretary of defense, this time with an offer to pay for seats on one of the C-141 transport jets. I still had faith.

Meanwhile, I decided the time had come to contact the American Pearys and find out whether they had had a change of heart. When I reached the family representative, I was once again met with a polite but cold tone. I talked about my recent visit with Kali and made it clear that he still hoped to meet his American relatives. After an extended silence, the spokesman said, "I guess if you give them free transportation, they would go anywhere with you."

"I don't think Kali and his family are looking for anything free, sir," I responded. "They just don't have the resources to pay for such a trip. The only way they will ever get to the United States to see Admiral Peary's grave is for us to help them."

"Well, we won't help," he replied. "You give them the free transportation if you want, but we will not help you bring them here."

I was disappointed that the Peary-Staffords had not softened their position and sad that I might inadvertently be hurting their family by insisting on inviting Kali to come along with Anaukaq. Nevertheless, I could not understand how they could reject Kali outright.

Around the same time, I heard from the Amer-Eskimos Hensons through the translator in Greenland. Anaukaq had taken ill and was being kept in the tiny Danish and Eskimo-run infirmary at Qaanaaq. The diagnosis was prostate cancer. Like most elderly people, Anaukaq hated hospitals and wanted to go back home to his family. When he entered the hospital, he told the translator that he would be well enough to return to his family in a short time but added, "Tell Allen if I am going to visit America, it will have to be soon. Please don't you leave the area before I get out of the infirmary, because I want you to go to America with Kali and me as our translator when Allen comes to get us."

When I contacted a Danish physician who had treated Anaukaq to inquire about his condition, he told me that his prostate cancer, like other cancers, was fairly unpredictable. "It is difficult to tell," he said. "In his present condition, he could go on living for years, or he could succumb earlier. I think he has a strong will to live now."

Understandably, Anaukaq's family also felt a greater sense of urgency about the trip. Fearful that Anaukaq's health might deteriorate quickly in the months ahead, they suggested that we plan the visit for the spring of 1987 rather than the ensuing fall. I agreed, even though the new timetable would make it even more difficult to work out our plans.

As a result of the nationwide publicity about my meeting with Anaukaq and Kali, I was receiving dozens of letters and telephone calls from journalists and film crews—all wanting me to tell them how to reach Anaukaq and Kali. From the articles that appeared in *Newsweek*, the *Boston Globe*, the *New York Times*, and other newspapers, Anaukaq and Kali had attained a kind of celebrity, and many in the media simply wanted to get their story. I could just imagine some of the callers descending upon their villages with their note pads, tape recorders, and cameras. Some reporters and photographers all but demanded that I reveal to them Kali's and Anaukaq's whereabouts. In fact, one U.S. wire-service reporter called me to say that he had received permission to travel to Thule by convincing the air force that he was going to do a story on the military in Greenland, but that he really wanted to do a story on Anaukaq and Kali. He insisted that I tell him how to locate the Amer-Eskimo families and expressed anger when I refused.

Even in Denmark, a number of newspapers carried articles on Anaukaq and Kali for the first time, prompting new interest in the Polar Eskimos. Some Danes tried to contact them. Others claimed that they had known of Anaukaq and Kali all along, but apparently never thought the information of interest to the public.

Perhaps the most disturbing news I received from Greenland during this depressing period, however, came a few weeks later. I learned from the Amer-Eskimo families in Greenland that some of the American Pearys had contacted them and had tried to dissuade them from traveling to America with Anaukaq and his family. The Amer-Eskimo Pearys were shocked, confused, and eventually angered by this effort. The American Pearys had never reached out to make contact with or even to acknowledge them as relatives in over eighty years. Now these same people, who had earlier tried to convince me that Kali was not Robert Peary's son, claimed to be acting with Kali's best interests in mind. The irony of this was not lost on the Eskimos.

The Amer-Eskimos told me that the Peary-Stafford family had enlisted the help of an adventurer who traveled to the area for Arctic photographic work. It appears that this man, like so many others, became aware of Anaukaq and Kali only after they had come to national and international attention in 1986. Eventually he put together a team of filmmakers from England and traveled to the area to film Anaukaq and Kali in the spring of 1987, just before they were to leave for America.

The Peary-Stafford family representative also sent letters and other materials to one of the Eskimo Pearys who spoke some English, suggesting that if Kali and his family came to America with me, they would be abused and midhandled, particularly by the news media. Even more disruptive, the family representative and his collaborator brought up the issue of race in an apparent effort to create a rift between the Eskimo Hensons and Pearys. According to the Eskimos, they suggested that my efforts in this project would only exalt Henson and discredit Peary, and that although they were part Eskimo, they were also part white. It would therefore be better if they waited and came to the United States at some future date. Kali later informed me that the explorer had tried to get him to wait and visit America with him.

Naturally, I became deeply concerned about the Pearys' interference with the plans that I had made with Anaukaq and Kali. The intervention of the Pearys and their associate had ended up pitting members of the Amer-Eskimo Peary family against one another, and I could see the potential for further confusion and discord if such meddling persisted. I felt I had no alternative but to call the family spokesman to investigate the allegations.

When the Peary-Stafford representative confirmed that he had been in touch with Kali and his family, I asked him why. He responded by saying that he and his family remained convinced that if Kali and his children came here, they would bring negative publicity on themselves as well as on the American Pearys, and he thought it was within his right to say this to them.

"Well, if you cared as much about this family as you're suggesting now, why haven't you been in touch with them before, just to introduce yourself or acknowledge them as family?" I asked. He seemed to squirm about for an answer, suggesting that the American side of the family might have done so one day in the future but that my efforts had really added impetus to their desire to talk to the Arctic Pearys.

"Well, just a few weeks ago you indicated to me that the Peary family members were not certain that Kali was in fact Robert E. Peary's son, and now you're contacting them and asking them not to come to America," I said. He struggled uncomfortably for a reply.

It became quite clear to me that this man was in fact attempting to sabotage Kali and Anaukaq's plans to visit America. It took all the strength I could muster to control myself. I assured him that I was responding to Anaukaq's and Kali's wishes in bringing them to America and that they were both elderly men who simply wanted this opportunity now because they did not know what the future held for them.

He suggested that it would be fine for Anaukaq and his family to come to the United States but that he still felt the need to let the Arctic Pearys know that they were probably being exploited. "If you felt there was exploitation," I responded, "then why were you not concerned about the Amer-Eskimo Hensons being exploited as well? Why didn't you contact the Eskimo Hensons as well to indicate that they too might be exploited?" Again he was unable to come up with an adequate reply.

He then explained his collaborator's role by saying that he had been working with him on a new project about Robert Peary's polar explorations and that the family was providing him with certain information from the Admiral's private papers. He admitted that he had asked this man to intervene on behalf of the Peary family in America with "the Eskimos who say they are Pearys."

Despite my anger, there was little I could do except urge him to stop interfering with our plans. I assured him that every activity I had planned for Anaukaq, Kali, and their families would be carried out with great dignity and respect for them, their privacy, and their well-being. I ended the conversation.

At this point so many issues and problems confronted me that I simply did not know which way to turn. I still hadn't been able to line up transportation to the United States for Anaukaq, Kali, and their families. I was uncertain just how successful the Peary-Staffords and their emissary had been in undermining my efforts. And, further complicating matters, I was receiving reports that the publicity surrounding the trip had attracted the attention of a number of influential people in Greenland who felt that they should be included in our plans.

There was, moreover, another matter that bothered me—and had bothered me for some time. Robert Peary had been buried with full military honors and had a beautiful monument in Arlington National

Cemetery, while Matthew Henson was buried in a simple grave in Woodlawn Cemetery. In many ways their graves symbolized the disparate treatment they had received in life from their fellow Americans. Peary's grave site boasted a massive monument from the National Geographic Society. Henson had received nothing from the society, which had ignored him in death as in life. Peary's grave site was situated on a hill carefully selected for its commanding position in Arlington National Cemetery. Henson's small gray headstone was simply placed in a common row of other equally simple grave sites. If Henson's service to his country had been given proper consideration at the time of his death, he too would have been buried in our most prestigious national cemetery. This was a tragic wrong that needed to be righted. I felt that moving Henson's remains to Arlington National Cemetery would in some measure make up for the lack of recognition he had received from his country during his life.

I shared my idea of the reinterment with several of the American Hensons, and they fully agreed. Next, I contacted Washington officials who could help me to arrange to have Matthew Henson's remains removed from the Woodlawn Cemetery and reintered at Arlington. I learned that only two people can assign individuals to burial sites in Arlington National Cemetery. One is the secretary of the army, who makes decisions about former military personnel whose families wish to have them buried in Arlington. The other person is the President of the United States.

At the very mention of this idea, some of my colleagues and friends laughed in disbelief. "You'll probably have to wait for another administration. This administration is not known for doing this kind of thing," one friend told me. Others suggested that such an effort would be virtually impossible under the present army hierarchy and that it was futile for me to try. But, as usual, such comments only hardened my resolve.

One evening in late 1986 I sat down and composed a letter to President Reagan requesting permission to reinter Matthew Henson among other American heroes in Arlington National Cemetery.

Later in the spring, I received word that Anaukaq had left the infirmary in Qaanaaq of his own volition, telling the nurses and translator that he was fine and ready to travel to the United States.

"Please don't forget that I want you to travel to Mahri-Pahluk's homeland with me and my family to serve as our translator, when Allen comes," he reminded the translator.

What Anaukaq did not know was that I still had not found a way of transporting the families. I had begun to explore the incredibly expensive option of using a Canadian charter airline, which hops from island to island across northern Canada, when I again heard from the Department of Defense. This time the news was good. The U.S. Air Force had granted my request to transport Anaukaq, Kali, and their families from Dundas Air Force Base in Thule to McGuire Air Force Base, provided that each passenger paid a fee covering air transport and lodging on the base. The cost of transporting all prospective passengers would run to at least ten thousand dollars. At this point, I was so thrilled at having surmounted a major obstacle that I did not worry about the money. I simply heaved a great sigh of relief and then ran through University Hall telling my students the good news.

Several of my students, fellow faculty, and friends at Harvard had been very helpful and supportive throughout my involvement with this project. Even the president of the university had met with me to express his special interest in my efforts and to offer his encouragement. But the students were a tremendous source of inspiration from the moment they heard the story. They saw this effort as a kind of victory for Anaukaq and Kali—a victory over prejudice and abandonment and the fulfillment of a lifelong wish. And they wanted to be actively involved in making that dream come true. I drew much of my inner strength from the enthusiasm of these young people.

We decided to form the "North Pole Family Reunion Committee," a group of Harvard students, faculty, and staff, along with members of the American Henson and, we still hoped, Peary families. As we began to organize the visit, we soon realized that the costs would be much greater than originally anticipated, and the complications manifold. In addition to the cost of air transportation from Thule, we would have to pay for air- and ground-travel in the United States as well as for food, lodging, guides, translators, and security in every city. We also needed medical and health insurance along with traveling medical personnel, in case of an emergency. We estimated the total costs to be in the tens of thousands of dollars. Like typical academics, we turned to granting agencies.

I approached several such agencies and known philanthropists about possible support for the project. While they all found the idea interesting, each had other funding priorities at the time. No support materialized. I had already decided that I would pay Anaukaq's and Kali's transportation and other expenses from my personal funds, but I was unsure about how to cover the other costs of bringing several members of their families along. Some of the committee recommended that we cut costs by reducing the number of family members traveling on this first trip. But we all agreed Anaukaq wanted his five sons with him and Kali wanted his only son and one grandson to join him. This meant a minimum of nine family members plus the translator. Also, Malina served as Anaukaq's nurse, so she would have to come along. And Aviaq did not want Malina and her father to leave without her. Reluctant as I was to leave Anaukaq's and Kali's sons and grandchildren behind, I had to concede it was unlikely that I could raise the thousands of dollars necessary to bring them along. The committee suggested a more modest plan of bringing Anaukaq, Kali, a translator, and one assistant on the first U.S. visit. We could try to bring other family members sometime later.

Just when we had all but given up hope of finding outside financial support, I remembered a chance encounter I had had some ten years earlier with a man who shared my admiration for Matthew Henson. This man, too, is one of my heroes, and he had told me about the role Matthew Henson had played in his own successful career. I had filed this remarkable story away in the back of my mind years ago. Now, as if by divine intervention, I retrieved it at a critical juncture.

The man was John H. Johnson, chairman of the Johnson Publishing Company and publisher of *Ebony* and *Jet*. Johnson and his publishing empire represent a historical institution in America. He is an icon in the black communities of the world. From very humble beginnings like Henson's he has risen to become one of the wealthiest and most accomplished men in America.

After fleeing racially oppressive Arkansas in the thirties, Johnson and his mother moved to Chicago. His mother encouraged him to become a businessman and, when he reached adulthood, she helped him borrow five hundred dollars to support his idea of starting the new magazine he named *Ebony*. Johnson launched his publishing venture in 1945, when postwar America was beginning to deal with civil rights, and black Americans were in the incipient stages of developing a substantial middle class.

Like all magazines, *Ebony* needed business advertisements to survive. But all the large wholesale and retail businesses in Chicago were owned by whites. So Johnson and his wife, Eunice, would go from business to business, door to door in Chicago, trying to obtain the necessary advertising to keep his magazine afloat. This kind of effort was unprecedented in 1945, and Johnson, like most black entrepreneurs, was unable to establish substantive business relationships with the white establishments of Chicago. He went as far as hiring white ethnics to try to sell the ads to white businesses in Chicago, but without success. He found that even those businesses that had a large black clientele would not purchase advertising space from him. In many ways, Chicago was as racially biased as his native Arkansas.

But Johnson and his wife persevered. She would often wait in the car while he tried, usually without success, to get past a secretary and meet with the head of a corporation to discuss advertising space in *Ebony*.

As Johnson tells the story, his luck changed one day in 1946 when he entered the headquarters of Zenith Radio Corporation in Chicago to meet with its chairman, retired commander Eugene F. McDonald. McDonald had agreed to give Johnson a brief audience to hear about his business venture.

When he entered the office, McDonald stood, extended his hand, and cordially welcomed the well-dressed young entrepreneur. He offered Johnson a seat in one of the dark leather chairs in his office. "Do you see those snowshoes there on my wall, Johnson?" McDonald asked. "Those snowshoes were given to me by one of the greatest explorers in the history of Arctic exploration. He was a better man than any three white men put together—and he happens to be of your race." McDonald explained that the snowshoes had been given to him by Matthew Henson after he returned from the North Pole with Peary. Rubbing the walrus-skin strings of the snowshoes as if they were precious gems, he asked Johnson if he had ever heard of Matthew Henson.

Johnson told McDonald that he had just done a story on Henson in his new magazine, *Ebony*. He handed McDonald a copy of the magazine, feeling proud that he had carefully researched McDonald's interests before the meeting and learned that Arctic exploration was one of his passions.

McDonald skimmed through the magazine until he reached the story on Henson. He quickly read over parts of the story, then looked up at Johnson. McDonald was impressed. He mentioned that Henson had written an autobiographical account of his North Pole experiences, which he had been unable to find anywhere. He asked Johnson if he would help him locate a copy, whereupon the well-prepared young publisher handed McDonald an autographed, hardcover edition of *A Negro Explorer at the North Pole* by Matthew Alexander Henson.

McDonald was flabbergasted. He thanked Johnson profusely as he thumbed through the book.

"Mr. Johnson, how can I help you?" McDonald asked.

Johnson told him that he wanted to sell Zenith some advertising space in his new magazine. He described *Ebony* as a human-interest magazine that featured educational, social, cultural, and political articles by and about blacks in America and other parts of the world, and he expressed confidence in its potential for success. Johnson had actually been trying for months to get ads from Zenith, but on each occasion he had been turned away, usually by McDonald's secretary.

McDonald pressed his intercom and asked his secretary to step into his office. To Johnson's—and the secretary's—surprise, he asked her to arrange to have Zenith ads placed in *Ebony* on a regular basis. McDonald also agreed to ask some of his business associates to have their companies buy advertising space in *Ebony*.

Johnson thanked McDonald and left. A few days later, he received his first substantial advertising account from Zenith. Soon other large white-owned Chicago businesses bought advertising space as well. Johnson Publishing Company was off and running, and Matthew Henson had unwittingly played a major role in another historic moment.

I wrote John H. Johnson and reminded him of our meeting and mentioned my recollection of this remarkable story. I told him about Anaukaq and Kali and asked whether he would consider defraying some of the costs of the North Pole Family Reunion.

Johnson telephoned me immediately upon receiving my letter. "Amazing," he said. "Dr. Counter, have you actually found a son that Matthew Henson fathered in the Arctic?" he asked.

"That's right, Mr. Johnson—and Henson's five grandsons, and twenty-two great-grandchildren."

"That is incredible!" he said. "How on earth did you find them?"

I told him the story from the beginning. I could tell from his voice that he was deeply moved.

"How can I help you, Dr. Counter?"

"Well, sir, I am trying to raise money to pay for the North Pole Family Reunion project. I am using my own funds for some things, but I need more money to make the project a memorable success. I wondered if you would be willing to make a contribution to the effort?"

"Dr. Counter, I support what you are trying to do. Matthew Henson is our hero, and it is just great to know that you are trying to keep his memory alive. You have brought this project this far, and I have all the faith in the world that you will carry it through. I want to help you in any way that I can. Just write me and tell me what you need."

"Thank you, Mr. Johnson."

I was bursting with joy and pride—joy that I had finally secured the necessary funds, pride that John H. Johnson, a man I greatly admired, had agreed to cosponsor the project. I drew up a budget and sent it off. A short time later I received a check and Johnson's best wishes for success. The North Pole Family Reunion was now closer to reality.

*   *   *

Anaukaq and his family wanted to visit in the late spring of 1987, and we agreed upon late May to early June as the best time for everyone. The only problem now was that this date gave us very little time for preparation. We needed passports, visas, and other documents that would normally take months to process. So we wasted no time in organizing the tour.

At our next committee meeting, we planned the official North Pole Family Reunion itinerary. We carefully selected the cities and sites that held special significance in the lives of Anaukaq's and Kali's fathers. Formal ceremonies were planned for each stop on the tour, involving local family and officials. Several students were selected as hosts and escorts for the tour, and other committee members were assigned various tasks. I would spend the next weeks on the telephone or in writing letters in an effort to implement our plans.

Perhaps our most important decision was to start the North Pole Family Reunion at Harvard. Our committee felt that we had such widespread support for the project in the Harvard community that it would be a good idea to hold the welcoming reception at the university. Such an arrangement would also protect Anaukaq and Kali from the uncertainties of a more public reception, where we would be less able to control events and people. In addition, we decided that a single North Pole Family Reunion Banquet involving Hensons, Pearys, and friends from all over the nation would be more practical than trying to hold several small banquets in different cities. This "neutral" venue was agreeable to most of the family members, although some still wanted small banquets in their hometowns. We chose Harvard's historic Memorial Hall as the banquet site.

Our committee raised concerns about possible actions of the American Peary family. We still had received no expression of interest from them, and we wondered if their apparent efforts to sabotage our plans in Greenland portended similar behavior once Kali and his family arrived in the United States. We were not even certain whether Kali and his sons would still want to make the trip in the wake of the family conflicts and dissension that the American Pearys and their associate had caused. But the committee shared my belief that if Kali still wanted to come along, we should bring him and his family, regardless of whether the Pearys would receive him. We would receive him and would see to it that he visited his father's grave site in Washington as well as Peary's old summer home on Eagle Island, Maine. Although we also knew that the American Hensons were prepared to welcome Peary's Eskimo family as their own, we agreed that I should try once more to reach other members of the American Peary family to see whether they might receive Kali or at least greet him at the Harvard reception.

By now, I had an extensive list of immediate Peary family members living all over the United States. I reached a few of them, but they all indicated that they did not want to meet Kali or take any part in our activities. One of the most revealing encounters occurred while I spoke with one of Robert Peary's great-granddaughters. We spoke by telephone and her voice suggested a very pleasant and kind person. I introduced myself and told her about the plans for Kali's visit. I also told her that Kali was a Peary and simply wanted to visit America and meet some of his relatives. She listened attentively, occasionally responding with polite remarks.

"I understand what you're doing, Dr. Counter, and I would like to participate, but I have to stick with the family." I implored her to consider Kali's feelings and his lifelong desire to meet his American family. I invited her to meet him at Harvard or in the privacy of her home.

"This is the first time I ever heard of any Greenlandic Pearys," she said. "I would like very much to have my children meet them."

I could feel her wavering a bit. I became hopeful. "I would be happy to bring Kali and his children to your home to meet you and your children," I offered, probably with too much enthusiasm.

"Mmm, I don't know," she said. "But there is something I would like to know. What is the name of the young man with the beautiful smile?"

"I beg your pardon?"

"You know, the young man in the *Newsweek* article—the one with the very beautiful smile. What's his name?"

I pulled out the copy of the *Newsweek* that featured my first visit with Anaukaq and Kali. "Oh, yes. You must mean Ole, Kali's nineteen-year-old grandson. He is a wonderful person—a little shy but very friendly. You and your family would enjoy meeting him, and he you."

The woman at the other end of the line seemed to acquiesce for a moment. "Yes, I would like very much for my children to meet him."

Then she added, "But no, I can't do that. I'm sorry, I have to stick with my family on this one. Good-bye."

*   *   *

Obtaining passports and visas for thirteen Greenlandic Eskimos to visit the United States was a formidable task. It involved coordinating activities with authorities in Greenland, Denmark, and the United States. The police inspector at Thule agreed to help me obtain passports for each of the Hensons and Pearys traveling to the United States, provided I could get photographs of each. Fortunately, I had taken photographs of each of the Hensons and Pearys when I was in Greenland. With the help of my translator Navarana and the police inspector, I managed to get the paperwork completed and passport applications for the thirteen members of the traveling party sent to Copenhagen. This effort was complicated by the fact that most of the men were away from the settlement for weeks on hunts.

The next hurdle was the visa office of the U.S. embassy in Denmark. Because of the unusual nature of the project and the use of military transportation, I had to request special visas for the group. I wrote the U.S. ambassador to Denmark, asking for his help in obtaining special short-term visas. Within about two weeks, the consulate had agreed to grant the group special entry visas. To save time, and because the members of the traveling party had no experience in this process, they even permitted me to complete the visa applications for each member of the group.

"In all my years of foreign service, I have never received a visa application on which the applicant's profession is listed as 'retired hunter,'" said Lynn Schiveley of the U.S. consulate office in Denmark, when he called to confirm that the applications were being processed. "We all have been very moved by your project, and we have taken a special interest in it here at the embassy. The ambassador and staff want to offer you all the assistance you need."

"Thank you, Mr. Schiveley. And please thank the ambassador for me."

CHAPTER ELEVEN

✳ ✳ ✳

Defeating Tornarsuk

In Polar Eskimo culture, when something goes wrong or when something interferes with the best-laid plans, it is often attributed to the evil spirit Tornarsuk. Such, of course, is the stuff of myth and legend, one of those features of traditional societies we find quaint and colorful. Or so I thought as I prepared to bring Anaukaq, Kali, and their families to the advanced technological world that is the United States of the late twentieth century. By the time our trip was over, however, I would become as much a believer in Tornarsuk as any of my Eskimo friends.

✳ ✳ ✳

The surface of the heavily packed snow glistened like ground glass under the bright May sun over Moriussaq. Even at a temperature of −20°F, the twenty-four-hour day gave a feeling of warmth. Dogs throughout the settlement barked at the crunch of my boots as I made my way through the snow toward Anaukaq's igloo.

Anaukaq met me along the path looking somehow different— younger and more vibrant than on my earlier visits. At first I could not figure out just what it was that made him look so changed. He greeted me with a big smile and his characteristic laugh. Then it dawned on me—Anaukaq had new teeth. While in the infirmary that winter, he had asked the Greenlandic health authorities to give him a set of dentures in preparation for his big trip. The infirmary had also provided him with glasses and a hearing aid to help overcome his typical hunter's hearing loss.

"Allen, I am ready to go with you to Mahri-Pahluk's homeland now. I look like a younger man now that I have teeth—and a haircut," he chuckled, rubbing his hand through his newly cropped hair.

"You look great, my friend. Your American relatives will be impressed with your new youthful appearance," I said, giving my first hint that the trip to America was imminent.

Anaukaq laughed and grabbed my hand. "Welcome back to Moriussaq, Allen. I have been waiting for you every day. Our settlement becomes so quiet when you leave."

There was a special excitement in the air throughout the settlement. Everyone knew that Anaukaq and his family were going to America, and they were happy for him. Yet Anaukaq was cautious in his optimism. His sealskin bag had been packed for weeks. But after waiting three-quarters of a century for this moment, he would not be certain of the reality of this trip until he set foot on American soil.

Little Aviaq and her favorite cousin, Malina, were also packed and ready to go. Everywhere I went around the settlement, Aviaq tagged along to be certain that I did not leave for America without her.

Anaukaq's sons Avataq, Ussarkaq, and Ajako were miles from the settlement, hunting for food that would supply their families and dogs during their absence. We had no way of contacting them or knowing when they would return. Kitdlaq and Vittus, the other two sons, were rushing to complete their work in time for the trip.

I hadn't the slightest idea about Kali's plans. I wondered whether the Pearys and their English associate had persuaded him not to travel to America after all or, worse, whether they had hurt his feelings. Anaukaq too was concerned about Kali. He had received word of conflicts among the Amer-Eskimo Pearys caused by the outside intervention, and he too had been approached by the Pearys' associate after my last visit to his settlement.

"No one has ever taken any interest in us up here. Now that you are taking us to Mahri-Pahluk's homeland to see our relatives, some have come up here to photograph us and to ask Kali and his family not to go with you. I do not understand this," Anaukaq said.

A week passed by without any word from Kali and his family. Anaukaq was also becoming anxious because his sons had not returned from the hunt. We bided our time recording stories of Anaukaq's impressions of his youth and explanations of Eskimo life.

Several days later, while outside stretching sealskins, we spotted a dogsled on the horizon, mushing toward us at great speed. Normally, the Eskimo children will recognize the driver of the sled hundreds of yards away, from his manner of driving or his dogs or his yells, and shout out his name for the other youngsters and villagers. In this case, however, the children of Moriussaq did not know the sled driver or dogteam.

As the dogsled came closer, we could see that the driver was dressed in full, traditional Eskimo garb, including polar bear skin trousers, anorak, sealskin boots, and a combination of sealskin and polar bear fur mittens. He was raising his whip high and cracking it just above the ears of his dogs. *"Wock, wock, wock,"* he yelled as he mushed the dogs up the hillside toward the village. When he reached us, he brought the excited dogs to a halt. *"Ha-shhh."*

The driver turned to Anaukaq and me and smiled. Even before he pulled back the hood of his anorak, I could tell from his radiant smile that it was Ole, Kali's grandson. "Whew! I thought I might be too late," he said, out of breath. "I was out hunting for food for my family and our dogs. Are we still going to America?"

"Of course we are," I responded, hardly concealing my delight at this first indication that Kali and his family would join us. "Where is Kali?"

"My grandfather left Qeqertarsaaq by dogsled some days ago. He is in Qaanaaq now, but he is coming," Ole replied.

"Great! *Ahunggweelok* [Fine]" I said, shaking his hand vigorously. "I am so happy that you are going to join us."

"Talilanguaq, my father, is coming here also. He wants to travel to America with you, but he is many days out, hunting for seals and walrus, and has not had much success. I hope we can wait for him."

"We'll wait for him," I said with a sigh of relief. "I am just happy that you are going to join us."

Anaukaq was ecstatic about the news. "I am so happy that my cousin Kali will join us," he told Ole. "We have waited for this opportunity all of our lives, and now the time is here."

When Ole parked his sled and secured his dogteam, we all went to Anaukaq's igloo and sat down to some hot tea, fresh soup, and seal meat.

A few days later, Avataq returned by dogsled to Moriussaq with his ten-year-old son Magssanguaq riding atop several seals they had killed on the hunt. Magssanguaq cuddled his pet puppy as he rode into the settlement.

"Allen!" Avataq shouted, as he and Magssanguaq unloaded the seals and about a dozen kittiwakes tied together. "I am ready to travel to Mahri-Pahluk's homeland. But Ajako is still out on the ice hunting seals. He should be here in a few days."

I noticed that the usually active and friendly Magssanguaq appeared sullen and distant. Though already an accomplished hunter, Magssanguaq was still a child at heart. Dressed in his polar bear pants and anorak, he looked like a miniature image of his father. He had taken his one-month-old puppy with him to the hunting grounds for company, and he was now focusing all of his attention on the pup in play and ignoring the people around him entirely. "What's wrong with Magssanguaq?" I asked Avataq.

"He is sad because I have told him that he cannot go to America with us on this trip," Avataq said. "I told him maybe he could go on some future trip."

I knelt down and tried to cheer up little Magssanguaq, but he was not in the best of moods. He did not want his father and grandfather to go away without him and he was sad. "My *ahtahtah* and my *ahtah* [grandfather] are going far away, over there," Magssanguaq said pointing toward Umanak mountain in the south, "and they may not come back."

"Oh, they will come back," I reassured him. "They will only be away for about two weeks, and then they will come right back to Moriussaq," I told him.

"Aviaq is going," he said, referring to his ten-year-old cousin.

"I know," I said sympathetically. "She was selected by your family to make this trip. But there will be other trips, and I promise to take you to America to meet your relatives on the next trip. Okay, my little friend?"

Magssanguaq nodded his head, staring down at the puppy in his lap, and softly, but unconvincingly mumbled, "*Eee.*"

Anaukaq put his arm on Magssanguaq's shoulder and said, "Come with me, my little *peeneeahktoe.*" He walked Magssanguaq behind the igloo, out of his father's sight, where the two of them sat down in old broken chairs. Anaukaq was very fond of little Magssanguaq, who lived in his igloo and whom he had helped to rear.

"Magssanguaq, you are a very good hunter. Your *ahtah* wants you to become a full-time hunter when you grow up," Anaukaq told the boy. "You should not try to work for the Danish people in any of these trade jobs—that would not suit you. You must promise me you will be a full-time hunter when you grow up, just like your grandfather and now your father."

"*Eee, ahtah,*" Magssanguaq murmured, still looking toward the ground and pulling at the polar bear fur on his trousers.

"Now the first thing a great hunter must learn, no matter how young, is responsibility," Anaukaq continued. "We would like to take you on this trip, but we cannot. I want you to stay behind this time and take care of the family and look after our dogs. That is a big responsibility."

"Yes, Grandfather," he responded.

"We won't be away long," Anaukaq said. "Do you think you can look after the rest of the family and the dogteams until your father and I return?"

"Yes, Grandfather," Magssanguaq replied.

"Allen has said that he will take you to Mahri-Pahluk's homeland on a future trip. He will keep his word with you just as he did with me."

Still looking down at the snow, Magssanguaq pulled anxiously at his polar bear fur. Anaukaq rubbed Magssanguaq's head. "You are a fine grandson," he said.

* * *

While we waited for Kali and the hunters to arrive, I went around the settlement and out to the hunting grounds conducting audiological tests on all the villagers. Everyone was cooperative and enthusiastic about the tests. It was common knowledge among the villagers that the hunters in particular had problems hearing, even in their twenties and thirties. Some young fathers complained about not being able to hear their children's voices well, a complaint most often made by grandfathers in our society. My results bore them out. I was finding that permanent, high-frequency, "nerve" hearing loss began in the teenage years and became progressively worse through age sixty. Many had severe hearing impairment in both ears by age forty. These were noise-induced hearing losses due primarily to the men's regular hunting activities with high-caliber rifles. The Polar Eskimo women I tested, who generally do not hunt with rifles, did not have such hearing losses.

I had brought along some special earplugs attached to a necklace that could be hung around the hunter's neck until he was ready to use them. When he spotted game and was about to shoot, he could put the plugs in his ears to attenuate the gunshot noise reaching his inner ear, then remove the plugs after each shot. By introducing this simple hearing conservation measure, I felt that I could reduce the incidence of hearing impairment in present and future generations of Polar Eskimos.

One afternoon some days later, while I was out on the hunting grounds conducting one of my tests, Ajako's sons Nukka and Jens came flying across the ice with their father's dogteam. "Allen, Kali has arrived in Moriussaq," they shouted as they approached me. "He is with Anaukaq."

"Fantastic!" I shouted back. "Let's go back to the settlement to greet your grandfather," I said to Ole, who had brought me out on his dogsled.

We packed my audiometer and other apparatus, and in no time we were off, sledding across the ice at high speed behind eight big running dogs.

Ole was beaming with happiness. He was pleased that his grandfather had chosen to join Anaukaq. On our way back to Moriussaq, he vented his excitement by racing Nukka and Jen's dogteam.

When we reached Moriussaq, Anaukaq and Kali were sitting outside on a log, basking in the sun and enjoying a cup of coffee. An older woman and friend from the neighborhood had joined them. As I jumped off the sled and ran toward Kali, he greeted me with his outstretched hands and a huge grin. We shook hands and embraced before Kali pulled back and looked me in the eye, saying nothing, just grinning from ear to ear.

"Oh my goodness! Kali, you have new teeth," I shouted as I finally grasped what he was trying to show me.

We all laughed.

"You didn't think I was going to let Anaukaq get new teeth and not get some for myself, did you?" Kali chuckled. "We might meet some new wives over there in the United States, and we have to look our best."

Kali continued to joke, and Anaukaq loved every minute of it. This was the old Kali he had known since childhood—his friend, his cousin. And now he knew for certain that they would fulfill their lifelong dream together.

Kali explained that he had stopped at the infirmary in Qaanaaq en route to Moriussaq to get his new dentures. That was the reason his arrival had been delayed.

"They ship these from Denmark for the old people up here, and the nurses shape them to fit our mouths."

They both grinned to show each other their new chompers.

* * *

Most members of the traveling party were now gathered in Moriussaq. The only ones missing at this point were Kali's son, Talilanguaq, and Anaukaq's sons Ussarkaq, Kitdlaq, and Vittus.

"I would only hope that all five of my sons can go to America with me," Anaukaq said. "This may be the last time we will all be together again."

"*Eeee*," Kali agreed. "I want my son to travel with us also. Maybe he will like it over there and take my other children and grandchildren someday."

I had arranged for a flexible departure schedule because of the unpredictable weather and other possible unforeseen circumstances. Nevertheless, we had only a small window of opportunity for travel.

We could not request the delay of a U.S. Air Force plane. If the sons did not show up in time, we would be forced to leave without them. I hoped that this would not be necessary.

Later that evening, we discussed our American itinerary.

"Our trip to our fathers' homeland now looks as if it is going to be a reality," Anaukaq said to Kali. "I don't know if I am prepared to meet such fine people. Allen, you will have to advise me on how to act," he said mischievously.

"Just be yourselves," I said. "Just be Anaukaq and Kali and everything will be fine."

"When we get to America and meet such fine people as our relatives, we will have to take off our hats and bow—like this," Anaukaq chuckled, removing an imaginary hat and bowing. He fell back on the bed, laughing. We all laughed. I had never seen Anaukaq in such a jocular mood.

"What about you, Kali?" I asked. "How will you act at our big family reunion banquet?"

Kali thought for a moment. "Oh, I get very emotional at gatherings, especially when there are speeches being made. I can't help that. I think when I meet my relatives and see my father's grave, I will get very emotional."

Kali showed us a small wreath of dried flowers he and his family had made for his father's grave. He was quite proud of the wreath. Only a few species of tiny flowers grow in northwest Greenland, but he and his children had collected many of them, along with shrubs, and tied them together to form a lovely oval.

While we waited for the rest of our traveling party, Anaukaq entertained Kali by showing him some of his prized possessions. One was a massive polar bear skin, which looked as if it had been pulled off the bear in one piece. Avataq had killed the bear not far from the settlement earlier that winter. But he said that his favorite new possession was a banner I had given him as a gift on an earlier visit. It was an Afro-American flag that I had designed some years earlier in the interest of instilling cultural and historical pride in young black Americans. I had used the flag on lecture tours and in classrooms to teach Americans of all races about the origins, history, and present-day makeup of Americans of black African ancestry. Anaukaq had put the flag up on the wall of his igloo so that his family and visitors could view it.

Like a teacher, he walked Kali through the symbols of the flag. "The dark brown represents the color of Mahri-Pahluk's people," he told Kali. "The red borders represent the blood of their ancestors who died to build their country; the green tree speaks of their ancestry from a place called Africa." And so on through each symbol, just as I had explained to him almost a year earlier. I was touched that this gift had meant so much to him and amazed that he had actually memorized everything I had told him.

Kali showed his interest in the flag by asking Anaukaq questions about each symbol.

"What does the star stand for?" he asked.

"That is the star the *kulnocktooko* people used to find their way to freedom," replied Anaukaq.

"And what is this?"

"That is *herrkahnook* [the sun]," Anaukaq answered. "It gave life and skin color to the first *kulnocktooko*."

Whether they fully understood what they were discussing, I shall never know.

*   *   *

The police inspector had received all the visas and passports from Denmark but one. Malina's passport had been lost. She was shaken by the news, which dampened everyone's spirits. Malina had been looking forward to this trip, especially since she was her grandfather's caretaker and personally very close to him. She did not want him to be far from her care.

Using the lone battery-operated telephone in the settlement, I reached the police inspector at Thule. He had no idea where Malina's passport was or whether it could be found in time for her to make the trip. The next flight from Copenhagen was over two weeks away. I asked him to wire Lynn Schiveley of the American embassy in Copenhagen and request a special visa for Malina in lieu of a passport.

A few days later, Schiveley sent word that the embassy would wire ahead to our U.S. point of entry to explain that if Malina had proper, official identification, she could enter the country on a short-term visitor's visa for the two-week visit.

The police inspector informed me that the only person in the area authorized to draw up identification papers for Greenlandic citizens was the Danish military commander at Thule. We made arrangements for me to meet with the commander as soon as we reached the air base.

Four days before we were to depart from Thule, we still had not heard from Talilanguaq or Anaukaq's other sons. We were all getting worried. Anaukaq went outside and walked through the village. A short time later he returned and told Kali and me, "We're in for some bad weather. It looks to me like a big storm is coming. It could last for several days."

We just looked at each other, knowing that we were powerless to do anything about it. We could only wait—wait out the storm, wait for the others to reach Moriussaq.

Everyone was packed and ready to go. The men busied themselves with chores, one of which was feeding the dogs. Both Avataq and Ajako were out stuffing their dogs with seal innards and blubber. When the dogteams were fully fed, the residual food was then taken to some of the female dogs with puppies. The nursing females were kept in small shelters built to protect the puppies from the extreme cold. It is not uncommon to find the carcasses of small pups that have wandered off from their mother frozen solid in the snow. With most of the chores completed, we were ready to travel to Thule.

The storm rolled in later that day, with heavy, wet snow and howling winds. It rapidly became a blizzard. We were trapped. Only Magssanguaq seemed oblivious to the storm and its implications for our trip, as he played with his puppy and ran around in the igloo. Outside, even the short distances between the little houses were difficult to negotiate in the blinding, wind-driven snow. The dogs, curled up into balls and totally covered by snow, posed another danger. If you accidentally stepped on a snow-covered dog, it was likely to tear off a piece of your ankle.

As the blizzard roared on into its second day, our hopes sank in the deepening snow. We wondered whether the storm had trapped the hunters out on the ice. The Polar Eskimos are accustomed to unpredictable snowstorms and generally seem undisturbed by weather-induced delays. This time, though, everyone was hoping for a rapid improvement in the weather.

It was three days before our scheduled departure from the air base, and the storm was still raging. The helicopter would certainly not come for us in this weather. Wearing my heaviest clothes, I stumbled through the blizzard to the government-run shop near the edge of the settlement. I wanted to call the police inspector to get a weather forecast and some word on the helicopter schedule. But the telephone—the only one in the village—was out of order. The batteries were dead. We now had no way of communicating with the outside world. Tornarsuk, it seemed, had put another hurdle in our way.

The telephone batteries were three massive, 10-volt units, like those used in large trucks. They were encased in a huge wooden box. New batteries would have to be brought in by helicopter; there were no replacements in the village. If the storm continued another day and the helicopter couldn't come to get us, dogsleds were our only hope for reaching the base.

I broached the idea of traveling by dogsled with the group, and they all agreed that this might be our only means. Dogsled travel, however, was not easy. It would require a mobilization of the entire Moriussaq community.

Then we discovered that Ajako had a large box of new 1.5-volt flashlight batteries. We tried connecting twenty of these standard D batteries in a series to get the equivalent of thirty volts and attached them to the telephone wires. It worked!

When I reached the helicopter control office, I was told that the storm was expected to leave the area in the next twenty-four hours, but the winds were forecast to be too strong for the helicopter to go aloft. Dogsleds it would be, then.

I also reached Qaanaaq by phone and learned that the other members of the traveling party had returned safely from the hunting grounds but could not leave the village because of the storm. I urged them to travel to Moriussaq by dogsled, but they pointed out that it would be difficult to bring their dogs there and leave them in the care of the others. Dogs are a very private and personal possession among Polar Eskimos.

The next day the storm finally blew over, and a period of calm descended. We were now only two days from our scheduled flight from Thule. I made a quick decision to transport the group already at Moriussaq to the air base a day before our scheduled helicopter flight, to avoid the possibility of being trapped there by another storm.

All day, we waited near our bags, ready to go. But the helicopter never came. When I telephoned the helicopter flight director at Thule, he said that the winds were still too strong for the helicopter to fly to Moriussaq, but that the moment the winds died down, they would come in for us. We waited for several more hours, and I called the helicopter pad again, only to be told the same thing. It was now four o'clock in the afternoon. I knew that the helicopter pad would close at five. Yet by this point, I had become concerned about the judgment of the helicopter control post. It appeared to us that the weather had calmed down enough to fly the helicopter in. I shared the helicopter people's concern for safety, but the Eskimos and I felt there was no reason why the helicopter couldn't fly in to get us while the weather was calm, even after regular work hours. After all, there were twenty-four hours of daylight this time of year.

Five o'clock. No word from the helicopter base. I tried to reach helicopter control, but no one answered. The managers had left the post for the day and would not be reachable until the next day. By now, everyone worried that we would not make our plane. It seemed that old Tornarsuk had done his worst.

Nukka, Jens, and a neighbor offered to take the ten of us to the air base on three large dogsleds, but we decided that this would be risky. We were contemplating their offer, however, when I remembered that I had met the helicopter pilot on an earlier trip and he had given me his telephone number at the pilot's barracks. The pilot was Swedish and used to enjoy my surprising facility with the Swedish language, something he seldom heard in Danish Greenland.

It's worth a try, I thought, as I dialed the number. To my surprise, the Swedish pilot answered the phone.

"Hej! Jag heterer, Allen. Hur star det till? [Hello, this is Allen. How are you?]"

He too was surprised to hear from me.

"Jag mar bra, tack [I am fine, thank you]."

I described our desperate situation and explained the special nature of our project, mixing in a little Swedish wherever I could.

The winds had been too strong to permit the helicopter to fly over the mountains into our area earlier that day, he said. But it was now after work hours, he reminded me, and the pilots were not expected to fly into areas such as ours unless there was an emergency.

He paused. "I will come to fetch you."

"Great! Tack sa mycket! [Thank you very much]," I said.

"I will call back in an hour or so to let you know when I am leaving Thule, so that you can be ready at the landing area. I must get in and out quickly while the weather is good."

I was ecstatic. I had taken a chance and something positive had happened. This was typical of Greenland. It seemed that nothing happened unless someone made it happen, and everything required a bit of luck. Clearly, had I not made the effort to reach the pilot that afternoon, we would have been stranded in Moriussaq for another day or two and would probably have missed our jet to America.

The phone rang. "We are on our way to Moriussaq," the pilot said.

I ran about the village and notified everyone that the helicopter was on its way. The news created quite a stir. We all grabbed our bags and put them on the sled for transport to the landing site. Everyone, including Anaukaq, said their good-byes and made last minute bag checks.

About forty-five minutes later, we heard the roar of the helicopter off in the distance. As always, the children of the village heard it first and started running about, yelling that the helicopter was coming.

Anaukaq and Kali led the crowd as we walked toward the landing area. Anaukaq, with his cane, moved through the snow as quickly as everyone else. Our bags and camping gear were being pushed to the landing site on a large sled.

As the helicopter landed, we had to turn our head to protect our faces from the heavy snow blown up by the blades. The Swedish pilot got off the helicopter and headed straight for me. "Hej, Allen. Der ar kallt [It is cold]," he said in the accent of northern Sweden.

"Ja, mycket kallt [Yes, very cold]," I replied.

"It looks like the weather has cooperated with us," he added.

"Yes! But I want to thank you for your special efforts in coming out to pick us up. You have contributed greatly to the success of this project."

"Don't mention it. I am glad to help you," he said. "I think you are doing a good thing. But we must hurry and board the helicopter," he added. "With the amount of luggage you have and the number of passengers, we will have to make two trips."

He had been in the area for a number of years but he had never heard of the Henson-Peary story or of the sons of Henson and Peary. But once he heard the story, he said, he was touched by my efforts to help Anaukaq and Kali, and he offered what help he could.

Unfortunately, the weather north of Moriussaq was still too inclement for him to fly up to Qaanaaq to pick up the other three members of our traveling party. He would fly our Moriussaq group on to Thule and wait for a chance to pick up the rest of the group the next day.

After we packed the luggage securely in the helicopter, Anaukaq and Kali were the first to board. They were grinning like two young boys. Seven of us, including Aviaq and Malina, left on the first shuttle. When the pilot lifted the helicopter above the ground, everyone looked at one another and smiled.

In the noisy chopper, everyone sat silently, staring out the window. I wondered what each person was thinking about. The silence was occasionally broken by the excitement of spotting a dogsled down on the ice, traveling at what appeared to be, in relation to a helicopter, an incredibly high speed. As we neared our destination, Kali pointed with excitement to the unusual mountain called Umanak, saying it looked to him like a teacup turned upside-down. This mountain had special significance to the older men. It had been the traditional home of many of their people before the air base was built at Thule, and the two old hunters had spent many of their eighty years in its shadows. Some of the young Polar Eskimos had begun to talk about reclaiming the area around the base. This, of course, did not sit very well with the military establishment.

Once we passed over Umanak, the military base came into view. The sight of the sprawling air base caused quite a stir among the passengers. As they marveled at its enormous size, I thought about how very different much of the outside world still must appear to the Polar Eskimos. They, more than any other Eskimo group, had adhered to the old cultural ways of hunting, preparing food, and making clothing. They still spoke their special Polar Eskimo language, and they think of themselves as true Eskimos. While nothing about the outside world seemed to overwhelm them, they were still awed by many things they saw. I could only wonder how they would react to New York City, Boston, and Washington, D.C.

"You are clear to land," we heard the military air-traffic controller tell our pilot. Very soon he was hovering just above the landing pad and slowly putting the helicopter down in its center. Everyone smiled as the rotary blades wound to a halt.

Anaukaq seemed especially cheerful. He looked happy and as healthy and strong as ever. We all helped each other down from the helicopter pad and headed off for our quarters. The pilot lost no time in unpacking baggage and heading back to pick up the others left behind in Moriussaq.

* * *

The huge dining hall was a novel sight for the Eskimos, and our group was something of a strange sight for the military staff too. Many wanted to know who we were and what we were doing there. When I explained who Anaukaq and Kali were and the purpose of our trip, everyone wanted to meet the "celebrities."

To my chagrin, the helicopter pilot told me that evening that the winds were still too strong up in Qaanaaq to pick up Talilanguaq, Ussarkaq, and Kitdlaq. I reached Kitdlaq by phone and told him that it looked as though the only way for his group to reach the air base was to travel by dogsled. Kitdlaq said this would be impossible, since they could find no one who could take time off to bring their dogs back. Moreover, they could not be assured of having enough food for the dogs' round trip, since their latest hunt had not been so successful as they had hoped. It now looked as if I would have to put them on a later U.S.-bound military jet or have them wait for another trip in the distant future.

The pilot said that regulations required him to get a certain number of hours of sleep before flying, but he would make another attempt at 4 or 5 A.M., weather permitting. I told him that I would go to my quarters and pray for good weather. And I did.

Later that evening, I received an urgent call from Maj. Quincy Sharp, chief of operations. He told me that the base commander wanted to meet with me, but that I had to wait until seven o'clock the next morning because he would be in meetings until late that night.

"Is there something wrong?" I asked.

Sharp said he was not sure, but it must be important if the commander had requested a meeting. He did, however, mention that the adventurer had visited the base. Understandably, I began to worry that some of the Peary family's powerful friends had convinced the commander to rescind our flight orders. I knew that such a decision would devastate the Eskimo families. Unfortunately, I could not find out for sure until the next morning, just before our scheduled departure.

I invited Major Sharp to meet Anaukaq, Kali, and their families at the residence hall where we were staying. When we entered the door, a loud cheer went up from the Eskimos, who all rushed forward to greet the major. Several crowded around him and asked that I take their photographs with him. They were thrilled to meet this impressive black American officer, and he in turn was charmed by their sincere warmth. They seemed to think that all blacks they met were in some way relatives. I sensed that he represented for them the first symbol of what their trip to America would be like. As the major left, he assured me that he would do everything he could to make certain that our flight orders were okay.

Despite his encouragement, I stayed up all night worrying. While my Eskimo friends slept, I busied myself with packing and various other tasks. I prayed that our flight orders had not been changed and that the weather would permit the helicopter to get through and pick up the rest of the traveling party at Qaanaaq.

At 3:30 A.M., I walked about a mile through the cold morning air and waited outside the hangar for the helicopter pilot. True to his word, he arrived at precisely 4 A.M. It was a go. The weather had miraculously opened a brief window of time for him to fly over the mountains to Qaanaaq and back, a trip of about two and a half hours. We had beaten Tornarsuk again, I thought.

The pilot lost no time getting the helicopter airborne. I left for the base commander's office.

Upon my arrival at 7 A.M., I was immediately escorted in and offered a cup of coffee. The commander greeted me as warmly as always. First, he said, he wanted to confirm the names of everyone in my traveling party. After we discussed this matter, he informed me that our flight to McGuire Air Force Base would be delayed because of activities there involving the secretary of defense. We talked about the reunion project in relation to the Thule air base, and he assured me of his support for the project. At last I could relax. He invited me next door to meet the air force public relations staff, who would do a story on its role in the North Pole Family Reunion.

I was relieved that my worst fears had not materialized. As I was saying good-bye, the commander said he would join us at the departure terminal to meet Anaukaq and Kali and to see our group off.

When I arrived at the hangar, I saw the helicopter sitting on the landing pad. I knew then that the other members of the traveling party had arrived. I ran up to the pilot, grabbed his hand, shook it, looked him in the eye, and said, "Tack sa mycket! [Thank you very much]." He looked me back in the eye and said in Swedish, "ingen orsak, ingen orsak [You're welcome, you're welcome]." We had just enough time to get the group together and over to the military airlift command hangar for the jet flight to the United States.

The waiting room at the military airlift command is rather austere in comparison to the waiting rooms at commercial airline terminals in the United States. When we arrived with our many bags, we were asked to stack them with others in a large pile in one area of the terminal. The bags would be taken and placed with the rest of the freight in the cargo section of the plane, just ahead of the seats. We waited and took our seats among thirty or so air force servicemen who were also traveling to the United States. As promised, Major Sharp and Colonel Knapp came out to bid us farewell.

Walking from the hangar onto the frozen tarmac, we saw the camouflaged green C-141 that would carry us to America. Its small tires and very low-slung profile made it look more like a large bomber than a conventional jet, while its large wings, extending from the top of the fuselage, seemed to droop like those of a giant vulture.

In no time we were all aboard and strapped into our seats facing backward, away from the cockpit. Everybody seemed very comfortable, and no one seemed especially frightened or uneasy about the flight. The flight sergeant started blaring instructions over the loud intercom system, which is designed to overcome the attenuation of the earplugs each passenger receives on the uninsulated jet. I had to get up with the translator and go from person to person to make certain that seat belts were fastened and earplugs were in.

The crew treated the Eskimo travelers rather like celebrities, passing out extra fruit and juice. The pilots invited us to the large panoramic flight deck, which is about four times the size of the cockpit of a regular commercial aircraft. Anaukaq and Kali enthusiastically accepted the invitation, and we headed up the steep stairs. Once in the room-sized flight deck, they were thrilled to see the sky around them at forty thousand feet and the vast snow-covered flatlands and mountain peaks below. The pilots and other officers on the flight deck were so impressed with the two old men that they pulled the military insignia from their uniforms and gave them to Anaukaq and Kali as a gift. The two old hunters accepted graciously the first gifts from their American journey.

"*Kooyounah, kooyounah,*" they repeated as they tried to stick the velcro insignia to the shoulders of their coats.

After seven hours of smooth, restful flying we started our descent for McGuire Air Force Base in the center of New Jersey.

On Friday, May 29, 1987, Matthew Henson's and Robert Peary's sons set foot on American soil for the first time. They stood together on the tarmac for a moment, surveying their surroundings in silence. Their faces registered pleasure and awe.

"It is now a reality. We have reached our fathers' land," Anaukaq said.

"Yes, after so many years," replied Kali. "But it sure is *Keyettoe* [hot]!"

As we feared, the temperature was a steamy ninety degrees, a hundred-degree differential from the temperature we had left in Greenland. The East Coast was experiencing one of the worst heat waves in decades, and the air was oppressive. But the group didn't seem to mind. We all just shed our coats as we stepped aboard an air force van bound for the terminal.

The air-conditioned terminal came as a relief. We filed through customs to the comfort of a waiting room. Everything appeared in order as the unsmiling, tough-looking customs official checked us through, one by one. There were thirteen Eskimos in the group, nine Hensons, three Pearys, and the translator. The Hensons included Anaukaq and his sons Avataq, Ussarkaq, Ajako, and Kitdlaq, who were all together for the first time in years. (I made separate, special arrangements to bring Vittus, the fifth son, into the United States from southern Greenland.) Also, Anaukaq's grandson Massauna-Matthew and his granddaughters Malina and Aviaq were with us. Kali had invited only his son, Talilanguaq, and his grandson Ole along.

Just when we thought it was going well, we hit a snag. The customs official called me over to say that Malina did not have proper identification and could not be permitted to enter the country. This could not be so, I assured him. After all, we had received special permission from the U.S. consulate in Denmark for her to use the document signed by the commander of the Danish military at Thule. But the customs agent showed me that the commander's document read in small print that it was valid only if the said Malina Henson could prove her identity with a birth certificate or other form of Danish/Greenlandic identification. Malina had no such identification. She had never been outside the Moriussaq region and had no need for it. No one had told us she needed further identification.

"I am sorry. The others may go through, but I cannot let her enter the country without proper identification," the customs officer said.

When the translator explained the problem to the group, Malina dropped in a chair and lowered her head. Tornarsuk had a long reach.

I pleaded with the customs officer, but to no avail.

"Well, she can't stay here at the base. What can we do?" I asked.

"We'll have to send her back on the next available plane," he replied. In the meantime, she would have to be confined to base.

I knew that the next plane would leave for Thule at 8 A.M. the following Monday. If that flight had no seats, she would have to remain on base until the air force could find her a seat on yet another returning flight.

The other members of the group, having cleared customs, sat in a second waiting room, separated from us by a large glass enclosure. They could see Malina slumped in her chair, staring at the floor. Their momentary joy had turned to despair.

I went over to console Malina, who was shaking with fear. She was hurt and embarrassed that she might have caused complications for her grandfather. I tried to reassure her that everything would be fine.

I asked for permission to call the State Department to request special approval for Malina to enter the country. My request was granted, but I knew that this would probably involve a great deal of red tape—and our staying on the base until the matter was resolved.

Returning to the customs officer, who by now had observed the sadness that had swept over the entire group, I appealed for understanding. I told him the story of Matthew Henson and Robert Peary, and the significance of their sons' visit. I showed him copies of the visa applications which I had brought along, including Malina's. I even shared with him reprints of newspaper and magazine articles about the planned reunion. He seemed unmoved.

"There is no way I can permit her to enter the country without the documentation called for in the commander's identification papers," he said. "I'm sorry, but I must put her on the next flight to Thule."

"Please sir," I implored. "Don't break this young woman's heart. Let her join her family for this two-week visit. I give you my word that I will have her back at this gate, ready to return to Greenland on schedule."

He did not respond. In fact he began to talk with others around the terminal.

I was on my way to the phone to call the State Department, when I turned to him and asked, "When will you be able to put her on a flight back to Thule?"

"In two weeks," he replied, smiling for the first time. "Take her on through—and good luck on your project."

We just looked each other in the eye for a moment and acknowledged our mutual appreciation. The gruff old guy had a heart after all. "We all thank you, sir," I said.

The group cheered Malina when she came through the customs door. Avataq and Ajako ran up to the customs officer and shook his hand saying, *"Kooyounah."*

CHAPTER TWELVE

✻ ✻ ✻

The North Pole Family Reunion

Outside the terminal, my students were waiting in a large, air-conditioned chartered bus. Our committee had chosen the bus over other forms of transportation because we felt it offered us the greatest flexibility and, in the long run, would cost less. The driver, a seasoned veteran, and the student escorts who had driven down from Cambridge earlier that day helped our guests get comfortable. Before long we were on our way to Harvard. Trying to avoid the big-city traffic, the driver took as many back roads as possible. Our Eskimo friends glowed with excitement as they gazed out the windows in utter amazement at their surroundings.

"Incredible," said Ussarkaq. "Look at all of these plants," he said pointing to the trees and shrubbery along the road. "I have seen these plants ever since we arrived. They're everywhere! I have never seen so many plants in my entire life."

"The pathways go on forever," said Kali, referring to the maze of highways. "They never end! Are they manmade? Maybe they were here when the earth was formed."

"*Eemuckkah* [Maybe]," responded Anaukaq, sitting beside him. "But look at the *pedde* [cars]—so many *pedde*. They look like a flock of little *cheemeahk*—little auks, flying all around you. They just keep coming toward us and coming toward us," he shouted, gesturing with his hands. "Endless! They never stop. So many *pedde*—it's just too much."

"Igloo, igloo, igloo, igloo, *quah, quah, quah, pah che* [So many igloos]," said Kali.

"*Eeee*, I see them," said Anaukaq. "Look! The tall ones have many little igloos inside where people live—like the cliffs above Moriussaq where the birds live in holes on the face of the mountain."

"Look at that large white igloo. I could live in that one," Ussarkaq shouted, pointing to a large white Victorian home.

Everyone laughed.

"It is hard to believe that we are now in America. A little while ago I was sleeping in Qaanaaq," Ussarkaq said.

As we passed through one town, Ole shouted, "Look at all of the people—where do so many people come from?"

"I don't know. They come and go down large streets which look like canyons," Talilanguaq commented.

"So this is America," said Kitdlaq. "The place we have always dreamed about. I can't believe we are here."

After a few hours of travel, we pulled into a highway rest stop. We all got off to stretch our legs and get a bite to eat while the bus refueled. The only restaurant at the stop was part of a well-known hamburger chain, so the Eskimos were treated to a classic American meal: a large hamburger, french fries, and a cola. They loved it. This would be just the beginning of many such roadside stops as we moved up and down the East Coast during the next two weeks.

We arrived at Harvard early that evening and were greeted by students, family members, and friends at Leverett House, where I had previously made lodging arrangements. After dinner in the Leverett dining room, we joined other students in the courtyard. The trees, birds, and squirrels around the courtyard all fascinated the Eskimos. No one wanted to turn in. They were all too excited about the strange new world around them.

Eventually we convinced Kali and Anaukaq that they should retire to their room and get some sleep. We then took the rest of the group to Harvard Square. The lights and sounds of the square dazzled them. There were people and cars everywhere. And now they were no longer viewing them from the window of the bus, but mingling among them. The Eskimos spoke with curious passers-by and sampled pizza, sausages, sandwiches, ice cream, and about every other tasty delight the Square had to offer.

When we returned to Leverett with late-night snacks to talk about the planned events, we found Anaukaq and Kali still up, talking in their room. Only utter exhaustion forced the group to retire in the wee hours of the morning.

The next day, everyone was up at six o'clock. For over an hour, the entire group stood in the courtyard and watched two squirrels put on what was, for the Eskimos, a fantastic show. The lively squirrels ran about the Leverett courtyard, climbing trees and scampering across telephone wires. Back in Greenland, no wild animal runs about so freely, especially if there are hunters around. Little things that we take for granted fascinated my Eskimo friends.

Anaukaq noticed a slight swelling in his leg and brought it to my attention. I had him examined immediately by our project physician, Dr. Louis C. Brown, who had served for many years as a physician to the Harvard University Health Services. Dr. Brown, assisted by Ann J. C. Daniels, R.N., determined that Anaukaq's leg was not draining properly. Like many elderly folks, he had a slight swelling in his legs from time to time because of poor circulation. His legs had been in one position for several hours during the long flight and later during the bus ride, and this had adversely affected his circulation and drainage. They also found that he had never removed the tight wool long underwear that he had worn since we left Greenland. They treated him and elevated his leg in a comfortable position for several hours. Dr. Brown and Nurse Daniels would spend the next ten days with us, checking Anaukaq's and Kali's blood pressure, heart, lungs, body temperature, sweat levels, and just about everything else on a daily basis.

The following morning, while Anaukaq rested his leg, we took the group shopping for clothes. We bought summer shirts, pants, jackets, shoes, and accessories for everyone. Aviaq and Malina bought dresses, along with earrings, headbands, sunglasses, and watches.

Our plans called for us to visit the Peary-MacMillan Arctic Museum in Brunswick, Maine, that afternoon. Since the museum is not far from the home of Robert Peary, Jr., before we boarded the bus I decided to make one final plea to the Pearys to see if they would meet Kali. This time, however, I bypassed the family spokesperson and telephoned Robert Jr. directly. His wife answered the phone. She listened patiently as I explained how much it would mean to Kali to meet his half brother, that we didn't mean to intrude but had planned to be in the area anyway, and so forth.

"Oh, all right," she said finally, in a grandmotherly way. "Bring him up to meet us."

I was no less delighted than I was surprised by her response. How ironic, I thought, that the two people who ostensibly needed to be "protected" most from the sensitive news of Kali's existence were the ones who first agreed to see him.

When we arrived, the Pearys, along with their son, Robert III, came out to greet us. Robert Jr. walked up to Kali with a big, warm smile and extended his hand. With an equally big grin, Kali shook his hand. They stared at each other for a moment.

"Now, are you my half brother?" Robert Jr. asked.

"Yes, I am Peeuree's son," Kali replied.

"And your name is Kali?"

"Yes, Kali Peeuree."

"Well, I'm a bit confused," Robert Jr. admitted. "I have never met you, but when I was up in Greenland back in twenty-six, I saw some Eskimos that were said to be related to me. I didn't meet them, but the name I remember is Anaukaq. Now I hear from my son that Anaukaq is colored—Matt Henson's son. I'm confused."

"You are confusing me with my older brother Anaukaq!" Kali explained through the translator. "He too was Peeuree's son. But he is dead now."

"Now I understand," said Robert Jr. "Now I understand."

"And who are all these fine people?" asked Mrs. Peary.

"Well, this is your brother-in-law," Robert Jr. said to his wife.

"How nice to meet you," she responded warmly.

Kali introduced his son and grandson, and we introduced ourselves.

"Well, come on inside," Mrs. Peary said. "I had my son go out to get some cool lemonade for you."

The house was filled with Peary memorabilia. Bearskins and other

Arctic trophies lined the walls of the rustic New England home. Robert Jr. took Kali on a complete tour of the house, explaining each item. Kali too explained some of the items that were indigenous to Greenland, such as old Eskimo implements.

"Do you have the classic Peary gap between your two front teeth?" Robert Jr. asked Kali at one point. "All Peary men must have the trademark of the family," he chuckled.

"Well," Kali thought for a moment. "I think I used to have that gap when I had my own teeth. But I can't rightly say that the ones I have now are mine."

Everyone burst into laughter.

As we all gathered in the living room to drink our lemonade, the joviality of the atmosphere moved Robert Jr. to play the old upright piano that was taken from Peary's ship, the *Roosevelt*—the piano that had been on the ship when Kali was born there.

After playing a delightful song for a few minutes, Robert Jr. cheerfully raised his hands to show Kali and the others that he had not been playing the piano after all. It was a player piano.

Kali and the rest of us laughed uproariously.

At Robert Jr.'s invitation, Kali, Talilanguaq, and Ole sat down at the piano to play as well. Three generations of Pearys, playing the admiral's piano. Talilanguaq and Ole beamed with pride at the warmth of the reception for their father.

With his hand on Kali's shoulder, Robert Jr. explained the piano to his half brother. They have finally come together, I thought, and they were enjoying each other like the long-lost brothers they were. I wondered just how much of the resistance to letting Kali meet his American relatives had come from family members who were out of touch with Robert Jr.'s feelings. Like many elderly people, Robert did not seem to care about all the fuss being made over what Kali might do to his father's image or family name. He seemed only to want to enjoy people and every moment of the rest of his life.

Robert Jr. and his wife were gracious hosts. The visit was brief, but it meant the world to Kali and his children. "For the first time in my life," Kali said to his brother, "I feel like a Peary." Robert Jr. stared at him but said nothing.

We gathered on the lawn for photographs before departing for the Peary-MacMillan Arctic Museum in nearby Brunswick.

* * *

On Sunday morning, we rose early and dressed for services at Harvard's Memorial Church. The Amer-Eskimo Hensons and Pearys looked quite spiffy in their new clothes. Anaukaq wore his new trousers, but not the shirt we had bought. He insisted on wearing the traditional white Polar Eskimo anorak he had brought with him from Moriussaq.

Knowing that Anaukaq and Kali had embraced Christianity and from time to time attended the missionary church in Greenland, I had asked my dear friend Peter J. Gomes, minister of Memorial Church, for a special "Service of Welcome" for the Eskimos and their American families. As a member of our committee, Gomes had expressed both concern and compassion for the Amer-Eskimo Hensons and Pearys, and he shared my desire to make their first American reception special.

The church steps were crowded with American Hensons who had come to meet Anaukaq and his family. Several of them ran forward to greet Anaukaq, including his cousin Olive, who warmly embraced him. Emotions poured forth from both sides.

"These are your American family members," the translator told Anaukaq and his sons.

"My family?" Anaukaq said, now glassy-eyed.

"Yes, they are all Hensons—and this is Olive, your cousin who sent you the blanket."

"This is Olive?" Anaukaq said. "I am happy to meet you. Thank you for the beautiful blanket."

"Oh, is this your cousin?" Kali asked Anaukaq. The American Hensons embraced Kali and his sons as if they were part of their own family.

At the sound of the bell, we moved from the enervating outdoor heat into the shady comfort of Memorial Church. Hundreds of students, faculty, and other regular parishioners stood as we took seats in the first pews.

With hands raised above the congregation, Peter Gomes declared a day of celebration and welcome in honor of our guests from Greenland.

"We are particularly honored and happy to welcome as visitors to this congregation this morning, members of the Henson and Peary families, who come to us from very far distant places indeed. We have done our best to provide you with as opposite and different weather as it is your custom to experience—we hope you will forgive us if it is too hot. We trust that should we in turn visit you, you would return the favor. . . .

"Now the books have long celebrated the achievements and discovery of your fathers, Matthew Henson and Robert Peary. They live in the pages of history. . . . And by dint of imagination and great courage landed at the top of the world. And one would like to think that it is their example of colleagueship and indeed fellowship that trickles down from the top of the world and embraces all the rest of us today. But what we celebrate today is not a mere geological survey or Arctic adventure—a simple cover story for *National Geographic*. Rather, we celebrate the story of an enormous human achievement and adventure, a tale of collaboration between black and white when that was neither fashionable nor familiar. And we celebrate as well the human spirit that knows no boundaries, either of race or place— a spirit that in the faces of these men and women unknown to us and each other for so long says we are all related, we are all your brothers and sisters. The distance between us is bridged by the human fellowship we now share with one another. We are all cousins. Dare we aspire to anything less than this? . . .

"We know the risks and charges of our history. The burden of it is with us every day of our lives. That is why it is so wonderful when we can celebrate a discovery whose human dimension enriches us all and redefines in the most appropriate and useful way, the whole meaning of the human family. That is why your visit to America is not purely a private matter—though that it is. It is a matter of the most immense public interest. For you by your presence help us define anew, and more generously, who we are and who you are. . . .

"And so in the spirit of that reunion, I am delighted that our brothers and sisters from the top of the world have taken the risk of reunion—have taken the risk of the journey, have taken the risk of the heat—to be with us today. And to help us celebrate with you the unity of the human family, under God. You are proof that it works— as are we to you. Why did it take you so long to come home?"

Peter preached eloquently throughout a service mixed with Scripture, poetry, humor, and wit. At one point, he reminded the congregation that "the Eskimos were in some ways like the Indians at Plymouth Rock. They had their own culture and history. And when they first came into contact with outsiders who claimed to have discovered them, they exclaimed, 'What do you mean "discovered" us? We were never lost in the first place!'" It was what we call at Harvard a classic Gomes sermon, at once fitting and deeply moving.

Following the service, the church held a brief outdoor reception attended by family, friends, students, and, of course, the press. Although the fierce midday heat forced us to cut it short, it was here that Kali met some of his other American relatives, albeit distant ones. The couple and their son were descendants of one of Robert Peary's paternal uncles. This line of Pearys had moved to Pennsylvania along with Robert Peary's father to set up a wood and barrel business in the mid-1800s, and they had remained there when Robert's mother moved back to Maine after her husband's death. Upon learning of my meeting with Kali in Greenland and my plans to bring him to the United States, the Pennsylvania descendants had written to ask if they might participate in the reunion activities. The committee, of course, was delighted to oblige. Before Kali's arrival in the United States, they were the only members of the Peary family who had shown any interest in meeting Kali and his family.

*   *   *

Later that afternoon, we headed to the town of Milton, a suburb of Boston, where the American Hensons had arranged a traditional backyard barbeque for their Eskimo kin. As I drove Anaukaq, Kali, and their families to Milton in a large rented van, they all sang traditional Eskimo songs—songs of joy and happiness.

To locate the family gathering, we had to find our way through the maze of curving streets and rotaries common to the Boston area. But the American Hensons provided very special directions. For the last few miles, all the way to the door of the house, they had tied yellow ribbons around the trees along the road to mark the way. The Eskimo families had never heard of this practice and were profoundly touched when I explained it to them. They delighted in helping me spot the trees with the yellow ribbons, cheering each as it came into view.

When we reached the Henson's home, there were the usual introductions, along with music, dancing, and, of course, lots of food—"soul food"—on the lawn of the beautifully landscaped backyard. Our hosts served barbequed chicken, cornbread, collard greens, black-eyed peas, yams, ham, corn, rice, okra, cakes, and even homemade ice cream.

"This is the special food of the *kulnocktooko* people," Ussarkaq announced to the others. " 'Soul' food—that is what they told me."

"What are collard greens?" Avataq asked.

"That is a traditional black American vegetable," I told him.

"Mmmm, it tastes good," he responded.

"Try a little vinegar on them," I told him.

"This is some of the best food I have ever tasted," Avataq offered.

"*Eeee*," Anaukaq replied. "This chicken tastes a little like our *cheemeahk* in Moriussaq—and the ham is a little sweet, like *nanook*."

To show their appreciation, the Amer-Eskimos sang several songs, after which Anaukaq and his children held a ceremony to present gifts they had brought from Greenland for their family and friends. They handed out authentic native carvings and other traditional Eskimo handiwork. Anaukaq and Kali surprised me with a gift they knew I really wanted: a beautiful pair of handmade, traditional sealskin hunter's mittens with polar bear fur tops. Nothing is more suited to the Arctic cold, not even the expensive synthetic gloves they saw me wearing in Greenland. Receiving these from Anaukaq and Kali, two *peeneeahktoe wah*, was a great tribute indeed.

Olive and the American Hensons presented Anaukaq and Kali each with a combination radio–tape recorder, with shortwave and AM-FM—something I knew they would enjoy back in their homeland. Greenland now has a radio station broadcasting in the Polar Eskimo language. Anaukaq, Kali, and their families were quite fond of listening to such radio programs.

"I am so happy to be here today—to look around me and see so many of Mahri-Pahluk's family here. I am also happy that my children and their children could come here to meet their relatives. We always thought we had relatives over here—and now we know. We are here now, and we can see you, and we feel good. We thank you for this celebration. I hope you will come to see us in our land. *Kooyounah.*"

Everyone cheered and applauded.

The celebration continued into the evening, with some family members retiring to the house, where they played the piano and sang.

One of the Hensons had a fancy van with dramatic designs on the exterior and an interior that looked more like an elegant studio than an automobile. The Eskimos were captivated by this unusual *pedde*, with its carpeted floors, colorful lights, and multistereo sound. And to their utter delight, they all got a ride in it—several times each.

As the reunion party continued into the evening, I overheard Kitdlaq say to his brothers, "This has been a great day for our family—perhaps the greatest ever. And the *kulnocktooko* people are very special—they have so much feeling." Talilanguaq, who was among the Amer-Eskimo Hensons, nodded approvingly, "Yes, they are very special."

* * *

The following evening, Harvard University sponsored the North Pole Family Reunion Banquet for Hensons and Pearys from all over the country. Anaukaq and Kali were the guests of honor in a gathering of some two hundred people at Harvard's historical Memorial Hall. I had initially planned a smaller get-together, but as word of the reception spread, more and more people wanted to come, and we had to increase the size of the function. Among those in attendance were Robert Peary III and Robert Peary IV, who at the last minute accepted our long-standing invitation to join in the festivities. They said Kali's brother, Robert Peary, Jr., was unable to make the trip from Maine to attend the banquet. Kali was, however, delighted to see his nephew and great nephew there, and so were the members of our organizing committee.

In spite of the heat and the formality of the occasion, the two retired hunters were gregarious and at times looked like royalty, as they were fanned and otherwise attended by family and friends. They sat at the head table with Harvard's president Derek C. Bok, and they spoke eloquently when introduced to the audience. Bok had earlier expressed a personal interest in the Amer-Eskimo families and was most helpful to the North Pole Family Reunion Committee. At my request, he agreed to act as host of the affair and present awards of recognition to Anaukaq and Kali, to herald their visit to the university and to honor their fathers.

At the podium, Bok addressed the gathering. "It is a great privilege to welcome to Harvard the sons of Robert Peary and Matthew Henson—Anaukaq Henson and Kali Peary—and the members of their families. This trip, as many of you know, represents the realization of a wish to see the land in which their fathers lived and died." His warm presentation was punctuated with spirited applause.

This was followed by a stirring speech from the keynote speaker of the evening, John H. Johnson, who several times brought the audience to its feet.

"I am delighted to be here tonight," Johnson began. "I usually have a speechwriter—and I had one this time. And I have a speech, but I'm not going to give it. I feel too much from my heart. This has touched me. I feel as if history has come alive here tonight."

Johnson was at his best, evoking both laughter and tears as he told us what Matthew Henson meant to his life and to the success of his business. "When they were trying to decide on who was going to go with him [Peary] on the last lap to the North Pole, Peary said 'I can't make it without Henson.' This is a man who had been with him for eighteen years—who had made eight trips with him. Imagine, eight trips. I think I would have dropped out at seven! But he made eight. This is a man who believed in his leader. I also think this says something good about Admiral Peary. It says that he was the kind of man who dared in 1909 to say that the best man for the job was a black man. That was a daring thing to do in 1909! Frankly, it's daring sometimes now."

Olive represented the Henson family. "I want to welcome everybody to this beautiful, happy feeling that I have in my heart right now," Olive said with choked voice and tearful eyes. "And I just wish everybody could feel the way I do. Thank you."

University marshal Richard Hunt joined Bok in making the presentations to Anaukaq and Kali.

"This award is presented to Mr. Anaukaq Henson to mark his visit to Harvard University and to salute his father's contributions to the discovery of the North Pole. Given this day, June 1, 1987."

Anaukaq, his pride not permitting any of us to assist him in walking, stepped up to the podium without his cane to receive his award.

"Also, from Harvard University, to mark his visit to the university and to salute the contributions of his father to the discovery of the North Pole, we present this award to Mr. Kali Peary."

The two old hunters were clearly moved. They stood together, erect with poise and dignity after walking up to the podium to receive the large, elegant engravings of the old Harvard Yard, with their names etched in shiny brass. They would gladly have accepted even the smallest token of recognition from any American, regardless of his or her position. They did not understand or even care about American hierarchy. But here they were tonight, being recognized by the president of the oldest and most distinguished university in America, receiving the same plaques customarily presented to royalty and heads of state.

Anaukaq never failed to amaze me. This little big man from the tiny village of Moriussaq addressed the Harvard gathering like a practiced statesman.

"I thank all of you for this reception you have given me and my family and Kali this evening. This is a special night for me," he said. "I thought that I would never have the opportunity to visit Mahri-Pahluk's homeland. And I believed that I would never have a chance to see my relatives in America. We are here now, and we are very pleased to be with our relatives."

The audience applauded. Thinking he had finished, I started to pass the microphone to Kali, only to be stopped by the translator, who reminded me that Anaukaq was "not finished yet."

"When people up in Greenland used to talk of Peeuree and Mahri-Pahluk, I would think about whether I had relatives over here. I used to tell my children, 'Maybe we have some relatives over there in Mahri-Pahluk's homeland. Maybe I have a brother or sister down there,' I would say. I had no brother or sister in Greenland. I was alone. And now I know that Mahri-Pahluk had no other children, and that I have no sisters or brothers in America. But I have lots of other wonderful relatives down here. I am just as happy to meet Olive and my other American relatives.

"I thank everyone who helped make this trip possible for me, my sons, and some of my grandchildren. I have finally made it to America, and here I am—Matthew Henson's son, Anaukaq, who has been hiding up in Greenland all these years." Then with a big laugh, he raised his arms, clenched fists above his head, and waved them defiantly. "I have finally come home in 1987 to proudly show everyone that I am the son of Matthew Henson."

His animation surprised everyone. During his long life, Anaukaq must have dreamed this scene over and over, many times. He must have fantasized about coming to his father's land and being received as a hero by family and admirers. He was ecstatic.

Kali spoke with confidence and eloquence. "I don't have words to express myself tonight. But I am reminded of the time when I was much younger and working in politics among my people. I learned an important thing. I learned the importance of cooperation among people. And I am thankful for that. Later, I was amazed when the first ships came up to the Thule air base, and we met other people. They wanted to cooperate with us, and we with them. And I thought that maybe the people have finally heard my words when I said that people must work together as people. It is very important for people to work together in achieving something. I can't keep going now because this is more than I can handle," he said with tears in his eyes. "Let some of the others take over. We are here with you tonight because we have all worked together—because of our cooperation. *Kooyounah.*"

The sustained applause testified to the powerful emotions that swept over the gathering. In a community where people typically depart quickly after a social affair, we were all surprised to see that most of the guests remained to talk with our Eskimo visitors and with each other long after the ceremony had ended.

The celebration continued at my house, where Anaukaq and Kali were later inspired to get up and dance to music they heard while watching television. They had everyone in stitches as they did old Eskimo dances to modern music.

The next morning, after a hefty breakfast, we boarded the bus for Charles County, Maryland, and Washington, D.C. A small group of friends gathered to see us off. I knew that Anaukaq and Kali charmed all who met them. But I never realized just how deeply the two men and their families had affected our community until I saw *Harvard Gazette* senior writer Marvin Hightower standing at the roadside, crying, as the bus pulled away. As a member of our committee, Marvin had helped us organize activities and chaperon the family. Like others who were involved with Anaukaq and Kali, he had also become emotionally very close to both families. The Eskimos fell silent when they saw Marvin's tears. Staring back through the windows, they slowly waved good-bye to him as the bus pulled off. He, like the other Americans, had had a profound effect on them as well.

* * *

In some sections, Charles County, Maryland, is as bucolic and verdant today as it was when Matthew Henson was born here in 1866. We were met at the county line by members of the Charles County Afro-American Heritage Society, with whom I had earlier arranged a public reception. The group's president, Mary Louise Webb, pinned black-eyed Susans on every member of our entourage and, with a motorcycle police escort, directed our long motorcade into the county seat. With sirens blaring, the police and motorcade led us down the main street to the town center. The Eskimo family sensed that this would be an important ceremony for them when they saw the parade of cars behind our bus, and the motorcycle police with lights flashing, in front.

"This is how they treat important people," Avataq said to Kali, who was sitting beside him. "This is to show us how much they appreciate that we are here."

I had also written the county commissioners to request an official reception for Anaukaq and his family. They welcomed us with a band and a flag-waving ceremony. The conductor led the band in "76 Trombones" as our entourage arrived.

Anaukaq and Kali stepped off the bus to loud applause from a gathering of more than two hundred citizens. Each of us received a small American flag from local officials as we were led to our seats behind the podium on the steps of the antebellum, white-pillared county courthouse.

Speeches by government officials and singing by local citizens rounded out the welcome.

"As a token of our appreciation for Mr. Henson's visit, we are presenting his family with the county flag," said the county commissioner, as she handed Anaukaq a large yellow banner with the Charles County insignia in its center.

"*Kooyounah,*" Anaukaq said, graciously accepting the flag and shaking the commissioner's hand.

In the tiny town of Nanjemoy, in the center of Charles County, we walked deep into the thick woods so that Anaukaq could view the spot where his father was born. We were guided by long-time resident William Diggs who, along with other members of the Charles County Afro-American Heritage Society, had located and marked the spot for posterity. Diggs had met Matthew Henson on some of his visits to Charles County to see his family.

"I thought that I would see the igloo where my father Mahri-Pahluk was born," Anaukaq said.

"Unfortunately, it is long gone," Diggs replied. "It was a log cabin. Only parts of the fireplace remain."

"It was over one hundred years old and made of wood," I added. "It simply deteriorated over time."

Anaukaq said he was pleased just to stand on the ground where his father was born. He took two bricks, part of the original fireplace, from the ruins of his father's home. These he would take back to Greenland as mementos.

As we drove along the narrow, rustic back roads, Anaukaq sat alone on the bus, staring out the window at the thick green forest around us.

"What a beautiful country!" he said. "This is Mahri-Pahluk's land.

I can see that he lived in a beautiful area. It seems like I am dreaming, but I'm not. I have never been to such a beautiful place."

∗   ∗   ∗

Next, we traveled to Washington to commemorate the meeting of Anaukaq's and Kali's fathers in that city a century earlier and to visit Robert Peary's grave in Arlington National Cemetery.

A few months earlier, I had contacted Mr. Raymond Costanzo, superintendent of Arlington National Cemetery, and told him about my plans. From the outset, Costanzo showed sincere interest in the subject and wanted to know how he could help. I requested that a small ceremony be held at Peary's grave, with a navy honor guard and chaplain to salute both Kali's visit and the memory of Robert Peary. Costanzo promptly contacted me to say that my request had been approved and that he would help arrange the ceremony. I then sent a letter to the White House, inviting the president or one of his representatives to join us for the ceremony.

About the same time, I contacted the Woodlawn Cemetery. Assuming that the president would not grant permission to transfer Henson's remains to Arlington in time for Anaukaq's visit, I requested a similar ceremony at Woodlawn, with a military honor guard, a minister, and a formal wreath-laying ceremony.

When our bus arrived at the gates of Arlington, uniformed soldiers snapped to attention and directed us up the winding road to Peary's grave. The stately tombs lining the pastoral lanes entranced everyone on the bus as we made our way up the curving hill. The monument marking Peary's grave sits alone on a spacious, hilltop site that commands a view of much of the cemetery.

About seventy-five Henson family members and friends greeted us when we reached the grave. The assembled guests were seated in front of the monument, under the branches of a large tree that shaded us from the afternoon sun. Standing to our left, behind a roped-off area, were some thirty members of the press, with cameras and sound equipment. Their cameras had started clicking the moment we stepped from the bus.

Costanzo greeted us with a warm smile. A man of gentle but firm demeanor, he had a special reverence for this cemetery, and he conveyed that feeling as he gave us a briefing on the procedures of the ceremony. Costanzo introduced me to Chase Untermeyer, assistant secretary of the navy, who attended the ceremony on behalf of the president of the United States, who was attending a summit meeting.

"I was sent to represent the president of the United States in the ceremony today. He has sent you a special message," Untermeyer told me. I was very pleased.

Next to Untermeyer was Comdr. Stanley DeLong, navy chaplain of Arlington National Cemetery. I could see many other high-ranking military officials in attendance as well. DeLong, Untermeyer, and Costanzo gave Kali and Anaukaq small gifts with military insignia.

Costanzo called the gathering to order. "We gather here today to honor Admiral Peary and Matthew Henson. Peary's and Henson's accolades were not won on the battlefield, but they were no less gallant. Their daring sacrifices in uncharted and treacherous territories rank them among our nation's most celebrated men of courage. They are linked to a long list of explorers and scientists who have been laid to rest here at Arlington. We are here to pay tribute to their immense contributions."

The ceremony was now under way. Dressed in white uniforms, a five-man navy honor guard marched before the assembly carrying the ceremonial U.S. flag, the U.S. Navy flag, and rifles. At Costanzo's signal, the entire gathering stood as the honor guard paraded before us. They stopped in front of Peary's monument. "Abou-uuut face! Attennn-hut!"

After DeLong delivered the invocation, the cemetery historian told the gathering about Peary's burial and the subsequent monument dedication. Although Peary was buried in Arlington in 1920 with full military honors, including airplane flights over his grave, the monument was given by the National Geographic Society and dedicated at an even larger ceremony by the president of the United States in 1922.

When my turn to speak came, I thanked the government officials for making this a special day for Kali. But I also reminded the gathering that we could not forget that Matthew Henson belonged in Arlington as well.

"Admiral Peary, the great explorer, deserves to be buried here. But Matthew Henson also deserves to be buried here among other American heroes. Henson and Peary were inseparable in their Arctic lives and accomplishments. They should be together in their resting places. I have written a letter to the president of the United States, asking him to consider reinterring the remains of Matthew Henson near those of his close friend and colleague Robert E. Peary here in the Arlington National Cemetery. This act would be appreciated by fair and patriotic Americans of all races, creeds, and colors."

Next, Chase Untermeyer stepped up to the podium and read a letter from the president:

> *Greetings to everyone gathered at Arlington National Cemetery for a service honoring the memory of Matthew Henson and Robert Peary, and a very special welcome to Anaukaq Henson and Kali Peary and their families, who have made the long journey from Greenland for the occasion.*
>
> *I am proud and happy to join with you in saluting the achievements of these Arctic explorers, who, with four Polar Eskimo companions, planted the American flag at the North Pole on April 6, 1909. Matthew Henson and Robert Peary worked together for twenty-three years and made eight Arctic voyages, during which Peary's leadership and Henson's interpreting and survival skills proved invaluable. The descendants and all the countrymen of these great Americans can be truly proud of their legacy of heroism and accomplishment in the service of science and our country.*
>
> *You have my very best wishes. God bless you.*
> *[signed] Ronald Reagan.*

After a round of grateful applause, Kali spoke from the podium.

"I thank the people here for this day. I have come this far to see the burial place of my *ahtahtah,* and here he sleeps in this beautiful place that I could not have imagined back in my homeland. My son and my grandson are here with me to share this day. And I have brought this wreath that my oldest daughter helped me make, so that our family and the Hensons of Greenland could honor Peeuree by putting it on his grave today. *Kooyounah.*"

A lone officer dressed in navy whites and standing among the tombstones some distance away, played a soft "taps" as Kali stepped up to Peary's monument and gently placed the wreath he had made for the occasion just beneath his father's name. Talilanguaq, Ole, and

Cousin Anaukaq then placed a second, larger wreath alongside the first. Kali asked me to walk to the monument with them. An honor guard escorted us.

After the ceremony, Kali bent over to try to read the inscription on the tombstone. I had it translated for him. It read: "Robert Edwin Peary—Discoverer of the North Pole—April 6, 1909." The side inscription read: "His beloved wife—Josephine Diebitsch Peary."

"This is Peary's wife's name," I told Kali and Anaukaq, who had joined him. "She is buried here also." He made no comment as he stared at the inscription.

This was the central ceremony planned for Kali in the itinerary. None of the American Pearys showed up. After the ceremony, he walked up to almost all the whites at the gathering, asking them one by one whether they were his relatives. They all said no. Sensing his loneliness, my Harvard students became very protective of him. They huddled around him and became his family. He never talked about it, but we hoped the Arlington ceremony was still a special event for him.

*   *   *

Between all the ceremonies, our guests had plenty of rest and relaxation. Their favorite pastime was playing in the swimming pool. The word "playing" is more appropriate than "swimming," even for the adults, since no one swims in polar Greenland. In fact, to the Eskimos, the very idea of plunging into a body of water is associated with death. This was especially evident from the face of Anaukaq, who had lost his eldest son to the icy northern sea. He watched with trepidation as Talilinguaq, Ole, Avataq, and the others entered the water for the first time and began thrashing about. They screamed and yelled at the thrill of their own buoyancy and their surprising ability to move about in water. Ajako, who was afraid to enter the pool, kept sticking his foot in the water to allay his fears, until he was finally pushed in. After this, it was difficult to get him to come out.

Eventually Anaukaq, too, overcame his fears. Although he never braved the water himself, he and Kali sat at the poolside, directing the others and laughing deliriously at their antics.

"Look at that!" Anaukaq said. "How can they move about in the water like that?"

"Ole looks like a big *pooeehee* under the water," Kali commented. "Look at him move," he chuckled, as his grandson dove beneath the surface in the three-foot section.

"Move your arms more like this," Anaukaq shouted to Malina, as he imitated swimming strokes.

With instructions from the experienced swimmers among our student escorts, Massauna-Matthew, Ole, Malina, and Aviaq, the youngest members of the group, quickly learned some strokes.

* * *

At 1237 Pennsylvania Avenue in Washington, a towering office building now stands where H. Stinemetz & Sons, Hatters and Furriers, stood a century earlier. As we passed the location, I pointed out to Anaukaq and Kali that this was the spot where their fathers had met a hundred years before.

The mayor had agreed to act as host at a reception for us at the Washington, D.C., Convention Center. Over a hundred guests, including American Hensons and friends, greeted us as we entered one of the reception areas of the massive building. In the center of the room stood a large ice sculpture of an igloo, surrounded by a profusion of elegant hors d'ouevres. The Eskimos cheerfully sampled everything until they were full.

We were officially welcomed by Washington Convention Center board chairman, and my old friend, Kent T. Cushenberry, who had arranged this affair at my request and who had been tremendously helpful to me throughout the project.

I had written Mayor Marion Barry about Matthew Henson's Washington roots and his contributions to the discovery of the North Pole, and I asked that Barry name the day of Anaukaq's first visit to Washington "Matthew Henson Day."

"I had never heard of the name Matthew A. Henson, to be frank with you, because it was left out of our history books," said Barry, surrounded onstage by Anaukaq, Kali, and their families. "And so I learned that Matthew Henson was a part of the North Pole expedition, that he was in fact chosen by Admiral Peary to actually, physically plant the flag at the North Pole. Never would I have thought in my wildest moments of fantasizing dreams that I would be here in Washington, D.C., today, as mayor of our nation's capital, meeting the sons of Peary and Henson. Now that is history being made. Actually, I really can't even write words to express what I'm talking about, I feel so touched."

The gathering erupted in emotional applause.

The mayor read from the proclamation. "And therefore I, the mayor of the District of Columbia, do hereby proclaim Wednesday June 3, 1987, as Matthew A. Henson Day in Washington, D.C., and call upon all the residents of this city in saluting this famous explorer. Signed Marion Barry, Jr., Mayor."

When the interpreter translated the mayor's words for the Eskimos, Ajako, who was holding his daughter Aviaq close to him, started to cry.

Detecting these feelings, the translator added a little humor to her translations.

"This day is Matthew Henson Day in Washington, D.C., until the great earthquake comes [Eskimo talk for the day of the end of the earth]. *"Bikdaoahgee* [Congratulations]," she shouted to the family.

Anaukaq, Kali, and their families cheered.

The mayor handed the proclamation to a happy and very appreciative Anaukaq.

Kent Cushenberry presented Anaukaq and Kali with U.S. flags that had been flown over the Capitol in their names at the request of Walter Fauntroy, congressman from Washington, D.C. The two Eskimo patriarchs and their children were visibly overwhelmed by these gestures.

I watched as Anaukaq and Kali, swarmed by family, friends, and well-wishers reveled in the moment. I recalled that a century before this day, Matthew Henson had sat down, not far from where we stood at the Washington Convention Center, and written Peary a letter expressing his desire to continue working with him in the future. He signed the letter, "From a friend—Matthew Henson." The friends who had met here in 1887 could never have dreamed that their sons, two very close friends, would be standing in Washington one hundred years later, being honored by the president of the United States, the mayor of the nation's capital, and a member of Congress.

* * *

Although Matthew Henson was born in Charles County, Maryland, and spent much of his youth in Washington, he lived for most of his life in New York City. He first moved there temporarily in 1892, when he rented a room at the home of Frederick Cook's mother while recovering from an Arctic eye ailment. Henson became enamored of the city and, after his estrangement from his first wife in 1897, he moved there permanently, remaining a New Yorker until his death in 1955. His last residence at 246 West 150th Street often buzzed with activity. A fireman who worked at a station near Henson's house in the 1950s recalled that one day, after having seen so many people visit the home, he was forced to ask the station chief who lived there. "In that home, my boy, resides the great Matthew Henson, who went to the North Pole with Peary," the chief told him.

Others remember Henson's legendary long walks, particularly those from his West 150th Street apartment to the Explorers Club on East 70th, in the dead of winter, without a topcoat. Henson enjoyed demonstrating his stamina and extraordinary ability to tolerate the cold.

I had told Anaukaq and Kali about the Explorers Club and their fathers' involvement with this select body. Peary served as president of the club from 1909 to 1911 and from 1913 to 1916, and Henson was elected to honorary membership in 1937. I arranged for the Eskimo families to have a tour of the club's house.

Just inside the entrance of the stately Tudor-style building, we were met by a ten-foot-high polar bear, standing on his hind legs, claws outstretched and teeth bared in a menacing snarl. The sight thrilled the old hunters, who rubbed the fur in amazement. They had never seen a stuffed polar bear, and the superb taxidermy made the animal look startlingly real.

"*Nanook,*" Anaukaq said to Kali. "What a huge thing. I don't think I have ever killed one this large. Have you?"

"No, not this large. And look at its *kokeet* [claws]," Kali replied.

Avataq, a hunter who has killed and eaten many polar bears, also marveled at the size of this "lion of the Arctic" that towered over him. "Look at the size of that mouth," he remarked, examining the stuffed beast as though he thought it might come to life at any moment. Even as Avataq walked away, he continued looking back at the bear in disbelief.

The bell taken from the *Roosevelt* is mounted on the wall of the club's main entrance. The family cheered as Anaukaq and Kali took turns ringing the bell, something they were too young to have done when the ship left Greenland for the last time in 1909.

Kali was particularly fascinated by the artifacts from his father's ship. During our visit to the Peary-MacMillan Arctic Museum in Maine, he spotted a replica of the *Roosevelt* and became very excited. "Is that the *Roosevelt*?" he asked. When the translator confirmed that it was, he became even more animated. "That is where I was born," he told me, gesturing toward the model. "Really, it is the truth. I'm not telling you a joke. That is what my parents told me. I was born in the *Roosevelt*'s machine room, and cousin Anaukaq was born in the coal room."

"Did you say Anaukaq was born in the coal room?" I asked in jest.

"*Eeee*," Kali replied. "We have known this since we were boys."

"Is that why Anaukaq is so dark?" I asked.

Kali and the other Eskimos burst into laughter. "Must be!"

On the walls, among the framed photographs of past presidents and honorary members of the club, were classic pictures of their fathers that made Kali and Anaukaq pause: Peary in a grand pose, wearing his military uniform and hat and sporting a thick, curled moustache; Henson, equally striking in his trademark anorak, the wind-blown fur of the hood outlining his features.

"Our *ahtahtah*," Kali said to Anaukaq, pointing at the photographs.

"*Eeee*," Anaukaq said solemnly.

"Who are all of these other men?" Kali asked.

"Past Explorers Club presidents," our guide told us.

"They all look so important," Kali said with a chuckle.

Yet what excited them most was the sight of one of the original sleds that Peary and Henson had used on their North Pole journey in 1909. Given to the club by the Peary family, the dark oak sledge (as sleds were once called) was about twelve feet long, two feet wide, seven inches off the ground, with three-foot upstanders. It was lashed together with sealskin thongs for flexibility and strength.

"Oh, this is a beauty. It suits this place," said Anaukaq. "It is the kind we had in the old days."

"Ahhh, look at this. This is very good workmanship," said Kali.

"Maybe Mahri-Pahluk used this one to give his boss a ride to the North Pole," Anaukaq said, teasing Kali.

"Maybe!" Kali laughed. "What are these bindings made of?" he asked Anaukaq as he rolled the lashings in his fingers.

"Aren't these thongs made of bearded seal?" Anaukaq replied, examining the tough leather cords with his experienced hands.

"I don't know," Kali said, still feeling the bindings. "Maybe they are made of something from this country."

The two old hunters explored every inch of the sled, like two old-timers examining an antique car from their youth.

After an extended tour of the club's several floors we departed, but not before Anaukaq and Kali had put their signatures on Explorers Club stationery, which I had dated to record their visit in the historical archives of their fathers' mutual fraternity.

* * *

Only the mountains of the Eskimos' world compared with the giant skyscrapers of New York City. Like all newcomers to the city, the two families were awed by the scale of everything around them.

"Igloo, igloo, igloo, *quah, quah, quah, pah che* [So many, many houses]," was again the cry of everyone on the bus. Ajako called his daughter Aviaq over to his seat and pointed out the tall buildings on his side. She lay on his lap, facing upward toward the ceiling of the bus so that she could appreciate the height of the skyscrapers.

After a shopping spree at Macy's and other stores, we pounded the pavement for blocks so that our friends could get a feel for Matthew Henson's city. At times their faces suggested that we were on another planet, as we crossed crowded streets, moved up and down elevators, looked down from skyscrapers, and stopped to touch police horses.

*   *   *

The sights, sounds, and smells of Broadway on a summer night are wildly alive and enticing. My Eskimo friends were taking it all in as we walked past street vendors and street hustler after gaudy street hustler.

"Hey, man! You wanna buy a watch?"

"Hey, you! Come here! See this ace of hearts? Now you find it among the three cards I just dealt on the table, and I will give you twenty dollars. If you don't select the right one, you give *me* twenty dollars. Deal?"

"Look here! I got some gold necklaces over here—cheap. I'll give you a good deal. What do you say?"

Some of the Eskimos bought items as gifts for their wives, children, and other relatives back in Greenland. Though they seemed somewhat puzzled by my efforts to bargain with the ravenous vendors, as we haggled over prices they were dazzled by the vast array of flashing neon lights and the open display of money—not to mention the legions of colorful, unusual-looking people.

"Look at all the people," Talilanguaq remarked. "Where do all the people come from? They are like huge flocks of birds."

On the next block, several young black and Puerto Rican teenagers danced to rap music blasting from a "boom box." Malina and Massauna-Matthew were spellbound by this impromptu street show. Excellent dancers themselves, the two eighteen-year-olds studied the steps intently and then mimicked them playfully.

The video arcade on Broadway was a big hit with everyone, youngsters and adults alike. The people playing the flashy electronic machines were as interesting to the Eskimos as the games themselves. And the old-fashioned mechanical claw that can be manipulated to pick up rings, watches, and other gifts behind a glass enclosure proved universally popular. I had never seen Ole or his father, Talilanguaq, laugh so much as when they tried, time and time again, to grab a prize with the claw. They became even more delighted when, to the cheers of the group, each succeeded in picking up a new watch.

As our group proceeded down the avenue, I felt Malina tugging vigorously at my arm. I turned to see sheer horror on her face as she mumbled something in Eskimo that I did not understand. Shaking visibly, she pulled me back to a spot we had just passed. She pointed to the ground, where an apparently homeless black man lay against the side of the building, his eyes glazed and fixed. The others watched in silence as Malina tugged at my pockets, beseeching me to give her some money, something she had never done before. I reached into my pocket, pulled out a five-dollar bill, and handed it to her. She stepped up to the man on the ground and handed him the money. He accepted, then looked up at Malina with a wide-eyed, blank stare and nodded his appreciation. She smiled slightly.

"Come along, Malina," one of the students said, pulling her along as she kept looking back over her shoulder.

As we continued along the busy New York streets, I could not help thinking of how Malina and the others must regard the stunning contrast of wealth and poverty in our country. She could not understand how people could walk past the obviously disabled man and not even acknowledge his presence, not to mention fail to help him. No one in her homeland would ever walk over a person in need.

* * *

Sunday morning. We are driving through Harlem. On one corner we see two apparently drunk young black men fighting. On the other corner stands an impeccably attired, elderly black woman in white dress and large white hat, seemingly oblivious to the violent clash across the street as she waits for her ride to church. Inside the bus, which has stopped at a traffic light, the Eskimos watch the incongruous scene in silence.

We were on our way to New York's historic Abyssinian Baptist Church. This was Matthew and Lucy Henson's church. They attended Abyssinian services regularly, and Lucy did civic and social work there. When Matthew died in 1955 and Lucy in 1968, their funerals were held at Abyssinian.

Knowing of the Hensons' long association with the church and two of its past ministers—Adam Clayton Powell, Sr. and Jr.—I contacted the current pastor, the Reverend Dr. Samuel Proctor, and asked whether he would hold a special service of recognition for my Greenlandic friends. Proctor enthusiastically agreed.

Anaukaq and his children had spoken frequently about their desire to experience various aspects of the culture of the *kulnocktooko* people, with whom they so strongly identified. I wanted them to experience the most enduring institution in the black community, the African-American church.

Abyssinian is a large Gothic church in the heart of the predominantly black community of Harlem, with a seating capacity of more than a thousand. The church was filled on this day. Two large choirs in flowing gowns stood in different balconies, singing a gospel song, when we entered the church. The uniformed ushers escorted us to reserved seats in the center of the congregation. By now the Eskimos were accustomed to large gatherings, but not so large or animated as this one. In our pews, the Eskimos sat in complete wonder throughout the service. There was singing and hand-clapping and foot-patting and contagious spirituality.

Proctor delivered a powerful sermon, his gravelly voice resounding throughout the church.

"Our circle is widening today, isn't it, Abyssinian?"

"Oh, yes! Yes, Lord," answered members of the congregation.

"We have people here today all the way from *Greenland*," Proctor stressed. "People who live in ice all the time. Speak another language. Eat another kind of diet. Dress differently. People whose lifestyle is different from our own. But here they are, smiling in our midst because Abyssinian has widened the circle today, and thank God for the friends who have helped us to widen our circle today."

"Amen," shouted the congregation in unison.

"Peacemaker, peacemaker. Learn how to be fair!" Proctor thundered. "You don't have to be so smart. You don't need to have a Ph.D. degree. Just have some *sensitivity* to what you are doing to people."

"Yes, Lord! Amen."

After the sermon, Proctor officially recognized and welcomed Anaukaq, Kali, and their families to the church.

"We welcome to Abyssinian today the son of Matthew Henson, who was a member of our church. Mr. Henson and his family are from Greenland. Will you bring Mr. Henson forward to speak with the congregation?" Proctor asked, his arm raised high in a magnanimous gesture.

As I escorted Anaukaq to the pulpit, I noticed that he moved swiftly, without reservation or discomfort about speaking before the congregation. At the pulpit, he stood proudly erect and addressed the congregation like a preacher.

"I am happy to be here, to share this ceremony with you today, in such a beautiful way. I am only a very ordinary person from far, far away, visiting the church of my father, Matthew Henson. And I thank you for receiving me and my family. *Kooyounah.*"

When the translation ended, the congregation erupted into applause. Anaukaq smiled in appreciation.

"We also welcome to our church this morning the son of Admiral Robert Peary. Will you please stand, sir?"

At the translator's signal, Kali stood to loud welcoming applause.

Following Proctor's lead, the congregation broke into one of the classic black American spirituals, accompanied by the choir and rhythmic hand-clapping.

I'm—so—proud that Jesus lifted me,
I'm—so—proud that Jesus lifted me,
I'm—so—proud that Jesus lifted me
Singing glory hallelujah,
Jesus lifted me.

This was a traditional Sunday song of fellowship. Members of the congregation turned to their neighbors to shake hands or embrace during the singing. Many came over to greet Anaukaq, Kali, and their families, welcoming them with a warm handshake or an embrace.

The congregation of the all-black church treated Kali and his sons with kindness and respect, as if they were longtime members of their spiritual community. Kali was moved to comment that he "felt good with the *kulnocktooko* people—like I'm one of them—and they treat me like I am one of them."

After the service, we were the church's guests at a lunch attended by hundreds of other parishioners in Abyssinian's large dining area. There we met many older church members who had known Anaukaq's father personally, one a well-known sculptor who had had Matthew Henson pose for a bust forty years earlier. To Anaukaq's delight, the old parishioners shared with him many stories about his uniformly admired father.

✳   ✳   ✳

Our last stop was Woodlawn Cemetery in the Bronx. This would be our last ceremony on the tour. As in Washington, the ceremony was attended by ministers, political dignitaries, Henson family members, and friends. Letters from the governor of New York and the mayor of New York City were read by their representatives. The Fordham College Choir sang and speeches were delivered. Four U.S. Marines in ceremonial dark-blue uniforms and white hats marched toward Matthew Henson's headstone in slow lockstep, then stood at attention with rifles shouldered and flagstaffs held high. Somehow a marine honor guard was fitting, I thought. Whereas the clean-cut, tailored, and suave Robert Peary in many ways epitomized the navy, the rugged and intrepid Matthew Henson seemed better suited to the navy's celebrated assault troops.

As Anaukaq and his family walked forward to lay a wreath at the grave, they were almost stampeded by a pack of disrespectful reporters and photographers. Although we had to stop the ceremony to move them back and give the family some privacy, Anaukaq remained unfazed. He placed the wreath on his father's grave and stared down at the headstone. After a long silence, he spoke aloud to himself.

"So it is here that my father is buried. . . . He must have had a tough life up in our land. . . . He must have been very cold up there at times. . . . My father. . . . My father."

He turned to us. "I too will be *sinnegbo* [asleep] soon. I am now ready to go back home to die and rest near my wife, Aviaq."

None of us knew what to say. Finally, I turned to him. "Anaukaq, when I visit Greenland next year or even five years from now, you will still be racing around Moriussaq with that old cane and laughing up a storm." He laughed.

* * *

The North Pole Family Reunion ended where it had begun ten days earlier, at McGuire Air Force Base. There was both joy and sadness as we all embraced and said our good-byes. Joy that the two worlds had been reunited—reconnected in both tangible and spiritual ways. Sadness that new friends and loved ones were about to be separated by vast distances and time.

Anaukaq and Kali were still in high spirits. Just about everything they could have imagined they had accomplished in the previous two weeks. Most important to them was meeting their American kinfolk and visiting their fathers' graves. They were now ready to return to the only world they had ever known.

But much had happened over the previous ten days. Eighteen-year-old Massauna-Matthew had become deeply infatuated with Suzanne Malveaux, one of the Harvard student escorts. He talked about her incessantly. When he reached the airplane, he started crying openly and did not want to leave. His father, Ussarkaq, had to persuade him to get on the plane.

Ole, the nineteen-year-old full-time hunter, had become equally enamored of Mariana Ortiz-Blanes, another student escort, who, upon sensing the Amer-Eskimo Pearys' loneliness in the absence of their American kin, had become a kind of protective mother and sister to them.

And Malina had been greatly taken with Kermit Alexander, the first young *kulnocktooko* man she had ever met. She joked that she wanted to marry him.

Both Eskimo families had fallen in love with Camille Holmes and Sean Brady and wanted to take them back to Greenland.

Ten-year-old Aviaq, who was already beyond her years in maturity, had grown tremendously. Entering the plane, she sported new sunglasses, watches, and other gifts she had received. She had always asked many questions about her American great-grandfather. Now she had some answers.

We had all become one big family.

As a final gesture, Anaukaq came up to me before boarding and handed me an official red-and-white Greenlandic flag, the recently inaugurated first flag of his nation. "This is a gift for you, Allen, from me and my family, and Kali and his family, to show you how much we appreciate what you have done for us. We hope you will come back to us in Greenland. *Kooyounah*, Allen, my friend."

"*Iddigdoo* Anaukaq, my friend."

We embraced and said good-bye.

Left to right: Kali Peary, S. Allen Counter, Anaukaq Henson, and Kali's son, Talilanquaq, in the village of Moriussaq, Greenland, in 1986.

Ajako Henson leads his sled dogs through Moriussaq on the way to the hunting grounds.

A Polar Eskimo family at a hunting camp in northwest Greenland (c. 1900). Though it is no longer a common practice, Polar Eskimo families traditionally traveled together during the hunting season, moving by dogsled from camp to camp across hundreds of miles of ice and frozen terrain. *Courtesy of the Explorers Club*

Ussarkaq Henson, Matthew Henson's grandson, hurls his harpoon at a narwhal. While most Polar Eskimos now hunt with rifles, many still resort to more traditional methods.

Ole Peary, great-grandson of Robert E. Peary, hunts for seals off the coast of northwest Greenland. The apparatus attached to his rifle is a white cloth blind, designed to conceal the hunter as he approaches his prey.

Avataq Henson and his son Massanguaq pack their dogsled for a hunt.

Returning from the hunt, Avataq Henson displays the tusks from a large walrus he killed. The ivory tusks will be sold to the government of Greenland, with all proceeds shared by the community of Moriussaq. The walrus meat will also be distributed among the villagers, although the best portions will be reserved for Avataq and his family.

Puto, wife of Ajako Henson, teaches her niece, Malina, to scrape the fat from the skin of a polar bear with a utility knife called an *ulu*.

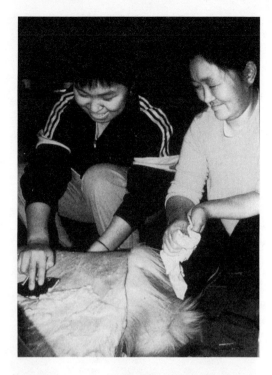

After dipping the bear skin in icy water and then covering it with snow, Ajako and Puto beat it with a stick to remove the ice. The skin will later be stretched and made into trousers for their son, Nukka, whose slaying of the bear entitles him to wear this traditional hunter's attire.

The late Peter Peary, Kali's oldest son, and his wife (c. 1960).

Mikkisuk Minge, Anaukaq's sister-in-law and close friend, who provided the author with an account of life in Moriussaq in the early decades of the century.

Kali and Anaukaq aboard the helicopter that will take them to Thule air base. From there they will fly by military transport to the United States (May 1987).

Anaukaq, Kali, and their families gather in Harvard Yard, May 1987. *Left to right*: Ole (*foreground*), Vittus (*background*), Ajako, Talilanguaq, Ussarkaq, Massauna, Malina, Avataq. Kali (*left*) and Anaukaq, wearing traditional Polar Eskimo anorak, sit in the front row.

Robert E. Peary, Jr., and his half brother Kali meet for the first time at Peary's home in Augusta, Maine (May 1987). In the center is Robert E. Peary III; to the left, the author.

Harvard's president Derek C. Bok (*second from left*) welcomes Anaukaq (*standing, center*) and Kali (*seated at far right*) at a banquet held in their honor. Seated between Anaukaq and Kali is translator Navarana Qavigaq Harper. Publisher John H. Johnson (*far left*), who co-sponsored the North Pole Family Reunion, and the author (*standing, right*) join in the applause. The banquet was attended by some 200 guests, including American members of the Henson and Peary families. *Photo by Hans P. Biemann*

Olive Henson Fulton displays a gift from Anaukaq at the Henson family picnic in suburban Boston (May 1987).

The Reverend Dr. Samuel Proctor welcomes Anaukaq, Kali, and their families to Abyssinian Baptist Church in Harlem.

Anaukaq Henson acknowledges the applause of the Abyssinian congregation. Seated to his right are Kali Peary and other members of the Amer-Eskimo Henson and Peary families.

Anaukaq Henson with Allen Counter at the grave site of Matthew Henson in Woodlawn Cemetery in the Bronx. When this photograph was taken, Anaukaq was telling the author that he had fulfilled his life's ambition and could now go home and join his wife, who had died several years earlier.

Accompanied by his wife Lucy and friends, Matthew Henson prepares to lay a wreath at the grave of Robert E. Peary in Arlington National Cemetery in 1954. Henson regularly visited the tomb of his longtime Arctic companion. *Courtesy of Virginia Carter Brannum*

Members of the Henson family join friends and officials at formal ceremonies marking the reinterment of Matthew Henson at Arlington National Cemetery on April 6, 1988. *James P. Blair, courtesy of National Geographic Society*

Matthew Henson's niece, Virginia Carter Brannum, poses near her uncle's newly installed monument in Arlington National Cemetery, adjacent to the grave site of Robert E. Peary.

U.S. postage stamp issued in 1986 to commemorate the conquest of the North Pole by Peary and Henson. *Copyright © 1986, U.S. Postal Service, Dennis Lyall, Designer*

Anaukaq Henson and his "cousin" Kali Peary in Moriussaq, Greenland (1986).

CHAPTER THIRTEEN

✳ ✳ ✳

Back Home in Greenland

The miracle of modern transportation again bridged two worlds in one day. Ten hours from the time they left America, Anaukaq, Kali, and their families were back in remote northwest Greenland. I did not relax until I received word that they had arrived safely.

They returned to families eagerly awaiting a full accounting of the American adventure, not to mention the distribution of all the gifts brought back from the United States. Avataq brought Magssanguaq a leather pilot's jacket. Kitdlaq brought his wife some jewelry. Ussarkaq and Ajako brought their wives dresses. Aviaq brought her mother a pair of sunglasses, and so on.

But they had also returned to the reality of their world, which even in modern times is a harsh one. They had many vital chores awaiting them: taking care of their dogs, hunting for seals, and, in this season, *kahlayleewah* to feed their families, readying themselves for the approaching fall and winter.

The Eskimos quickly readjusted to their customary way of life. Anaukaq went about Moriussaq as he had always done, visiting friends, eating fresh seal, drinking tea and coffee, and sharing stories, although they were now of his visit to America. His sons successfully hunted seals and birds, while Malina and Aviaq collected eider-duck down and eggs. The down would be sold to the government for communal income. The eggs would be consumed.

After a brief visit with other family members in Qaanaaq, Kali, Talilanguaq, and Ole returned to Qeqertarsaaq. Within a week, Ole had gone out to sea and slain his first narwhal of the season.

When I contacted Navarana, my former translator, a few weeks later, I learned that everyone was doing well.

*   *   *

One morning, about three weeks after returning to Moriussaq, Ana-ukaq got up, ate, did a few chores about the igloo, and followed his usual routine. Sometime later, he told his son that he felt like getting some fresh air. He put on his heavy coat, went outside, and walked around the entire settlement. He walked to the sea to look at Avataq's boat. He went to Ajako's little general store. He saw his grandchildren Malina, Aviaq, and Magssanguaq.

He returned to his igloo, walked up to Avataq, and told him that he had done everything that he wanted to do in his life and was now ready to sleep next to his wife, Aviaq. Anaukaq lay down on his bed. A few hours later he died of complications from prostate cancer.

The translator reached me at four o'clock in the morning to tell me the news. All telephone rings at 4 A.M. signal bad news. One reaches for the receiver with a numbing apprehension, knowing that something tragic has taken place. As I lifted the phone, I was prepared to receive sad tidings about someone in my own family. When I learned it was Anaukaq, the effect was the same.

I got up and started making arrangements to travel to Greenland. I had received the call on Thursday. The earliest available air force flight to Thule would leave the following Monday. I confirmed my reservations and made plans to travel to McGuire. But on Friday night, I learned that Anaukaq's family and friends had decided on an earlier burial. They would bury him the next day. I canceled my plans.

In a combination of traditional Eskimo and Christian funeral ceremonies, Anaukaq Henson was laid to rest under a white Christian cross next to his wife, Aviaq, in the little cemetery where he and I had stood just a few months earlier. Covering him was the African-

American flag that I had given him and that he cherished so dearly. He had asked his sons that the flag be draped over him when he died.

The weather in Moriussaq that day was extraordinarily beautiful, and the sun shone brighter than anyone could ever remember, the family said. After the ceremony, family and friends gathered outdoors to celebrate Anaukaq's life. They all felt he had lived a long, happy life, and they wanted no sadness because Anaukaq had rarely been sad.

At Woodlawn Cemetery, he had told us that he was going back home to die and join Aviaq. We hadn't believed him. Yet the Danish physician who had treated him in the past and Dr. Brown, the reunion committee's consulting physician, both said they were surprised he had lived as long as he had, given the advanced state of his prostate cancer. They shared with others a belief that the hope of fulfilling his lifelong dream had sustained him in recent months.

His sons said that Anaukaq had not shown any signs of illness before his death. In fact, he was actively looking after his dogs and doing other chores around the settlement. Had he been visibly ill, they said, they would have taken him to the nearby infirmary at Qaanaaq, but no one noticed any change in him. One Eskimo woman who had seen him back home in Greenland put it another way. "When I looked in Anaukaq's face, I could see that he was ready to go," she said. "I have seen that look before on the faces of the old ones who have done what they wanted to do in life and wanted nothing more than the final rest."

Anaukaq was not forgotten in the United States. The obituary pages of several American newspapers carried the announcement of his passing under the heading "Anaukaq Henson dies in Greenland."

Anaukaq's sons had anticipated his death. They asked Navarana to convey a special message to me from all of them: "Thank you for bringing all five of us together with our father for one last time."

"It was my privilege," I responded. "I am honored to have known Anaukaq."

* * *

A few weeks after his death, I received a somewhat unsettling message from some of the Eskimo Hensons. Anaukaq, they said, had

come back to them. At first I did not understand. Then I was told that
Anaukaq's twenty-five-year-old granddaughter Equilana had just
given birth to a boy and named him Anaukaq. In the Polar Eskimo
tradition, Anaukaq had truly returned to them.

CHAPTER FOURTEEN

❋   ❋   ❋

Welcome Home, Matthew Henson

Why did Peeuree have an impressive tomb in Arlington National Cemetery and Mahri-Pahluk a simple grave in New York? I had the difficult task of explaining to my Eskimo friends the nature of American racial prejudice and the disparate treatment of their respective fathers. Rarely has a man given so much of his life to the honor of his country and received so little in return as had Matthew Henson. Rising from the lowly background of a sharecropper with only six grades of schooling, he had become one of the most accomplished explorers of all time. He deserved a permanent place of honor in recognition of his achievements.

Before our final parting, I told Anaukaq that I had written to President Reagan and requested permission to transfer Matthew Henson's remains to Arlington National Cemetery. I promised that even if I were at first turned down, I would continue to petition until I succeeded.

"If you do move him, I want my children to see it," Anaukaq said.

Several weeks after I sent my first letter to President Reagan, I received a reply from the office of the secretary of the army. The letter explained that the White House had passed along my request to those military officials responsible for burials in Arlington National

Cemetery. An extensive discussion of the regulations governing burials at Arlington followed. Then came the verdict:

> Although Mr. Henson rendered great service to this country, I
> regret that the established criteria preclude me from granting your
> request. I am sorry that my response cannot be more positive. It is no
> reflection on Mr. Henson to say that to make an exception in his case
> would be unfair to the many others who have been denied burial at
> Arlington under today's restrictive criteria. Undoubtedly, he contrib
> uted much to the nation, but the Army is obliged to administer the
> rules of eligibility strictly and consistently. We do appreciate your
> bringing this matter to our attention.

Unwilling to accept this routine response, I continued my campaign by sending letters to cabinet members, prominent members of
Congress, and even the First Lady. But the outcome did not change.

In the meantime, my efforts attracted the attention of the *Boston
Globe*, which printed an excellent story, "Seeking Honor for an Explorer," on the treatment of Matthew Henson (April 22, 1987). This
article stimulated so much interest that people of all races wrote me
to offer their support. On April 27, 1987 the *Globe* also followed up
with a lead editorial on the subject, "An Explorer's Overdue Tribute,"
suggesting that the president should make a special effort to reinter
Henson's remains in Arlington. Several other newspapers ran similar
stories as well.

In response to this spate of publicity, officials at Woodlawn Cemetery contacted me to express their displeasure at what they perceived
to be my "complaints" about Matthew Henson's present grave site.
Understandably, the Woodlawn staff took great pride in having Matthew Henson in their cemetery and, indeed, took care that the plot
remained tidy and had flowers planted around it. I assured the
Woodlawn people that I had not intended to belittle their cemetery or
the condition of Henson's grave. But I also told them that I thought it
only fair to try to have him buried in our most prestigious national
cemetery. They seemed to understand.

My research on the proposed reinterment revealed several interesting things. I learned, for example, that some people had been
working to have Matthew Henson buried in Arlington ever since

Peary was buried there in 1920. After his death in 1955, a number of people had recommended that he be buried in Arlington instead of Woodlawn. But, then as now, some people in the military opposed reinterment because Henson had never officially served in the armed forces of the United States. Others objected because they did not believe that Peary had ever reached the North Pole and consequently felt that neither he nor Henson deserved to be buried at Arlington. Still others seemed to have had no other reason for opposing Henson's reinterment except considerations of race.

As I pointed out in my letters to the White House, to disqualify Matthew Henson from burial at Arlington because he had never served in the military was to perpetuate a past injustice in the guise of a bureaucratic technicality. During the period that Henson worked for Commander Peary (1887–1909), the U.S. Navy severely restricted, as a matter of official policy, the jobs and ranks that African Americans could hold. As someone who had served as a valet for a naval officer in the field and as a messenger at the Philadelphia Navy Yard, Henson had filled two of the few roles reserved for blacks in the navy at that time. Moreover, he had served his nation no less courageously than Peary and had brought it honor.

Whether such reasoning proved persuasive, I will never know. But in October 1987 I finally received word from the Department of the Army that President Reagan had granted my request to move Henson's remains to Arlington. I immediately wrote the president to thank him.

My joy was tempered only by the fact that Anaukaq would not be there to see it. Nevertheless, I was determined to fulfill my promise and bring his children back to America to witness the reinterment. I notified the Greenlandic and American Hensons of the good news. We all found it hard to believe.

I now had to deal with a host of problems raised by the prospect of the reinterment. First, I was told that the expense of the reinterment would not be handled by the government. I would have to pay the costs of disinterment and reinterment. Second, I had to go through the courts to obtain legal permission to disinter the remains from Woodlawn Cemetery. Third, I would have to recommend a burial site. Fourth, there were regulation caskets to be obtained. And so on.

I began by contacting Superintendent Raymond Costanzo at Arlington. As always, he was cordial and encouraging. He agreed to meet with me to discuss a burial site and headstone.

In the interim, I set in motion the legal proceedings for Henson's disinterment. New York law requires special permits from the city's Department of Health and the local court before any disinterment can take place. While the staff of Woodlawn Cemetery understood that I had the president's permission to transfer Henson's remains, they informed me that they would contest the disinterment in court. This, they explained, was simply a matter of policy, something they did with all disinterment cases, to protect the cemetery. I was left with the impression that they would not strenuously oppose the removal.

When I arrived at Arlington, I met Costanzo and his assistants at the marble administration building just inside the gates. I requested that Matthew Henson be buried with full military honors, his civilian status notwithstanding. I also asked that Matthew and Lucy Ross Henson be buried next to Peary and his wife, Josephine. This site, I felt, would give them equality in their resting places. Anaukaq and Kali too had said that "the old friends should be together."

I wanted to erect a fitting headstone, one that would make all Americans knowledgeable and proud of Matthew Henson. Costanzo and his staff listened carefully to my proposals but pointed out that there were new rules governing the size of all headstones in the cemetery. No longer were grave sites permitted to have the giant monuments of the past, such as the one the National Geographic Society had erected for Peary. All new monuments were restricted to a height of five feet, a width of four feet, and a thickness of one foot. Moreover, he noted, the cemetery preferred that the new headstones be even smaller.

Back in Cambridge, several members of the North Pole Family Reunion Committee, including Henson relatives and others, joined me in forming a new committee to oversee the reinterment. I was chosen to chair the committee, and John H. Johnson was elected honorary chairman. The "Matthew Alexander Henson–Arlington National Cemetery Reinterment Committee" met weekly to discuss every aspect of the project, including the possible dates for the disinterment and reinterment, guest lists, the program, the invitations, the headstone funds, and so on. Because the military was to be involved, officials at Arlington took responsibility for organizing the memorial ceremony. But the committee would be responsible for planning the memorial service.

My next task was to arrange for the return of the Amer-Eskimo Hensons to the United States to participate in the ceremony. The experience of the North Pole Family Reunion helped, but the requirements of obtaining special visas, arranging helicopter and air force flights and American accommodations were no less exhausting than the first time around. Committee members, students especially, also helped with the voluminous paperwork involved in getting the Amer-Eskimo Hensons back down to the United States.

A few weeks later, Costanzo wrote to say that the burial site next to Peary had been approved along with my request for full military honors. Lucy could also be buried next to Matthew. I would have to return to Washington to discuss the memorial service and the design of the headstone.

The committee decided that the monument should be as large as the current regulations would allow. I recommended a five-foot-high, four-foot-wide, one-foot-thick slab of polished black Vermont granite, with gold lettering and an attached three-foot-square gold-colored brass plaque with Henson's face in bas-relief. Both Arlington National Cemetery and the reinterment committee approved.

I spent the next several weeks drawing the design for the bas-relief, checking it over each night before I went to bed. For the facial bas-relief, I drew from the classic photograph of Henson in his Eskimo anorak. Just beneath the face on both sides of the bronze plaque, I included a globe showing the "American route" to the Pole, with a bronze star at the top.

I also felt that Henson would have wanted the Eskimos who traveled with him and Peary to the Pole included on the monument as well. For the Eskimos, I selected a photograph of them standing with Henson on a mound of ice at the North Pole, with an American flag in the background.

Last, I thought there should be a dramatic depiction of the struggle to reach the North Pole that included Peary and the other five men on the last leg of the journey. The opposite side of the headstone would read:

MATTHEW ALEXANDER HENSON
Co-Discoverer of the North Pole
His Beloved Wife Lucy Ross Henson

As I have mentioned, one of the memorable statements attributed to Peary and etched in Latin on his monument reads: "I shall find a way or make one." For Henson's headstone, I selected the last statement in his book of 1912: "The lure of the Arctic is tugging at my heart/To me the trail is calling/The old trail/The trail that is always new."

When I completed my drawings and proposal, I submitted them to the committee for review. They were approved unanimously. None of us, however, was prepared for the cost of high-quality headstones and caskets. The cost of the headstone alone would run into the tens of thousands of dollars. The cost of disinterment, transportation of the remains, and new caskets would also be in the thousands. I had already committed a substantial amount of my own money to the effort, but we needed more help to cover the rest. Unfortunately, the Henson family was in no position to help defray such expenses. But our honorary chairman, John H. Johnson, offered a contribution that made possible the reinterment and the monument we hoped for.

We chose April 6, 1988, as the date of the reinterment—the seventy-ninth anniversary of the North Pole discovery.

Rev. Peter J. Gomes would serve as our reinterment ceremony minister. Col. Guion S. Bluford, America's first black astronaut in space, agreed to deliver a memorial salute. Bluford, like Henson, was an explorer of uncharted worlds. John H. Johnson was selected to deliver the memorial address. Dorothy Height, head of the National Council of Negro Women and an old friend of Lucy Henson (who belonged to that organization), was asked to eulogize Lucy during the service. I was asked to deliver the eulogy for Matthew. Hampton University, a traditionally African-American university in Virginia, offered to provide the ceremonial band and choir.

Meanwhile, the Vermont granite cutters and the company making the bronze bas-relief rushed to meet our deadline. Several models of the bas-relief were sent to the committee for review and modification before final approval.

My court appearance in New York City was nothing short of bewildering. My attorney, a young Harvard graduate, ran into stronger-than-expected opposition from the three Woodlawn attorneys, one of whom was a Yale graduate who seemed eager to carry out the traditional rivalry of Harvard and Yale. The two men fought in legalese and postured for what seemed an eternity, both in and out of the courtroom. After listening to all the arguments, the judge, who happened to be black, ruled that he saw no reason why Matthew and Lucy should not be removed from Woodlawn and reinterred in Arlington. The Woodlawn lawyer tried to appeal the ruling, but to no avail. As he spoke, the judge looked over at me and, almost imperceptibly, nodded his head. In a silent expression of gratitude, I nodded back.

To represent the family at the ceremony, the Amer-Eskimo Hensons chose Mahri-Pahluk's oldest living grandson, Avataq; his youngest grandson, Kitdlaq; Ajako and his oldest son, Jens; and Magssanguaq, the ten-year-old son of Avataq and Anaukaq's favorite little hunter.

As he had been promised, Magssanguaq got to travel to America. After he and his family arrived at McGuire Air Force Base, we proceeded by train to Washington. It was now Magssanguaq's turn to stare at the new world. He was glued to the window of the train. Large lakes and boats astounded him—not to mention all the cars, igloos, and people.

In the days before the ceremony, Magssanguaq and his family toured the nation's capital. We took him and the family to the Cherry Blossom Festival, watched a large parade, and, to the family's extreme delight, saw a circus.

At the Air and Space Museum, the Eskimos were particularly interested in the Black Aviators section. But over at the Museum of Natural History, Magssanguaq and Avataq were utterly surprised to see life-size models of Polar Eskimos in kayaks.

"They look so real!" Magssanguaq said.

"Yes, but their kayaks are poorly built," said Avataq. Seeing their culture represented in lifelike mannequins behind glass was very strange to them. It gave them a chance to evaluate and criticize an exhibit about which they as Eskimos were the authorities.

On a visit to the Washington Zoo, Magssanguaq saw seals in captivity for the first time. He was mesmerized by their antics. Instinctively the hunter, he several times raised an imaginary gun, took aim, and "fired" at the seals.

* * *

April 6 arrived quickly, but with everyone and everything in place. At noon on that day, we were picked up by limousines and driven to the administration building at Arlington, where everyone on the program gathered for the preceremony check. The assembled group included the Greenlandic Hensons, Olive Henson Fulton, the honorary pallbearers, John H. Johnson and Col. Guion Bluford, Rev. Peter Gomes, and Superintendent Costanzo.

At 1:45 P.M. the limousines and hearses left the administration building for the site. Some two hundred people, mostly family and committee members, awaited our processional in the private guest area. Across the road were another fifty or so invited guests and a platform filled with members of the press.

We walked the last yards to the grave, with the Henson family leading the way. When we reached the monument at two o'clock, the reinterment ceremony officially began.

Magssanguaq and I each took a rope on top of the velvet cloth and on cue unveiled the new monument. Everyone applauded. The cloth draping the Henson monument had also been used for the monument to the astronauts who died in the Challenger disaster.

Ushers led the family and other official participants to the site of the open graves, where Matthew's and Lucy's caskets were to be suspended on cords. We held our hands over our hearts while the military pallbearers, wearing dark navy dress uniforms and white caps, removed the caskets from the hearses and marched them to the graves.

Peter Gomes performed the act of committal. "We have brought the explorer home. For here is where he belongs. To all of us, and to the nation."

I then stepped up on the platform next to Matthew Henson's casket and delivered the eulogy. "Welcome home, Matthew Henson. Welcome to the hearts of black Americans, and persons of all races who beam with pride in the knowledge that you are finally here.

"May your presence here inspire generations of explorers yet unborn as they seek new horizons. Welcome home, Brother Matthew. Welcome home."

After I had delivered the eulogy, ceremonial volleys from a twenty-one-gun salute echoed through the stillness of the cemetery. With the playing of "Taps," the honor guard ceremoniously folded the U.S. flag that had covered Matthew Henson's casket. The triangular, folded flag was then given to Comdr. Charles W. Marvin, the presiding navy chaplain, who presented it to Avataq.

"On behalf of the president of the United States, the nation is grateful for Matthew Henson's service and patriotism," the chaplain said to Avatak. "We present this flag to show our great appreciation for his faithful and loyal service."

Following the initial ceremony, the memorial service began with welcoming remarks by Gen. Julius Becton, representing the president of the United States.

Next, Johnson delivered the memorial address:

> Matthew Henson taught us all a great deal. He taught us to be independent. He taught us to achieve. He taught us to make the most out of whatever opportunities are before us, while trying at all times to improve those opportunities.
>
> Henson was a proud man. He did not receive the recognition that he deserved, but he never complained. I remember reading about his speech to the Chicago Geographical Society in which he said he had only sought to serve—that he was not bitter—that he knew what he had done—and that he had his own particular kind of pride. And so I would say, the world is better for Henson. The world has a better feeling about achievement—about a man who was willing to pay the price—a man who once said nothing had ever been given to him. He had always earned it. Matthew Henson has earned the recognition he is receiving today.

"Today, a grateful nation salutes Matthew Alexander Henson," Col. Guion Bluford said, "an Arctic explorer and a black American. May all future explorers follow in his footsteps."

Kitdlaq represented the Hensons.

"We Hensons from Greenland are very proud and honored to be here among our relatives and other people from the United States on this very important day in the history of America. We are thankful from our hearts. We are sure the Eskimos Egingwah, Ootah, Ooqueah, and Seegloo would be very proud if they knew Matthew Henson was being buried here in Arlington. They are the Inuit who went to the North Pole with Peary and Henson. Thank you."

The Hampton University band played "The Battle Hymn of the Republic" while the wreaths were placed at the grave.

The ceremony ended with the playing of "Lift Every Voice and Sing."

"Now the old friends are together again. They can talk about old times," Kitdlaq said.

Welcome home, Matthew Henson.

EPILOGUE

* * *

The Controversy: Did Peary and Henson Reach the North Pole First?

Perhaps no other claim in the history of modern exploration has been so controversial as the 1909 announcement by navy commander Robert Edwin Peary that he, Matthew A. Henson, and four Polar Eskimos had reached the North Pole on April 6 of that year. Some questioned the navigational accuracy and validity of the distances Peary claimed to have covered. Others dismissed his claim because he did not have any "reliable" witnesses. Still others believed that Frederick Cook, Peary's onetime assistant, had successfully reached the Pole a year earlier than Peary.

The dispute was never resolved. As a result, the widespread publicity surrounding the North Pole Family Reunion project in 1987 and the reinterment of Matthew Henson in 1988 sparked the controversy anew. Within months after the reinterment, articles appeared in national periodicals once again seriously questioning whether Peary and Henson had really made it to the North Pole.

The most direct challenge came from Dennis Rawlins, a Baltimore-based writer and longtime Peary critic. Rawlins claimed to have found a previously unexamined slip of paper in the National Archives with Peary's actual 1909 calculations as well as references to it hidden among the private papers of former Johns Hopkins and American Geographic Society president Isaiah Bowman. Rawlins maintained that this evidence proved that Peary never got within a latitude 121 miles of the Pole. Even more contentiously, he argued that when Peary realized his navigational error, he faked his records to show that he had reached the actual Pole.

It was not the first time that Rawlins, who is not a field explorer or navigator, had made such accusations. As far back as 1970, Rawlins claimed to have found conclusive evidence that Peary had never reached the North Pole.[1] Even though his alleged evidence of Peary's "hoax" was later shown to be nothing more than unsubstantiated conjecture, his 1988 challenge was taken seriously by some. Most notably, Boyce Rensberger of the *Washington Post* gave Rawlins's interpretation extensive coverage on several occasions, even after it had been questioned by professional scientists.[2] In defense of Rawlins's position, Rensberger quoted one expert, who said: "Rawlins has cracked a code that's been sitting there for eighty years. I couldn't be more convinced that he's right."[3]

A second, more widely publicized challenge to Peary's claim appeared in an article by Wally Herbert, a British explorer, in the September 1988 issue of *National Geographic*. The magazine's publication of this challenge ("Robert E. Peary: Did He Reach the Pole?") came as a surprise to many because the National Geographic Society has long been viewed as the main bastion of Peary's support. But when one considers the widespread interest in the topic, coupled with long-held suspicions that the society was "hiding" some of the facts in this case, it is understandable that the magazine's editors would permit another point of view to be aired in that, their centennial year. Nevertheless, to some the article seemed to signal the official abandonment of Peary after nearly eighty years of steadfast support.

Many African Americans were also troubled by the new challenges to Peary and Henson's claims. They could not help wondering whether it was pure coincidence that the new, "damaging evidence" against Peary just happened to surface some six months after the president of the United States had granted permission to reinter Henson in Arlington National Cemetery as "co-discoverer" of the North Pole. It was as if someone had said, "Okay, we'll show you that neither of them made it."

Wally Herbert, the author of the 1988 *National Geographic* article, had himself traveled to the North Pole in 1969, using back-up airlift support and airplane navigation for verification. Like Rawlins, Herbert had long held the view that Peary and Henson did not make it all the way to the exact Pole. In preparing for the article, however, he examined Peary's written records of the 1909 expedition, which are housed in the National Archives in Washington.

Although Herbert found "no simple yes or no" answer to the question of whether Peary reached the pole, the tone of the article and the character of the evidence he puts forth leave no doubt about his verdict. "The burden of proof . . . generally lies with the explorer," Herbert writes, and "Robert E. Peary failed to provide conclusive evidence that he had reached the North Pole." Herbert places particular emphasis on Peary's personal diary of the final expedition, which has "blank pages, an inserted leaf, and an incomplete cover title" and on "Peary's astonishingly slack navigation." He also expresses doubts about the distances Peary claimed to have covered on his final series of "marches" and subsequent return journey from the Pole.

In the end, Herbert characterizes Peary as a man so obsessed by his quest for worldly renown that he simply could not face the fact of his failure. "In all probability," Herbert writes, "during those last five marches northward Peary was being driven not by the rational mind but by a conviction that the Pole was his and that he had the divine right to discover it and return to proclaim his achievement."

*　*　*

I also contributed an article to the same one-hundredth anniversary edition of *National Geographic* in which Herbert's essay appeared. Although my piece did not directly address the issue of Peary's claim, I too had access to Peary's diary and other expeditionary records in the National Archives. The conclusions I reached, however, were quite different from those of Herbert and Rawlins.

Herbert's charge of "astonishingly slack navigation," for example, rests heavily on the fact that Peary did not take longitude readings, or at least did not record them in his diary, during much of the 1909 expedition. As a result, Herbert hypothesizes, he was probably detoured from the actual Pole some "30 to 60 miles."

What Herbert fails to point out is that Peary and Henson recorded navigational information in several places, not just in the small pocket diary on which Herbert bases his conclusion. Further, and more important, he does not sufficiently take into account the circumstances in which they found themselves. Racing against the elements, in constant danger of finding themselves marooned by a break in the ice, they could not afford to stop to take unnecessary measurements—and longitude readings were unnecessary.

On the morning of March 1, 1909, Peary, along with six American assistants and eighteen Polar Eskimo assistants, left his land base at Ellesmere Island, Canada, for the North Pole, which lay 413 nautical miles (475 statute miles) ahead of them. This is approximately the same as the distance between Richmond, Virginia, and Boston, Massachusetts. Once they set their line of travel along the seventieth meridian of west longitude, Peary and Henson used a simplified navigational technique that experience had taught them was equally accurate and much less time-consuming than conventional marine navigation, which involves ex-meridian observations and longitude sights. In fact, there is evidence that they had used the latter method on the unsuccessful 1906 North Pole expedition, when it nearly cost them their lives.

Using their compasses, sextants, and heated mercury sinks as an artificial horizon, the two men made frequent latitude observations and azimuth observations. Their navigational technique for steering north was based on the simple fact that the sun is due south at its noon high point and due north at its midnight low point, and that it is virtually impossible to steer a sledge closer than five degrees to a compass. They made midday latitude determinations, noting when upper culmination (the maximum elevation angle) of the sun occurred as it passed the meridian; the position of the sun is lower earlier and later in the day. Longitude lines narrow to within a few miles apart at latitudes near the Pole and are not critical to measurements of location. They checked their compasses for deviation every noon and midnight. The margin of error using this technique is self-correcting, not cumulative. In describing this navigational system, which is well known to professional explorers, *Polar Record*, a publication of Scott Polar Research Institute of Cambridge University, observed that it demonstrated "precision and elegance."[4]

There is also considerable evidence that Peary and his assistants calculated for ice drift due to the changing winds. Although we have only recently gained enough bathymetric (ocean-depth) data to predict Arctic ice drift with any precision, Peary and Henson were both aware of the "Nansen rule," which has long been used by navigators to provide a rough estimate of drift.

For a more objective assessment of my conclusions, I consulted several established authorities in the field of navigation. One of my primary sources was Terris Moore, former president of the University of Alaska, a decorated pilot, a navigator, and an Arctic bush pilot with the Canadian International Geophysical Year. Moore has studied Peary's navigational techniques for years and has written extensively on the subject. According to him, "Even if you have no idea what longitude meridian you're on, you can still continue to steer north in this way, wandering five to ten degrees in your 'pointing' back and forth, but pulled back constantly to averaging true north by your compass and by the periodic check of the sun to correct for any observed change in the magnetic deviation." Moore added, "I have done it innumerable times."

It is interesting to note that Peary's simplified navigational technique was precisely the same as that used by the Norwegian Roald Amundsen and his navigators in their attainment of the South Pole on December 14, 1911. Yet Amundsen's feat is today accepted universally. In fact, Amundsen "borrowed" Peary's system of navigation. Amundsen had planned to join the race for the North Pole, but when he received word in 1909 that it had already been claimed, he changed his plans and aimed for the South Pole. When Amundsen reached the South Pole, like Peary at ninety degrees north, he also measured his position with a "sextant" and an "artificial horizon" (a tray of mercury).[5]

Like Peary, Amundsen met with disbelief when he first reported that he had reached the South Pole. Like Peary, too (and all other polar explorers, for that matter), he had only his own word as proof. From the time of his announcement on March 7, 1912, in Hobart,

Tasmania, until months later, Amundsen's claim was treated with great suspicion and distrust, especially by the British, whose favorite son, Captain Robert Falcon Scott, was in a race with Amundsen (similar to that between Peary and Cook) for the national prestige and personal honor of reaching the South Pole first. Scott's wife publicly scoffed at Amundsen's claim, and much of Europe simply refused to accept his records or proofs as authentic. This treatment so angered Amundsen that he publicly charged that the British "are bad losers" who "feel obligated to detract from the success of an explorer just because he is not of their own nation."[6] Amundsen wrote in his autobiography: "The year after the capture of the Pole, the son of a prominent Norwegian in London came home from his classes at an English school one evening, protesting to his father that he was being taught that Scott was the discoverer of the South Pole."[7]

The scientific article in the January 1979 edition of *Polar Record* reported that with his "system of navigation" Amundsen "took no longitude sights during the whole polar journey, depending instead on a single longitude fix. . . . Thereafter he trusted to latitude observations alone, combined with dead reckoning based on compass courses and distances run."[8] *Polar Record* goes on to point out that "in contrast, Scott used conventional marine navigation as employed at lower latitudes, . . . made ex-meridian observations and longitude sights, spending considerable time and effort on calculations for a few kilometers, sometimes a few hundred metres of meaningless accuracy."

When Scott finally reached the South Pole, he found Amundsen's Norwegian flag and a tent containing jettisoned paraphernalia, a letter for the king of Norway, and a message addressed to Captain Robert Falcon Scott. Fortunately for Amundsen, the South Pole has stable, solid terrain and does not shift like the ever-changing ice floes of the North Pole. Amundsen's flag and other materials left behind as proof remained permanently in place.

Tragically, Scott and his men perished on their return journey. It was only after a search party found his body and his diary, along with some of the proof Amundsen left behind at the Pole, that the explorers and scientific societies accepted Amundsen's claim. It is ironic that the deceased Englishman became the verifier of Amundsen's

South Pole discovery. If Scott's remains had not been found, it is possible that there might have been years of bitter dispute about whether Amundsen reached the South Pole with such an "astonishingly slack" navigational system.

The second argument used by Peary's critics since 1909 is that it was impossible for him to have covered the distances he claimed— more than 296 miles from Bartlett's farthest north camp to the Pole and back—in the time he was gone. This charge is also erroneous.

Let us examine the points on which most observers agree. First, Peary had five "credible" witnesses on the North Pole trek, in addition to Henson and the Eskimos. Dr. J. W. Goodsell, the surgeon from Kensington, Pennsylvania, and Donald B. MacMillan, a mathematics and physical training instructor from Worcester Academy in Massachusetts, verified that they traveled north with the Peary expedition on the first leg, along the Cape Columbia meridian, for two weeks, ferrying Peary's supplies to 84° 29' (about the distance from Richmond to Washington, D.C.). MacMillan, who later became a U.S. naval commander and a famous explorer in his own right, never recanted his support of Peary's North Pole claim. MacMillan might have been permitted to travel with Peary and Henson closer to the Pole had he not injured his foot. George Borup, a recent graduate of Yale and an outstanding athlete, testified that he and his Eskimo assistants traveled with the expedition farther north, carrying supplies to 85° 23' (about the distance from Washington to Philadelphia). Ross Marvin and his Eskimo assistants then took fuel, food, and other supplies to 86° 38' (say, Philadelphia to New York), where he wrote and signed a message for Peary saying he had taken a measurement showing "Latitude at noon March 25th 86 degrees 38' north. Distance made in three marches, 50 minutes of latitude, an average of 16 2/3 nautical miles per march. The weather is fine, going good, and improving each day."[9] Unfortunately, Marvin lost his life on the return trip.

Finally, on April 1, 1909, Robert Bartlett, captain of Peary's ship the *Roosevelt* and an experienced navigator who had been a member of Peary's 1906 expedition (which came within 175 miles [87° 6'] of the Pole) wrote, "I have today personally determined our latitude by sextant observations. 87 degrees 46 minutes 49 seconds north. I return from here in command of the fourth supporting party. I leave Commander Peary with five men, five sledges with full loads, and forty picked dogs. The going fair, the weather good. At the same average as our last eight marches Commander Peary should reach the Pole in eight days."[10] This meant that according to the best instrument readings of that time and at the end of a line of five reliable witnesses, they were "133 nautical miles [153 statute miles] from the Pole." This is about the distance from Stamford, Connecticut, to Boston.

It is unlikely that all five men would falsify their records. Moreover, even if the expedition had traveled no farther north than Bartlett's position, they would still have achieved the record for "farthest north."

From this point, Peary and Henson—each with two Eskimo associates and with five sleds loaded with food, fuel, and scientific instruments—headed north. They traveled as rapidly as possible, with Henson leading and breaking the trail most of the way. On April 5, 1909, after several "marches" (uninterrupted sledge travel before rest) north, Peary "took a latitude sight and indicated [their] position to be 89° 25', or thirty-five miles from the Pole" (about the distance from North Providence, Rhode Island, to Boston).[11]

After a rest and before midnight on April 5, they "were again on trail." According to Peary, "In twelve hours of actual traveling time we made thirty miles. The last march northward ended at ten o'clock on the forenoon of April 6. I had now made the five marches planned from the point at which Bartlett turned back. Our average for five marches was about twenty-six miles." In other words, since leaving the point where Bartlett turned back, they had covered about 130 miles in about six days. Then Peary noted, "at approximate local noon, of the Columbia meridian, I made my first observation at our polar camp. It indicated 89° 57'."[12] He called this reading out to Henson, who wrote it down. According to Peary's records, they were now only three miles south of the theoretical exact spot of the North Pole (or the distance from South Boston to, say, Beacon Hill, a point they would have seen from such a distance). Peary and his team then traveled five to ten miles in different directions, taking latitude and meridian observations with what was then state-of-the-art technol-

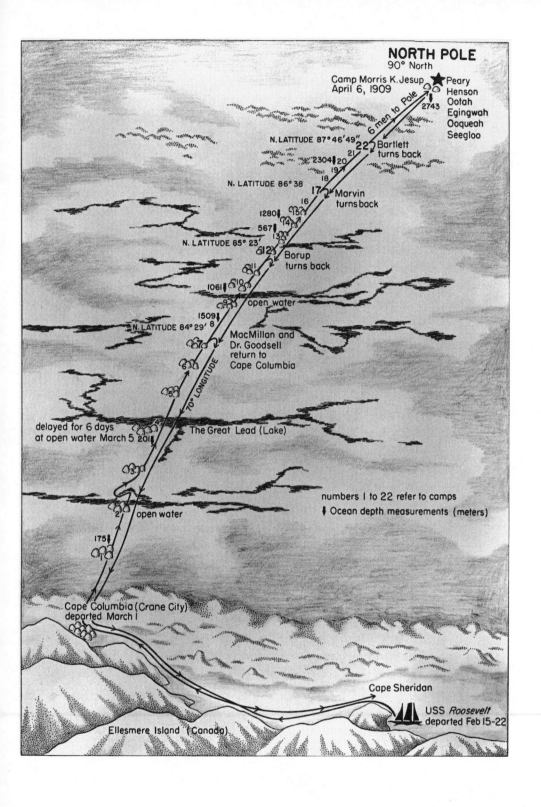

ogy (a sextant and an artificial horizon). With the sextant one can measure positions to an accuracy of one to three minutes of arc (or nautical miles). Peary and Henson were both quite capable of using a sextant proficiently.

At this point, the two Americans and four Eskimos had literally reached the top of our planet. If the North Pole were a fixed geographic feature, as Hispaniola was for Columbus, Robert Peary, Matthew Henson, Ootah, Seeglo, Egingwah, and Ooqueah would have been the first human beings to lay eyes on it. But, of course, this is the problem. The North Pole is a point on a vast, ever-shifting expanse of ice—a sort unverifiable by the human eye. Its exact position can only be measured by modern electronic instruments. Any other measurement is imprecise. Yet if, as Wally Herbert surmises, Peary and his party were some thirty or so miles from the actual Pole, they were still the first Americans (and Greenlanders) to have reached the very top of the globe. Or, as retired glaciologist William O. Field told me, "I feel that Peary and his group got close enough to the Pole to be given credit for reaching it first." Field, a member of the American Geographic Society, a scientific group, has conducted research in the Arctic regions for many years. In personal communication with me George Michanowsky, a historian-explorer and member of the Explorers Club, added, "as a partisan of the concept of sufficiency, I would say that the Peary expedition came close enough to the exact North Pole to be credited with discovering it."

After about thirty-six hours of measurements and rest at the Pole, the expedition set out at about four o'clock on the afternoon of April 7 for the land base at Camp Columbia. According to Henson, they traveled at "the break-neck pace that enabled us to cover three of our upward marches on one of our return marches."[13] On much of the return trip, they simply had to follow their outward tracks back to the next camp, which made their travel comparatively easier and faster. According to some experienced explorers, there are fewer pressure ridges (giant hills of broken ice blocks) and more smooth ice in the area near the Pole than near land, thus making it easier to travel at faster sledge speeds far out in the Arctic Ocean. "Our return from the Pole was accomplished in sixteen marches," wrote Peary, "and the entire journey from land to the Pole and back again occupied fifty-three days, or forty-three marches." This means that Peary, Henson, and the Polar Eskimos, using five sleds, covered about twenty-six nautical (twenty-nine statute miles) per march on the return trip and approximately nineteen miles per march for the entire round-trip to the Pole and back. Each march involved eight to fourteen hours without rest.

These figures are not as unreasonable or unprecedented as Peary's critics would have us believe. In a 1983 article in the *American Alpine Journal*, Terris Moore points out that the Alaskan "Iditarod" race of 1,047 miles from Anchorage to Nome is in some ways comparable to the thousand-mile distance the Peary expedition traveled from Cape Columbia and back, and that "many drivers . . . including women, have consistently done over 75 miles per day carrying sleeping gear, tent, and the necessary food provisions" in this race. Moore also points out that the 1981 Iditarod winner, "Rick Swenson, set the course record of 12 days, 8 hours, 45 minutes and 2 seconds. This would seem to be 84.8 miles per day, day after day. The times and distances have all been publicly verified."[14]

There are still other examples, such as one dogsled driver who traveled fifty-two miles in thirteen hours while rushing diphtheria serum to Nome in 1925. More recently, American explorer Will Steger, leading his first expedition on the Arctic ice, reported making thirty-eight miles in eighteen hours en route to the North Pole.[15] Again, Herbert seems to have overlooked or ignored these facts and figures in the course of his research.

Another equally important factor is that in 1909, Peary, Henson, and the four Polar Eskimos had more experience in dogsledging across the Arctic ice than probably anyone else on earth. During their years in the Arctic, Peary and Henson each had covered over ten thousand miles by dogsledge, under some of the worst conditions imaginable, and sometimes in complete darkness. Moreover, Peary, Henson, Ootah, Seegloo, and Bartlett had had the experience of traveling out on the Arctic Ocean in an attempt to reach the Pole in 1906, and had come within 175 miles (87° 6') of their goal, only to be turned back by shortages of food and supplies. Certainly, this extraordinary experience at sledging lends some credence to Peary and Henson's distance claims.

Most of Peary's modern-day critics simply ignore or fail to mention Henson's or the Eskimos' navigational skills. Henson was never treated as a "reliable" witness in the entire North Pole affair. Because of the racial attitudes of the times, he and the Eskimos were viewed by many whites as incapable of comprehending even the most fundamental technical concepts of navigation. This belief, often expressed in his presence by whites, hurt Henson deeply. He was particularly demoralized when the well-known general Adolphus W. Greely said in a major newspaper article that he did not believe Peary had made it to the Pole, especially since his only witness was an "ignorant Negro."[16] Greely, who had led an Arctic expedition to Fort Conger in northern Canada to set up a research station during the first International Geographical Congress in 1881, loathed Peary. Greely and his twenty-seven crewmen were left marooned for two years in the Arctic when, because of ice and other difficulties, the relief ships could not reach them. Most of his men perished of starvation as they traveled south on foot, trying to reach the rescue ships. When they were finally rescued, it was learned that the seven who survived had resorted to cannibalism. Peary (and Henson) later criticized Greely by suggesting that had he been a competent Arctic explorer, he would have found abundant game in the area to keep the group alive. Greely's racial attitudes may have prevented him from working with the local Polar Eskimos, who could have helped his men survive the ordeal. Greely never forgave Peary or Henson for this criticism.

But Henson knew how to determine latitude and longitude, and he confirmed Peary's sledging distances. Terris Moore, who knew Henson for close to twenty years, interviewed Henson on several occasions about his knowledge of navigation and the expedition's journey from Bartlett's farthest point north, at 87° 47', to the Pole. I asked Moore, "Are you fully satisfied from your many discussions with Matthew Henson that he knew enough about navigation to have gotten to the North Pole and back, and to have confirmed Peary's sledging distances and direction?"

"Yes, absolutely," Moore replied. "Matt knew how to determine latitude and longitude from solar sights at the noon and midnight meridian passages. He fully understood the use of Greenwich Mean Time, Greenwich Hour Angle [G-H-A], and the equation of time to obtain longitude at simple meridian passages. The Eskimos too knew that the sun is due south at its noon high point and due north at its midnight low point." Moore added that Henson had been taught navigational skills aboard the *Roosevelt* by Ross Marvin, a professor of engineering at Cornell University.

Unfortunately, through his own racial naivete, Peary may have contributed to the credibility gap that has plagued him since the North Pole discovery. For example, he wrote in *The North Pole* that Henson "would not have been so competent as the white members of the expedition in getting himself and his party back to land. . . . He had not, as a racial inheritance, the daring initiative of Bartlett, or MacMillan, or Borup."

Comdr. Donald B. MacMillan, on the other hand, would later write in *National Geographic* (1920) that Matthew Henson "was indispensable to Peary and of more real value than the combined services of all four white men."

What made the public so incredulous of Peary? There were several reasons, but a summary answer may be that Peary made so many wrong moves. He knew, for example, that Bartlett, a skilled navigator as well as a white man, was an especially "credible" witness. So he permitted Bartlett, rather than one of the four young white Americans, to lead the last support party and travel to a record north which surpassed that of the then-current record holders, Fridtjof Nansen of Norway and Umberto Cagni [under Duke Abruzzi] of Italy. This put Bartlett in the record books. But why did he not let Bartlett travel above the eighty-eighth parallel, say, to within seventy-five miles of the Pole—or fifty miles or twenty-five miles?

Peary said that Bartlett would have been nothing more than a "passenger" if he had taken him farther. But Peary also felt that no one would ever question his ability to travel the last one hundred miles, especially with Matthew Henson, Ootah, and the three loyal, younger Eskimos.

Peary was also well aware that any distance beyond the eighty-eighth parallel would not only establish a record distance north; it would also essentially put him at the top of Earth. Thus, to carry Bartlett farther meant that he would have to share the glory of the victory with him. The same did not apply to Henson. Like the four

Eskimos, he would never be accorded the status of "co-discoverer," on racial grounds alone.

Yet that was not the principal reason why Peary selected Henson to accompany him on the final leg of the journey. As Peary confided in MacMillan at the outset of the 1909 expedition: "Henson must not turn back. I cannot get along without him."[17] This was true for several reasons. First, Henson had more sledging and Arctic naviga-tion experience than any of the other Americans. Second, he was the man who built and repaired sledges and alcohol stoves and who drove the dogteams with the skill of an Eskimo. Third, he was the only man on the expedition who could speak the Eskimo language fluently and who could persuade the Eskimos to travel so far out on the ice. The Eskimos trusted him thoroughly.

Much has been made of the fact that on the return trip to Cape Columbia, Peary barely spoke to Henson. Wally Herbert, for exam-ple, interpreted this silence as evidence of Peary's bitter disappoint-ment and personal "anguish"—a tacit admission, as it were, that he had failed to reach the Pole. But Henson himself offered a different explanation for Peary's behavior. In a 1910 article in the *Boston Ameri-can*, he revealed that on the last leg of the journey he and two of the Eskimos had pushed on to the final campsite in defiance of Peary's specific orders. Although they thought they had stopped at a point just short of their ultimate goal, Peary's subsequent calculations showed that the camp was situated virtually at the Pole itself. It was this realization that left Peary despondent and provoked his anger toward Henson. "For the crime of being present when the Pole was reached Commander Peary has ignored me ever since," Henson explained.

In any event, looking back, it seems clear that Peary would have been better off had he taken both Bartlett and Henson to the Pole. In this way, he would have had his "credible" white witness to satisfy the Americans and Europeans, and Henson, the master explorer and expert in Eskimo sledging, culture, and language, to get them there.

Yet of all the sources of mistrust in Peary, none looms larger than Frederick Cook, the affable doctor who had served as Peary's assis-tant on an earlier expedition and who claimed to have reached the North Pole in 1908. Cook was a popular and charismatic all-American boy. By contrast, Peary was viewed as arrogant, distant, well connected, and heavy-handed. The great Danish explorer Peter Freuchen, who knew both men, once remarked that "Cook was a gentleman and liar; Peary was neither."

Objective examination of Cook's records would lead even his most ardent supporters to conclude that he never got within several hundred miles of the North Pole. It took four support groups, 133 dogs in seven teams, and tons of food, fuel, and other supplies to get Peary, Henson and the four Eskimos to the Pole. Cook would have us believe that he reached the North Pole and returned with two Eskimo assistants, two dogteams, and two sleds of food and fuel.

One is hard put to find any serious scholar, explorer, or scientist who believes that Cook came within four hundred miles of the North Pole. But strangely, some of Cook's supporters are willing to overlook his many inexplicable and weak excuses for acts unbecoming of a serious explorer. Cook's explanations for his lack of proof of his "attainment of the Pole" always seemed a little too convenient. For example, he claimed to have left the "proof" of his attainment of the Pole (i.e., papers and instruments) behind in Greenland in the care of a friend, while he traveled to Denmark to celebrate his victory. In the minds of the world public of that time, reaching the North Pole was tantamount to reaching the moon in our time. And how much "proof" was required? Notebook? Compasses? Peary is today being challenged on the basis of his "proofs" in a small pocket-sized notebook kept in the National Archives. Rawlins even used scribbles of Peary's notes on a single scrap of paper as "proof" for his claim that Peary faked the discovery. And yet Cook did not have in his possession even a single pad of navigational measurements. He "left them behind," where they are said to have been buried (and later destroyed by the elements) by his friend because Peary would not let him bring them to the United States aboard his ship.

Rather than attempt here to present the numerous other reasons that make it extremely improbable that Cook reached the Pole (many arguments have already been presented by Arctic historians), I will cite what in my opinion is one of the strongest arguments against his claim.

One of Cook's biggest mistakes was that he, like Peary, thought of the Eskimos as an inferior race of people. He was convinced that they would be unable to understand or report his movements around the islands of northern Canada in his so-called attainment of the Pole and that they would not be credible witnesses among white people. Cook, who had maintained little or no contact with the Polar Eskimos since his visit to Greenland in 1891, would also have us believe that he simply appeared in their villages seventeen years later and convinced them to travel with him on foot and by dogteam some 300 nautical miles from their village at Etah to the northern tip of Canada and an additional 413 miles to the North Pole (a round-trip of about 1,800 miles). Even Peary and Henson, who had known every Eskimo member of their team since they were youngsters, had great difficulty getting them to travel out on the dreaded Arctic Ocean ice. The Eskimos almost never traveled out of view of land on the sea ice, and they feared the ever-present danger of accidents on the ice, which they referred to as being swallowed up by the evil spirit of Tornarsuk. Although Peary paid each man handsomely with material goods and promises, a number of the Eskimo assistants deserted the expedition after a few days out on the ice. Others tried to abandon Peary as the expedition traveled farther north, but were persuaded by Henson and MacMillan, through promises of exorbitant pay, to remain.

By all accounts, Cook could not even speak Eskimo except to babble a few words, let alone enough to persuade them to travel out on the Arctic Ocean. Also, for some strange reason, after being dropped off near Etah by a fishing schooner, Cook left his single white assistant, Rudolph Francke, behind in an Eskimo village. He then set off "for the Pole with four Eskimos." After traveling about twelve miles out on the Arctic Ocean, two of the Eskimos returned to their village, leaving Cook, Etookahshoo, and Ahpellah alone in a snow house (igloo) they had built. There, Cook is believed to have raised the American flag over the snow house and taken a photograph of what he later called the North Pole. Cook then traveled south to one of the upper Canadian islands and found an old abandoned earthen igloo, where he and the two Eskimos wintered. In early spring, he made his way back to Etah to announce his "Attainment of the North Pole." His two Eskimo assistants later said during questioning that they did not know whether they had traveled to the North Pole with Cook, but they were certain that wherever they traveled they were "never out of sight of land." No land can be seen from the North Pole.

The two Eskimos were later interviewed by the Eskimo–Danish explorer and anthropologist Knud Rasmussen, who reported their story. The highly respected Rasmussen had initially believed Cook's claim of having reached the North Pole, but after talking with Cook's Eskimo hirees and reviewing the records of his journey, he concluded, "I realized it was a scandal." Rasmussen's interview of Peary and Henson's Eskimo assistants, on the other hand, corroborated their report of the polar journey.

It is worth nothing that Cook may have first conceived the idea of challenging Peary for the Pole around 1901 when, at the request of Peary's friends, he gave Peary a medical examination and found him in such poor health that he was not likely to be able to continue his polar quest. In any event, he did more than anyone to deprive Peary and Henson of the North Pole prize they rightly earned.

Peary also alienated many Americans with his aloofness and his catering to narrow, special-interest groups. For example, he carried the flags of the Daughters of the American Revolution and his Bowdoin College fraternity to the Pole, and he raised them along with the American flag. Some have even suggested that Peary was perceived by many Americans as being too closely allied with big-name Republican interests, making him a target for Democrats who traditionally supported underdogs like Cook. Predictably, he also overreacted to Cook's ruse, appearing to the American public to be mean-spirited and despotic, while Cook came off looking magnanimous. "Two records are better than one," said Cook when he heard that Peary had reached the Pole. Peary responded by calling Cook a "liar" who had "sold the American public a gold brick."

Some of Peary's critics also charge him with treating the North Pole as if it were "his domain" and calling the Greenland–Canadian route to the Pole "his" route. Indeed, Peary and Henson had spent eighteen years searching for and reporting in public journals the best route to the Pole. Moreover, Peary was not unusual or irrational in his insistence that he was the American representative in the race to the North Pole and that the Cape Columbia meridian route was his. Every nation involved in the race usually had one man who was by reputation and experience its sole representative in the North Pole contest, and that nation threw its support behind its man. In Italy, for example, the duke of Abruzzi with his associate Umberto Cagni were the "official" contestants for the North Pole. In Norway, until 1900, it was Fridtjof Nansen. One cannot imagine any other Italian attempting to compete with Cagni and the duke for the prestige of the North Pole or any other Englishman challenging Scott for the South Pole. In the explorers' world of that era, it was considered dishonorable for one explorer to invade the ongoing exploration of another. But in America, the land of opportunity (and opportunists), Cook did not have to adhere to these unwritten gentlemen's rules.

Most of Peary's detractors use a simplistic and time-tested formula: if you discredit Peary's character and motives and make him appear to have been an irrational, dishonest, and blindly ambitious man, and you then eliminate Henson and the Eskimos as "credible" witnesses, you can sow enough "reasonable doubt" to deprive Peary of his claim.

No one, however, can impugn the courage of the men who undertook the historic 1909 expedition. Every successful polar expedition since that time has required the use of aircraft or other advanced technology for backup and resupply. It is well known to psychologists and physiologists that such security serves as a source of comfort and physical resilience, enabling a person to husband special psychic and somatic resources for a dangerous and difficult task. This was an advantage that Peary, Henson, and the other members of the team did not enjoy. They knew that once they ventured out onto the Arctic they could not be rescued. The loss of a supply sled through a break in the ice, the opening of an impassable sea lane, a sudden violent storm, a broken or frostbitten limb—any of these or countless other accidents could result not only in disappointment and delay but in death. Yet somehow they overcame these obstacles, found their way to the Pole, and returned to the same spot on land.

* * *

Or did they? To settle the dispute once and for all, the National Geographic Society commissioned the Navigation Foundation, a highly respected private association of navigation specialists based in Rockville, Maryland, to review all the evidence related to Robert Peary's claim. The foundation spent more than a year poring over some 225 cubic feet of documents contained in the Peary Collection at the National Archives as well as other relevant papers collected at the American Geographical Society, the National Geographic Society, the Explorers Club in New York, and other institutions. It also solicited testimony from a range of experts who had studied the evidence. I, too, submitted my findings.

Among the first conclusions reached by the Navigation Foundation was that Dennis Rawlins's analysis of Peary's data was "completely erroneous."[18] Far from cracking some hidden "code," the foundation reported, the equations Rawlins used to prove Peary's failure were actually drawn from the serial numbers of Peary's three navigational watches. The report went on to suggest that anyone with even a modicum of navigational experience would not have made such errors in analyzing Peary's notes, which were apparently taken on an earlier expedition and from land.

William E. Mollett, a navigation expert who flew ninety-one polar missions with the U.S.A.F. Weather Service between 1952 and 1955, delivered an even more stinging indictment. In material submitted to the National Geographic and the Navigation Foundation as part of their investigation, the retired U.S. Air Force colonel wrote:

> The complete amateur, Dennis Rawlins, and the Polar stunt man Wally Herbert were very critical of Peary for not taking transverse sextant sightings (unnecessary), frequent soundings of ocean depth, variation figures, constant wind speed and direction of cloud conditions. Peary was intent on only one thing: reaching the Pole. To call his efforts to obtain a lot of scientific data perfunctory would be an exaggeration. Soundings and unnecessary sextant sightings when the temperatures were so cold to say the least are activities that can easily be skipped. . . . There was a serious error made in the September 1988 article [in *National Geographic*] when it was assumed that Peary was attempting to navigate the Pole without any celestial references for longitude. His celestial reference was almost constantly available, and only slightly less accurate than references made with a sextant. They could be done without bothering with logarithms and spherical trig-

onometry and a miserably cold sextant operation. Why use a bubble
horizon when the sun is right on the real horizon?[19]

The Navigation Foundation agreed with Mollett. "We are persuaded," the foundation reported, after systematically presenting
the available evidence, "that Peary's system of navigation was adequate to get him to the near vicinity of the Pole without taking
longitude observations along the way."[20]

The foundation also found that the distance and speed Peary
claimed to have traveled during the expedition, including the final
dash to the Pole, "are entirely credible. Dogs and sleds with far less
skillful drivers than Matthew Henson and Peary's Eskimos have often maintained or exceeded these claimed speeds over much longer
distances."[21]

Additional confirmation of Peary's claims was provided by a comparison of recently established Arctic Ocean depths along the seventieth meridian with measurements recorded during the expedition
and by "photogrammetric rectification"—a technique involving the
mathematical analysis of shadows on photographs to determine the
sun's elevation when the picture was taken. After applying this
technique to a series of photographs that Peary claimed to have taken
at the Pole, the foundation concluded: "The pictures were taken very
close to the vicinity of the Pole. . . . probably within four or five miles
of the reported position." This the foundation regarded as its "final
and most conclusive" evidence that Peary, Henson, and the four
Eskimos were "essentially at the Pole."[22]

Several months later, in April 1990, the foundation issued a "Supplemental Report" after discovering two more photographs from the
1909 expedition.[23] Unlike the other thirteen pictures that had been
analyzed through photogrammetry, these photographs showed the
position of both the sun and the horizon, making it possible to
determine even more precisely the position of the photographer.
Analysis of the new photographs moved Peary and Henson's proba-
ble location even closer to the exact Pole.

The Navigation Foundation's reports should put the matter to
rest. But somehow I doubt it. As Robert Peary himself observed, the
North Pole was the "Last Great Geographical Prize." Yet unlike so

many other such "prizes"—the South Pole, Mount Everest, even the moon—the North Pole remains shrouded in uncertainty and mystery, a point surrounded by an ever-shifting sea of ice and unidentifiable by the human eye. Perhaps that is its most enduring legacy: it continues to represent human striving for what is approachable but never fully attainable.

NOTES

Chapter 6. Black and White Partners

1. Matthew Henson's date of birth is commonly believed to be August 8, 1866, but is listed as August 8, 1868, on his marriage license issued on April 13, 1891, by the Clerk of the Orphans' Court of Philadelphia County, Pennsylvania.
2. Robert E. Peary diary entry, in Robert E. Peary Collection, Record Group 401-1, National Archives, Washington, D.C.
3. Robert E. Peary, *Northward over the "Great Ice"* (n.p., n.d.), p. 508.
4. Ibid., p. 47.
5. Matthew Alexander Henson, *A Negro Explorer at the North Pole* (New York: Frederick A. Stokes, 1912), p. 3.
6. Robert E. Peary Collection, Record Group 401-1, National Archives, Washington, D.C. Unless otherwise noted, all personal letters that I quote from in the text can be found in this collection.
7. John M. Verhoeff diaries, in Robert E. Peary Collection, National Archives, Washington, D.C.
8. Ibid.
9. T. S. Dedrick, Jr., diaries, in Robert E. Peary Collection, National Archives, Washington, D.C.

Chapter 7. The Struggle for the Pole

1. Donald B. MacMillan, "Peary as a Leader," *National Geographic*, April 1920; and Donald B. MacMillan, "Matthew Henson," *The Explorers Journal* (official journal of the Explorers Club), Fall 1955.
2. MacMillan, "Matthew Henson"; and Bradley Robinson, *Dark Companion* (New York: Robert M. McBride, 1947), p. viii.
3. Henson, *Negro Explorer*, pp. 113, 114.
4. Ibid., p. 124.
5. Robinson, *Dark Companion*, pp. 261–62; Harold Harwood, *Bartlett: The Great Explorer* (Toronto: Doubleday Canada, 1977), p. 87.
6. Robert E. Peary, *The North Pole* (New York: Frederick A. Stokes, 1910), p. 269.

7. "Matt Henson Tells the Real Story of Peary's Trip to the Pole," *Boston American*, July 17, 1910.
8. Peary, *North Pole*, p. 273.
9. Robert H. Fowler, "The Negro Who Went to the Pole with Peary," *American History Illustrated*, May 1966 (this article was based on interviews with Henson that Fowler conducted in 1953). Also, personal communication to author from Terris Moore.
10. MacMillan, "Peary as a Leader."
11. "Matt Henson Tells the Real Story."
12. Letter-article by Peter Freuchen, "Ahdolo, Ahdolo!" dated March 18, 1947. Sent to James Zarlock, Robert McBride Co. (publishers), New York.
13. "Cook's Route Far from Pole, His Eskimos Say" and "Map of Cook's Arctic Voyage Containing No Dash to the Pole—Traced by His Two Eskimos," *New York Times*, October 13, 1909.
14. Telegram from Peary to Henson, October 17, 1909: "If, as papers state, you have pictures of North Pole and sledge journey they must not be shown. Wire me"; and letter from Peary to H. C. Bumpus. Both in Robert E. Peary Collection, Record Group 401-1, National Archives.
15. "Matt Henson Tells the Real Story."
16. "Matt Henson Mourned by Thousands," *New York Amsterdam News*, March 19, 1955.

Chapter 9. Growing Up Eskimo

1. Henson, *Negro Explorer*, p. 183.

Epilogue

1. Boyce Rensberger, "Debunking Peary Myth," *Washington Post*, September 18, 1988. According to Rensberger, Dennis Rawlins had put forth his case against Peary in a report to the Navy Institute Proceedings in 1970 and had reiterated his challenge three years later in *Peary at the North Pole: Fact or Fiction* (Washington, D.C.: Luce, 1973).
2. Boyce Rensberger, "Peary's Notes Show He Faked Claim: Suppressed Document Places Explorer Far from North Pole," *Washington Post*, October 12, 1988.
3. Boyce Rensberger, "Explorer Bolsters Case against Peary," *Washington Post*, November 2, 1988.
4. D. J. Drewry and R. Huntford, "Amundsen's Route to the South Pole," *Polar Record* 19, no. 121 (1979): 329–36.
5. Roald Amundsen, *The South Pole* (London: John Murray, 1912), p. 112; and Roald Amundsen, "Expedition to the South Pole," *Annual Report of the Smithsonian Institution*, 1912, pp. 701–16.

6. Roald Amundsen, *My Life as an Explorer* (New York: Doubleday, Doran & Co., 1928), p. 72.

7. Amundsen, *South Pole*, p. 112.

8. Drewry and Huntford, "Amundsen's Route," pp. 329–36.

9. Peary, *North Pole*, pp. 319, 356. Marvin's note was found in a small canvas pouch attached to the upstanders of his sledge when it was returned to the ship by his Eskimo companions, Kudlooktoo and Harrigan. They had apparently overlooked this item when they pushed his body and all his personal belongings into the Arctic Ocean to hide the evidence of his murder.

10. Ibid., p. 360.

11. Ibid.

12. Ibid., pp. 285, 286.

13. Henson, *Negro Explorer*, p. 140.

14. Terris Moore, "Charge of Hoax against Robert E. Peary Examined," *American Alpine Journal*, 1983, pp. 114–22.

15. Will Steger and Paul Schurke, *North to the Pole* (New York: Times Books, 1987).

16. "Neither Peary nor Cook Found Pole, Is Gen. Greely's Belief," *Washington Star,* January 25, 1926.

17. MacMillan, "Matthew Henson"; also Robinson, *Dark Companion,* p. viii.

18. Peary North Pole Interim Report, No. 1, January 13, 1989, Navigation Foundation, Rockville, Maryland.

19. Letter/report, October 1988, from Lt. Col. William E. Mollett, submitted to National Geographic and Navigation Foundation.

20. "Robert E. Peary at the North Pole," report of Navigation Foundation, December 11, 1989. See also "New Evidence Places Peary at the Pole," *National Geographic,* January 1990.

21. "Robert E. Peary at the North Pole."

22. Ibid.

23. "Robert E. Peary at the North Pole: A Supplemental Report," Navigation Foundation, April 16, 1990.

GLOSSARY

This glossary gives the phonetic spellings of common Polar Eskimo words and phrases used by Matthew Henson. These spellings and their pronunciations served Henson well in his dealings with the Eskimos, and he was the only American on the Peary expeditions who was able to communicate with the Eskimos in their own language. Not all the words given in this list appear in the text, but the sampling is intended to offer the reader an introduction to words in everyday use. The selection proved helpful to the students and staff involved in the North Pole Reunion Committee.

Ah-dok	Bottom of feet
Ah-ee-who-ghia	I am fine
Ah-hahn-nah	Aurora borealis
Ah-hock key-et-toe	Hot summer
Ah-kah-lik	Rabbit
Ah-kai-gu	Tomorrow
Ahk-duk	Killer whale
Ah-key-show	Ptarmigan or grouse
Ah-mak-de-hee-oh	Many
Ah-muck-kah	Maybe
Ah-nah-kah-ting-woot	Sister
Ah-nah-kah-ting-woot-neeya	My sister
Ah-nahn-na	Mother
Ahn-nah	Woman
Ah-poot	Snow
Ah-she-de-shot	Camera

Ah-tah	Grandfather
At-tah-tah	Father
Ah-tow-toe	Yawn
Ah-ung-gwee-lok (Greenlandic)	Fine
Ah-vuk	Walrus
Ah-who-ghia	Fine, okay
Ak-day-you-ahk-toe	Shy
Ang-goot	Man
An-new-ee	Wind
An-no-wah	Hooded jacket, anorak
Bik-check	Good
Bik-doo-ah-gee	Congratulations
Cah-nock-toe	Falling snow
Cah-nook	Mouth
Chair-ree-in-yah	Fox
Chee-me-ahk	Bird (general)
Chee-me-ahk-toe	Airplane
Chee-tok-we	Cup
Chi-bag-ee	Tobacco
Ching-mia	Bird (general)
Cobve	Coffee
Dah-ho	Fighting between two people; a fight
Day-mah	It is finished
Dough-ko	Dead
Du-wah-hok	To hear
Ear-ee-ah-nock-toe	Beautiful
Ed-de-hahm-ah-neet-cho	Crazy
Eeee	Yes

Ee-hee-kah-kah	[My] feet
Ee-helk	Eye
Ee-nuk	Person
Eh-nah-hock-toe	Yawn
Err-nahk	Son
Foo-he-ah	Membranous sack in bird's throat; crop
Foo-who-chee	What are you doing? What's happening with you?
Ha-ah-chew-go	Ouch
Hah-vik	Iron or metal
Hav-oc	Sheep
He-ah-wah-whah	Sugar
Hee-ah-ko	Knee
Hee-oou-nee	Ear
Herr-kah-nook	Sun
He-tak-toe	Sling shot
Hi-nay [Hi-nah]	Hello; Hi
Hi-nay-nuk-who-nay	Hello. How are you?
Hi-nic-toe	Sleeping person
Hin-nik-doo-ah-gee	Good night
Hin-nik-toe	Sleep
Hu-qua-gah	Candy
Id-dig-doo	You are welcome
I-ding-nook	Bad (weather)
I-du-di-ah	Iceberg
I-hee-ga	Foot
I-hook-ko	Little finger
Ik-kil-nock-toe	Cold, or to be cold

Ik-pill-nah	Mosquito
Ing-mung-wah	A little, as in "a little coffee"
In-nook	Water
In-nuit	Person
I-nook-du-yak	Good-bye
Ir-riah-nock-toe	Beautiful
Kaa-be-ho	Coffee
Kah-do-nah	White-skinned person
Kah-kok-tok kah-lay-lee-wah	White whale (Beluga)
Kah-lay-lee-wah	Narwhal
Kahl-nock-tok kah-lay-lee-wah	Black narwhal
Kah-mah-toe	Angry
Kah-tuk	Cup
Kah-ou	Forehead
Ka-miks	Boots (made of animal skin)
Kang-wah-chee	Binoculars
Kar-rah-hah	Brain
Ka-toong-wah	Children
Kay-cheek-toe	Dancing
Kee-chuck-dah	Middle finger
Keen-yah	Nose
Key-ah-see-oak-dua	I'm sweating.
Key-et-toe	Warm, hot, heat
Key-net-chee	What is your name?
Key-you-tee	Teeth
Kim-milk	Dog
Kod-dee-pah-luk	Stove
Ko-do	Thumb
Ko-keet	Claws

Kong-new-we-ho	Snore
Koo-you-nah	Thank you
Kul-nock-to	The color black
Kul-nock-too-ko	Dark-skinned or black [person]
Ku-mah-ah-ho	Puppy
Kute (cute)	Tooth
Nah-mak-toe	Good tasting or tasty
Mee-kee-lil-rahk	Ring finger
Nah-ahn	No
Nah-do-oh-hoy-ah	I don't know
Nah-mock-toe	Fine, as in okay
Nah-pah-ham-a-wick	Infirmary; hospital
Na-nook	Polar bear
Nay-goo-hock	Doctor
Nee-shock-toe	Great, as in "a great person"
Neh-we-ah	Seagull
Net-do-ve	When were you born?
New-nah	Earth, land
New-yah	Hair
Nock-toe-ho	Pregnant
No-dia	Wife
No-low	Rear end; buttocks
Oh-mia-hahm-me	On board ship
Oh-mia-hock	Big ship
Oh-you-ah-hock	Rock
O-miak	Ship or boat
O-ming-mak	Musk ox
Om-mik	Moustache
On-ee-yee-cheech	Stop here

Ooh-kah	Tongue
Ooh-wang-gah	I
Peed-de	Car
Pee-nee-ahk-toe	Hunter
Pee-nee-ahk-toe wah	Great or master hunter
Pee-shah-hah	Strong
Poo-ee-hee	Seal
Puto	Hole
Pu-you-tee	Pipe
Qeqertarsaaq	Herbert Island
Quah, quah, quah, pah che	So many
She-neck-tah-ko	To sleep forever; to die
She-neg-boo	Sleep
She-you-tee	Ears
Tad-dok	Chin
Tah-ku-huk	To see
Tah-tah-rah	Black-legged kittiwake
Tee-de-ord	Teapot
Teek-yuk	Index finger
Tee-nee-vok	To fly or flying (as in "the bird is flying")
Tie-ee-ok-toe	Sneeze
Tock-toe	Dark, darkness
Took-too	Caribou
Too-lu-gah	Crow
Tu-pik	Tent
U-lu or Ooh-lu	Small utility knife
Who-we	Husband

ACKNOWLEDGMENTS

Many fine people of all races, colors, and backgrounds contributed to the success of the North Pole Family Reunion and the reinterment of Matthew Henson. I have named some in the text; here I wish to thank them and others who made exceptional contributions to this project.

I am especially grateful to John H. Johnson, chairman of Johnson Publishing Company. The North Pole Family Reunion and the reinterment of Matthew Henson were made possible by his moral and financial support.

I thank the members of the Amer-Eskimo Henson and Peary families, especially Anaukaq and Kali, for their friendship and supportive efforts. I also thank the members of the Polar Eskimo communities of Moriussaq and Qaanaaq, northwest Greenland.

I thank the members of the Harvard community, the North Pole Family Reunion Committee, and the Matthew A. Henson Reinterment Committee for their support and encouragement, especially President Derek C. Bok, Rev. Peter J. Gomes, L. Fred Jewett, dean of Harvard College, Marvin Alvert Hightower, David L. Evans, Dudley Herschbach, Kent Taylor Cushenberry, Chester Pierce, Richard Hunt, Josephus Long, Lynn Thompson Long, Edwin H. Kolodny, John E. Dowling, Sisella Myrdal Bok, Erik Borg, Mimi Aloian, Kermit Alexander, Sean T. Brady, Mariana Ortiz-Blanes, Camille Holmes, and Suzanne Malveaux.

I am also grateful to the government and military officials who contributed to this project, including President Ronald Reagan, Samuel R. Pierce, Frederick J. Ryan, Jr., Raymond J. Costanzo, Gen. Julius Becton, Marion Barry, Jr., Col. Guion S. Bluford, Navy Chaplain Charles W. Marvin, Col. Philip Bracher, Col. James Knapp, Maj. Quincy Sharp, Sgt. Theodora Hart, Kay Cormier, the Department of Defense, the Military Airlift Command (MAC), and the U.S. Air Force.

I owe special thanks to the project associates and the Henson family: Ann J. C. Daniels, R.N., project nurse; Dr. Louis C. Brown, project physician; Regina O. Counter, project assistant; Navarana Harper, primary translator in Greenland and America; Ned Johnston, cinematographer; Anthony B. Jacobs, sound recordist and technician; Hans P. Biemann, photographer; Olive Henson Fulton; Virginia Carter Brannum; and Audrey C. Mebane.

I would also like to thank the following individuals and organizations for their special efforts and contributions to the project: Rev. Samuel D. Proctor and Abyssinian Baptist Church, Thobius Danielsen (second translator), Ruth Hamilton, Dr. Robert Screen, William R. Harvey and the Hampton University Band and Choir, Dr. Bo Klarskov, Police Inspector Karl Peterson, Carlos Vallechio, Cherie Cushenberry, Ann Willoughby, Mr. and Mrs. Marvin Hightower, Sr., the Washington, D.C., Convention Center, the Afro-American Heritage Society of Charles County, Maryland (especially Louise Webb and William Diggs), Terris Moore, Nicholas Sullivan, William F. Looney, Robert C. Barber, Jeanne Capodilupo, John, Jean, and Brian Powell, Melvin B. Miller, the Fordham College Choir, the National Archives, First Air of Canada, and the Explorers Club.

I wish to thank Bruce Wilcox and the University of Massachusetts Press for their genuine interest in *North Pole Legacy,* and especially Clark Dougan for his excellent editorial advice.